Geoffrey Bould was born in Yorkshire in 1920. After service in World War II, he worked in the civil service until retirement in 1982. In addition to working as a freelance journalist, he established and edited for several years the ecumenical newspaper *Interfaith News*. An active Quaker, Geoffrey Bould is a member of Amnesty International's Religious Affairs Panel.

Conscience Be My Guide

Dedicated to Eloise Joanne

Conscience Be My Guide

An Anthology of Prison Writings

edited by
Geoffrey Bould

Zed Books Ltd
London and New Jersey

Conscience Be My Guide was first published by
Zed Books Ltd, 57 Caledonian Road, London N1 9BU and
165 First Avenue, Atlantic Highlands, New Jersey 07716 in 1991.

Copyright © Geoffrey Bould, 1991

Cover design by John Marsh
Typeset by AKM Typesetters, Southall
Printed and bound in the United Kingdom by
Biddles of Guildford and King's Lynn

ISBN 1 85649 010 6 hbk
ISBN 1 85649 011 4 pbk

A catalogue record for this book is available from the British Library.

U.S. C.I.P. is available from the Library of Congress.

*All royalties on the sale of this book will be donated to human
rights organisations.*

Contents

My prison shall be my grave before I will budge a jot, for I owe my conscience to no mortal man; I have no need to fear, God will make amends for all; they are mistaken in me. I value not their threats nor resolutions, for they shall know I can weary out their malice and peevishness, and in me shall they behold a resolution above fear, conscience above cruelty.
William Penn, writing from the Tower of London, 1668

Give me the library to know, to think, to believe, and to utter freely, according to conscience, above all other liberties.
John Milton

Introduction

Prisoners of conscience have been with us since time began. No doubt the first leader of the first tribe made rules for their conduct, and enforced sanctions against those who resisted. More established governments make laws that inevitably produce opposition because no government is perfect, and minorities and individuals alike search out ways to change what is insufferable. Those in authority argue that any injustice done to the individual by the state is a necessary service to the state. Not unnaturally those who suffer the injustice see it differently. They are likely to see it as a misuse of the overweening power of the state machine.

In a democracy the individual has some redress, and thus less reason to claim the right to rely on conscience in defying the state. But even a democracy can stray, or fail to react to changing forces within society. And power, even in a democracy, is a tempting fruit. The weight of government can all too easily stifle the voice of the lone citizen under the guise of security, law and order, confidentiality, or the 'national interest'.

Under repressive governments whole groups of people, even whole races such as the Kurds, can suffer under the use of state-legitimized force. In a totalitarian regime the entire nation is imprisoned and the individual lives in a miasma of doubt and fear. The one who speaks out for truth and freedom becomes a threat to the state's all-pervading authority, and must be silenced, all too often by imprisonment, or worse.

Throughout human history there have been those who express in themselves that defiance which seems embedded in them more than others. They are the conscience of us all. All of us can express defiance to a point, but prisoners of conscience seem to draw this spirit of defiance from a deeper well. They stand for the conscience that exists in each of us, and for the values to be found in the moral standards of the larger group. On their shoulders they carry the burden of society, for their protest can right the wrongs of society. Their challenge can be the focus of an existing but unarticulated discontent, as well as opening the floodgates of a discontent which then grows to engulf a whole nation, as in Eastern Europe in 1989.

Without their chained hands lifting up, the fallen world would not be lifted up.

The internal drive in the prisoner of conscience has been called by Christians a 'divine stubbornness'. Certainly it is that, but it is found also in the non-religious, so that it is perhaps not proper always to call it 'divine'. What is sure is that there has to exist an ethical faith or belief beyond the bounds of human comprehension. It is beyond normal understanding to know or to name what it is that drives otherwise ordinary human beings to submit themselves to the suffering of the prisoner of conscience, for no reward and against all earthly logic.

In refusing to serve in Hitler's army, Franz Jägerstätter held out alone against the persuasion of his bishop, his army recruiting officers, his fellow villagers, his affection for his family and the arguments of his military tribunal. He knew that in so doing he would be executed, but he continued to pit his bravery against this enormous pressure, and went to his death, alone. Many others in the German Reich had his religious faith, but found a way to square their consciences. In so great a matter, Jägerstätter would not. There is something in the hearts of such women and men which makes them say with their lives 'I can do no other'.

What it is, I do not know. I can only admire it, and suggest that some of that conscience is in all of us. If we are human, it is there, and I think this is why prisoners of conscience evoke a response in others. Something in their actions touches a spark in us. Their consciences burn like a flame, ours are less visible. But it is their example that challenges us, as the Chinese student challenged the tank in Tiananmen Square, and imparts to us some of their virtue. Such actions enrich humanity.

It is for that reason that I consider this anthology uplifting, not depressing. This may seem odd in the context of the deprivation and suffering that is the lot of these prisoners of conscience. And beyond that, there is the torture undergone by so many of the prisoners, the dehumanizing of individuals that is so plainly evil yet issues from the actions of human beings to fellow human beings. These sufferings make one turn away in revulsion, a first reaction which is entirely normal.

But it is my view that in reading the passages in this book there comes a second reaction – gratitude for the fortitude displayed, admiration for the superior human qualities exemplified and awe at the dedication to a cause beyond personal advantage. It is the idealism to which we respond, an idealism which rises above their sufferings, so that, as in Greek tragedy, we feel raised up as human beings, proud to be of the same species as those with such rare courage. We are assured that, in spite of all our frailties, there must be hope for humanity yet.

Such statements as that by Seremane in the introduction to the torture section evoke a response to his lack of bitterness, his gentle astonishment at the real presence of evil in others. The impassioned piece by Mangakis in which he speaks with eloquence of human dignity and trampled honour reminds us that an individual's human dignity is a part of that humanity to which we all belong. We should be proud that such human dignity surfaces again and again, in spite of all the torments to which humanity subjects itself.

For we are responsible for our society and what we build in it. Even if we build human torments into it, we are still free to read and empathize with those who have suffered the slings and arrows of outrageous governments. If we can accept that they have suffered vicariously for us, then it can only arouse a determination to better our society.

Those who talk of democracy like to state that an appeal to conscience is no justification for breaking the law. That is the view of people who criticize those who refused to serve in the Gulf. But such a view ignores the great historical precedents, some of which are cited in this volume, and is propounded by lawmakers who wish to perpetuate the legal myth that their laws are perfect and immutable. Whatever the society, there will always exist a need and a duty for individuals to oppose that society in some respect; there is no perfect society, and there will always be contrary opinion. Whilst every cause espoused by a prisoner of conscience will not necessarily be a just cause, the right to object strenuously must be sacrosanct. Hence the cardinal place of freedom of expression, hence the cardinal place of the prisoner of conscience whose moral duty stands above the law. If this freedom to oppose is attenuated, a democracy becomes unhealthy, in some countries turning into a one-party state, then into a repressive government.

Democracy is not just a vote at election time; it is a voice with which to express dissent against unjust laws. At times the prisoner of conscience becomes that voice. The suffragettes, conscientious objectors resisting service in the armed forces, the press and the trade unions, among others, have shown how injustice under the law can exist. This does not argue a disrespect for the institution of the law. Rather, it argues a respect for the law, in that the prisoner of conscience wants the law to be respected as the embodiment of the highest possible moral standards.

Equally prisoners of conscience have a moral obligation to face the full consequences of their lawbreaking. If they have a moral duty to object, they have a moral duty to bear the brunt of their actions. It is not a matter of expostulating from the safety of an armchair, it is a matter of staking one's freedom in a cause which is not only one's own. The protest of prisoners of conscience is not personal, though they are often as alone as it is possible to be when in their cells wrestling with their consciences, as Martin Luther King found when writing his letter from Alabama's Birmingham jail to fellow ministers.

It is said that there is an element of attention seeking in the actions of prisoners of conscience, of seeking after martyrdom. They are said to go to their deaths in the hope or expectation that they will achieve posthumous fame. Apart from the illogicality inherent in the argument, for the dead can never know of their historic fate, the sort of person who seeks out martyrdom is not made of the stuff of martyrs. T.S. Eliot has the truth of it when he says: 'To do the right deed for the wrong reason is the greatest treason.' To act out of the motive of seeking fame would be a treason of the conscience, and not the action of the true idealist.

Many of the prisoners featured here remarked how they hated the thought of prison. Its rigours are no light yoke. Daniel Berrigan described graphically his abhorrence at the thought of prison but, as he said, he 'could not *not* do it'. So, while it was abhorrent, it was more bearable than compromising his conscience and living with that compromise for evermore. Archbishop Cranmer, for example, struggled to avoid the necessity of his sacrifice. Here is a prime example of a sensitive intellectual who, fated with the ability to see both sides of an argument, struggled to find a way to an honest recantation which might save him from the fire. He, like others, sought the truth above the argument, even when he knew his opponents were seeking not the truth, but his death. Such women and men know when their consciences have won the day, and when they must, like Cranmer, extend a hand to the flame.

Paradoxically, some prisoners suggest they would rather be in prison than out of it. Not for the comfort, but for the peace of mind in knowing that their integrity is safe. They feel an inner freedom, having answered the call of conscience. As William Dewsbury put it, they 'esteemed the bolts as jewels'. They feel free from the daily travail of battling the state, the censor, the security police and other organs of repression in pursuit of their vision of the truth. And sometimes they express a feeling of relief that they have come face to face with the worst that can be meted out to them.

Then there begins another fight, the struggle to survive. Simply to lose one's freedom is a deprivation, the first and perhaps the worst of many. To be confined is to risk losing one's self-hood and sense of individuality. The prison bureaucracy knows this, and helps the prisoners along by the prison garb, shaven heads, use of numbers instead of names, purposeless tasks, rules against talking, singing or smiling, and as many other impositions as the vindictive mind can conjecture. On the Yugoslav prison island of Otok a famous writer, Venko Markovski, was given a new identity so that neither his guards nor his countrymen knew that he still existed. Being imprisoned incommunicado or in solitary confinement adds to the assault on the psyche, as does such physical ill-treatment as a starvation regime, degrading living conditions and brutality.

This dehumanizing process is worst under torture, where prisoners are blindfolded and led to the torture room to suffer such pain that the pain is all they are. Their disorientation is complete. What Ngugi wa Thiongo calls the 'hot knives of torture' can reduce a prisoner to a suffering body without control over its natural functions. Natural dignity vanishes, the animal-like remnant of a person loses consciousness, and we who read of it breathe a sigh of relief.

It is virtually impossible to comprehend the evil that often seemingly ordinary individuals can perpetrate on their fellows, especially when the torture becomes banal and routine, performed by men who listen to pop music the while and then go home to wives and children. They treat it as just a job, and can do so because they are in a group which creates of itself an acceptable consensus, a group consciousness. This aura of sanctioned respectability is perhaps even more dangerous than the act of torture itself, for it makes evil respectable. The culture of the concentration camp guards sustained itself in this bubble of self-deception; not a conscious rejection of normal values, but an internalized assumption that there was nothing there to reject. In this manner, Hannah Arendt's 'banality of evil' becomes normality. Fortunately for humankind even such a system is not perfect. For there have been instances, as this selection reveals, of guards who repented their ways, who showed kindness, whose humanity rose above the system.

Against this evil, prisoners of conscience have to pit their will to live. Once they have lost that, they are lost altogether, for they then accept death as a human being, as Bettelheim states in his study of concentration camp prisoners. They die slowly of inanition, destined for death by their failure of will. If prisoners of conscience are to survive, they have somehow to keep alive a determination which burns itself into their self-identity so that it becomes a part of them. For most it was that spark of faith or that belief in a cause which prompted their incarceration in the first place. In a religious person, it would be their faith or some aspect of it which spoke to the depths of their being. Sharansky turned to the psalms, Levi was determined to live to tell of the mad horrors of the camps, Kromberg challenged the humanity of her accusers and triumphed by establishing a personal rapport with them. With Thomas More it was a great principle to which he clung: 'I am the King's good servant, but God's first.' For some, their guiding determination was to put aside regrets for the past or thoughts of the future and insulate the mind. Edith Bone manufactured an activity to make the time pass, while Koestler concentrated on mental problems. This adaptation to the limits of their situation was not resignation, but part of their mental struggle to cope with and rise above the situation. Interestingly, hatred was very rarely the motive; hatred is not an easy bedfellow.

For the writer and artist in prison the urge to communicate overrides all else and gives them the will to live. Paper or material upon which to create become priceless commodities. Even in their absence, the artist triumphs and creates. Prisoners have written between the lines of other books, on soap or on linen sheets; Breytenbach wrote in the dark. In the extreme they compose in the head, memorize what they have written and put it on paper when released. When allowed paper, but subject to censorship, their words are smuggled out. Bonhoeffer used a friendly guard, and Chenier his laundry. Arango says notes were left on the ground to be picked up and passed on, a method known as 'the way of the rats'. Others doomed to die, as in the case of Victor Jara, dictate their last messages to colleagues who faithfully release them to the world, thereby defeating the efforts of their persecutors to silence dissent.

To the creative mind it is essential to communicate in order to live. To many more, imprisonment awakened a creativity born of the need to sort out their feelings in the unprecedented experience of captivity. The heightened emotion sometimes extracted from those who were not practised writers poetry and prose of telling effect and formidable talent. Not all of it, of course, was of high quality. But even so, writers struggling to reach the truth of their experience form a bridge between themselves and the reader, as in the personal letters to befrienders. When someone is writing from the death-cell, there is little desire to impress with elegant prose. Such letters may be written for posterity, but when facing death, as was Dostoevsky, truth and honesty are probably paramount.

Prison has produced much poetry, but I have tried to choose only poems which stand on their own merits as good verse. Attempts at prison verse which miss the mark seem to do so by a bigger margin than prose. This is not to demean the writers or the suffering which inspired them; perhaps the aim is higher, and the fall greater. Perhaps prose is a more natural vehicle for the tyro. At all events, prison poetry which does hit the mark can touch the heart and remain etched in the memory quite as much as poetry of other genres. 'Stone walls do not a prison make' has now entered into popular use.

The prison experience is unique to those who have suffered it, and cannot easily be comprehended by those who have not. But the truth of expression springs from emotions which are common to us all, and to read these deeply felt passages may arouse some empathy with the prisoner of conscience. The more so when we realize that life itself consists of many kinds of constraints, be they of colour, race, disability, sex, language or our own social background and upbringing. Society can be a prison for those who live in a dictatorship or under an apartheid system. So it is that these prisoners' accounts echo our own, though with a deeper note. We can share both in their despair and their elation, so that they become a paradigm of ourselves. Whilst we cannot possibly grasp the actuality of the 18 years incarceration of Hikmet or the rigour of Morales' torture, we can touch the edge of their sufferings through their words.

The evil wrought on man by his fellows can never be rationally justified, though the attempt has been made. The Inquisition called itself holy, and Nazism enunciated a bastard philosophy to support its genocidal policies. But it is our part to look to the courage of the prisoner of conscience, which is never mysterious, but a 'clean different thing' to the behaviour of his guards and torturers. We must be ever thankful that through all history there have always been human beings willing to turn the base metal of the human flesh into the gold of the human spirit.

Editor's Note and Acknowledgements

In selecting these extracts, I have adhered to Amnesty International's definition of a prisoner of conscience, namely, any individual detained anywhere on the grounds of belief, ethnic origin, sex, religion or language who has neither resorted to nor advocated the use of violence. The only exceptions are where prisoners have been subjected to torture; Amnesty opposes the use of torture in all cases without reservation.

Many passages have been abridged in the interests of brevity and in order to include as many excerpts as possible so as to illuminate the total experience of prisoners of conscience. For the sake of readability, I have mostly dispensed with the use of ellipses while square brackets have been used to indicate the occasional insertion of words into passages.

On occasions it has been necessary to preserve the anonymity of contributors. The original source for each selection is listed separately under 'Sources'.

I should like to express my deepest gratitude to my wife, Kathleen, and to my family for their support during the preparation of this anthology. Likewise, I would like to thank the many friends who have helped and encouraged me, especially Joyce Selby, Kate McCusker, Heather Ford, John Brown, Krystina and Mark Leach, Wolf Mendl, Norman Marrow, Roy Hoather, Fr. Michael Evans and Helen Vale.

I greatly value the support of Marigold Best, the staff of Friends House in London, the Quaker Abolition of Torture Group, Jenny Stephenson and the Amnesty International (British Section) Religious Bodies Liaison Panel, the Watford Branch of AI (British Section), Penny Jones and the Campaign against Psychiatric Abuse, Philip Spender of *Index on Censorship*, Siobhan Dowd of PEN (Writers in Prison Committee), Dorothy Birtles of the Quaker Befriending Group, and Drs Philip Walters of Keston College and John Andrews of Lancaster University.

The staff of the following libraries have been most helpful: Society of Friends, London, and particularly its librarian, Malcolm Thomas; Watford Central Library; Lancaster University Library; St Albans

Abbey (Hudson) Library; the Catholic Central Library; and the Mennonite, Wiener, Dr Williams and British Libraries in London.

Finally, I am happy to acknowledge with gratitude the financial assistance received from the Joseph Rowntree Charitable Trust, the Edward Cadbury Charitable Trust, the W.F. Southall Trust, the Puckham Trust, the Richard Cadbury Trust, and the Watford Branch of Amnesty International (British Section).

1. Creativity

One written word in the political cell is a more serious matter than having a pistol. Writing is more dangerous than killing, doctor.

Prison guard to Nawal El Sadaawi *Egyptian writer and activist*

Any firearms or books?

South African customs officer

I have lost my freedom. I have lost my family. I have lost my work. I am a writer. That is all. I want to write and one day I will write.

Pramoedya Ananta Toer *Arrested in Indonesia in 1965, Pramoedya was held for 15 years. Denied access to paper, he 'wrote' several books by dictating passages to fellow inmates who wrote them down upon their release*

Peter Abelard (1079–1142) was born in France, of a minor aristocratic family. A teacher in the cathedral schools of the time, he was eventually known throughout Europe as a philosopher and theologian. He and one of his students, Heloise, fell in love and married secretly. Her guardian was enraged and had Abelard castrated. Heloise and Abelard separated, but wrote a series of love letters to each other which are now famous. Abelard was arraigned before a canonical council in 1121 and accused of heretical writing.

Book burning

On the last day of the council the legate and the archbishop deliberated with my rivals and sundry others as to what should be done about me and my book, this being the chief reason for their having come together. And since they had discovered nothing either in my speech or in what I had hitherto written which would give them a case against me, they were all reduced to silence, or at the most to maligning me in whispers.

But my rivals went to the legate, and succeeded in so changing his opinion that finally they induced him to condemn my book without any further inquiry, to burn it forthwith in the sight of all, and to confine me for a year in another monastery. The argument they used was that it sufficed for the condemnation of my book that I had presumed to read it in public without the approval either of the Roman pontiff or of the church, and that, furthermore, I had given it to many to be transcribed. Methinks it would be a notable blessing to the Christian faith if there were more who displayed a like presumption.

Without further examination or debate, did they compel me with my own hand to cast that memorable book of mine into the flames. Thereupon, as if I had been a convicted criminal, I was handed over to the Abbot of St Medard and led to his monastery as to a prison. And with this the council was immediately dissolved.

The sorrow that tortured me, the shame that overwhelmed me, the desperation that wracked my mind, all these I could then feel, but even now I can find no words to express them. Comparing these new sufferings of my soul with those I had formerly endured in my body, it seemed that I was in very truth the most miserable among men. Indeed that earlier betrayal had become a little thing in comparison with this later evil, and I lamented the hurt to my fair name far more than the one to my body. The latter, indeed, I had brought upon myself through my own wrongdoing, but this other violence had come upon me solely by reason of the honesty of my purpose and my love of our faith, which had compelled me to write that which I believed.

The Flowery (from 'flowery dell', Cockney rhyming slang for 'cell') was an underground newspaper produced by World War II conscientious objectors in Wandsworth Prison, London. Any discovered association with the paper was punishable. The editorial below appeared in August 1942.

Swallowed in two large gulps

The Editor wishes to apologise right away for the writing, the spelling and the syntax. He apologises for the paper, the nib, the ink, and the binding. He apologises for all the contributors who have 'started the ball rolling' but he thanks them most gratefully for risking it. What he does not apologise for is the spirit in which it was conceived, and which was one of cooperation with all those 'inside' with him, and who are standing together against war. This effort has helped him. May it also help its readers.

It is suggested that:

A reader, as such, agrees to accept responsibility for *Flowery* if he is discovered.

It is to be retained one night or dinner-time only, and passed on to a known CO.

It is only to be read in the cell, with the door shut, and should not be taken if there is a possibility of special release or similar danger.

Please do not fold it, but keep it under your shirt, or sock—and the whole idea 'under your hat'.

If a certain PO with a reputation for seeing even the ridge of a cigarette paper under a convict's jacket should be about, we can only say that *Flowery* should be hastily swallowed in two large gulps.

An Afrikaans poet and writer, **Breyten Breytenbach** (1939–) left South Africa for Paris in 1960. In 1975 he returned secretly to South Africa to work politically but was arrested and sentenced to nine years imprisonment. He spent over a year in solitary confinement. He was released in 1982 and returned to Paris. He is an active member of the African National Congress (ANC).

Elbow-room in hell

The guards control your thoughts, you become part of their experiment. The interrogator and his quarry are delivered over to each other. Camus once said '*la résistance est une forme de collaboration*'. That also applies to the relationship between prosecutor and victim. You start to become interested in the humanity of your interrogator and realise that both of you are part of the same terrifying situation.

I was in an exceptional position. The security police were confronted with a well-known Afrikaans writer. If I had not been able to write in prison, I would have gone insane. It was the only way in which I could assimilate my experiences. The publication of my volume *Footwriting* [after imprisonment] occurred without my super-vision. I had dedicated the poems with the motto, 'No, colonel, I'm just trying to find some elbow-room in Hell'. That was a reference to the circumstances under which the texts had come into being. At the time all I intended to do with that book was to cry out: I'm here, I'm alive. Don't forget me. It was my only chance to make contact with the outside world.

I remained in maximum security, in the same section where the condemned to death were kept. The only ones who walked out of it by themselves were those prisoners who were under observation; the rest, 98 per cent, left in a coffin. In the background you could always hear the singing of those who were condemned to death, like the murmuring of the sea. Two weeks beforehand they were notified, and then they sang in a different strain, you could hear it. They sang in a kind of ecstasy, to benumb themselves.

The lights went out at eight o'clock in the evening and afterwards I lay for hours writing in the dark. I could not see my own lines and therefore could not change or scrap anything. I wrote in a sort of new language that I could not read back any more; lyrical poetry, *écriture automatique*.

The most important distractions were provided by the eternally recurring interrogations. I had to answer for everything I had ever said in an interview. They also took my writing literally. One of the most bizarre interrogations had to do with their interest in an imaginary character from my book *A Season in Paradise* — my alter-ego. 'Who is Panus?' they kept asking me. 'Where does he stand, politically?' They never forgave me for calling the men of the security police 'people with chewing gum brains and dark glasses' in that book. Their power is total, absolute, yet they are as touchy about their image as a young girl in love about her appearance.

There are scenes I shall never forget. In the little yard where I took the air, only 15 by 20 feet, a tomato plant was growing. I cherished that plant as if it were a child. Once after a white man had been hanged there in the morning very early (I could sometimes communicate with my fellow-prisoners by shouting) the guard who had just attended the execution plucked a deep red tomato for himself and for me. Together we ate the cold, dewy-fresh fruit. The warm corpse was still lying within reach. It was as if I were eating that heavenly fruit on behalf of the dead man. I have already said that the relation of persecutor to victim is very complex.

I am suspicious of demagogues who demand from their comfortable armchairs that you pay the highest price for the satisfaction of their desires. I know very well that there are people who would have preferred that I not be allowed to write, who would rather have seen me hanged so they could venerate me as a martyr. Someone who never went through it will never understand the kind of hideous game that is played between the questioner and the questioned.

Writing and meditation kept [me] going. You can only survive in such a situation if you manage to abolish the physical and spiritual limitations of life in a cell. I did my best not to cling to my previous identity. I tried to forget everything that had been idyllic in the past, to become part of the new rhythm. What I did do was produce piles of manuscript.

André Chénier (1762–94) was a lyric poet who opposed the Terror of Robespierre during the French Revolution. Arrested in March 1794 and imprisoned until guillotined in July 1794, his last poem was written when he had accepted the imminence of his death.

One farewell burst of light

One farewell burst of light, or final rush of breeze,
Prolongs a sunny summer's day;
So is it that my lyre grants me a moment's grace
As I draw near my bloody end.
The clock on which I fix my eyes now strikes the hour;
Perhaps before the minute hand
Has made another round and stands once more at twelve
I'll know that I must surely die.
Perhaps before I end the verse which I now chant
I'll see within these prison walls
The messengers of death and hear them shout my name.
They'll find me walking up and down,
My mind in search of words more sharp and venomous.
They'll bind my arms behind my back

And rudely hush the rhyme that lingers on my lips,
While my companions all withdraw,
Afraid to show that I have been their passing friend.

Why care? I've lived too much — too much!
What signs of righteousness, what trace of constancy
Worthy of honest manliness,
What evidence of justice feared by criminals,
What benefits bestowed by fate,
What tears aroused by pity for man's misery,
What acts of friendly faithfulness —
Alas, what proof is there in all the universe
That I should hesitate to die?

The gods men serve are fear, pretence, and savage greed.
What cowards are we all — yes, all!
Adieu, O Earth! Come, Death, benign deliverer!
Oh, come, and take my hand in yours!

No, no! My heart is not yet crushed by weight of ills.
I must live on for Virtue's sake!
The honest man who has the mastery of words,
Though victim of conspiracy
And dweller in a prison cell, may raise his voice
And proudly speak for honesty.
If fate decreed that I should never fight with sword,
I have a stronger blade — my pen!
I still can strike hard blows for sinking humankind.
O Truth, O Justice, gods beloved,
If ever heedless deed of mine, or word, or thought
Has met your disapproving frown;
If ever criminal by scornful act, or stench
That rises from a rotten soul,
Has pierced your hearts and left them with tormenting
    wounds —
Save me, I pray, and give me strength.
I have an arm well skilled to hurl dread thunderbolts,
And I'm your lover, your revenge.
To die while still my quiver holds a dart? No, no!
I'll force into the foulest pits
The executioners of law, the bloated ghouls
Who gorge themselves on fallen France!
I hold a never-failing weapon — treasured pen!
By offal, bile, secretions, merde!

O Truth, O Justice, gods adored, as you give breath
Convert my words into a scourge!
I suffer, yet I live. Though you are far away,
You're not too far to transmit hope.

Thomas Cooper, a Chartist schoolteacher, was sentenced to two years imprisonment in 1843 for sedition, i.e. encouraging labourers to strike 'until the People's Charter became the law of the land'. In gaol he wrote an epic poem of 350 pages, 'The Purgatory of Suicide'. He later became a journalist and Methodist preacher.

A Chartist poet

I vowed that I would break down the system of restraint in Stafford Gaol, and win the privilege of reading and writing, or end my life in the struggle. And if I could not write the poem on which I believed my whole future on earth depended — it was not worth enduring two years' dismal and unrelieved imprisonment, to come out in rags and with a ruined constitution.

During the first two months I could not get at my books. As I could not recover them, and did not know whether they would ever yield or allow me the use of my books and papers, I thought I could defeat their purpose by composing the poem and retaining it in my mind. So my thoughts were very much intent on making a new beginning — and on the night of 10th June, 1843, when we had been one month in the gaol, I felt suddenly empowered to make a start; and when I had composed the four opening lines, I found they rhymed alternately. It was a pure accident — for I had always purposed to write my poem in blank verse. Now, however, I resolved to try the Spenserian stanza. So I struck off two stanzas that night: they are the two opening stanzas of my poem.

I heard the feet of several persons in the passage, and could tell that they were sweeping it. They drew near the door, and I heard a whispering. Soon one of them whispered through the large keyhole.

'Mester Cooper! dooan't yo knaw me? I cum thrum th' Potteries; an' I heerd yo speeak that day, upo' th' Craan Bonk. Dun yo want owt? We can get you owt yo like, throo th' debtors. There's a chink i' th' wall where we get things through.'

'Can you get me some sheets of writing paper, a few pens and a narrow bottle of ink? Can you get me a letter sent out to the post office?'

'Yes,' they said. 'We knaw them among th' debtors that'll see it sent safe to the post office.'

I drew up a petition to the House of Commons asking that I might be allowed to write what I pleased, for my own purposes, during my confinement.

When I obtained the use of writing materials, at the end of those two months of struggle, I very soon had a fair copy written of the, perhaps, thirty stanzas I had by that time composed. The creation of my 'Purgatory of Suicides' I have called my 'great business' in the gaol. And so it was — for it employed a great part of my thought, and absorbed some mental effort, of almost every day I spent in Stafford Gaol.

Czech playwright **Václav Havel** (1936–) was a co-founder of the human rights organization, Charter 77, and a member of VONS (Committee for the Defence of the Unjustly Persecuted). In 1979 he was gaoled for four and a half years for these activities, and his work banned. He was again imprisoned for four months in February 1989 for participating in a demonstration to commemorate the death of Czech martyr Jan Palach in 1969. Within a year, he had become president of Czechoslovakia.

Gaoled for the truth

For several years I was forced to live in an environment where every effort was made to break people, systematically to get them to inform on others and to act selfishly: in an atmosphere of fear and intrigue, of mindless discipline and arbitrary bullying, degradation and deliberate insult, being at the same time deprived of even the simplest positive emotional, sensual or spiritual experience, like let us say a pretty picture, a kind word, or a sincere handclasp. Again and again I became aware that prison was not intended merely to deprive a man of a few years of his life and make him suffer for that length of time: it was rather intended to mark him for life, destroy his personality, score his heart in such a way that it would never heal completely. Prison thus seems to me something like a futurological laboratory of totalitarianism.

I wasn't even allowed to have a notebook or paper, much less to make notes. I was once even punished when they found me in possession of some drafts of letters I had legally sent home. The one thing they did not — and could not — stop me doing was to write the officially permitted, naturally censored, letters to my wife. That was my legal right: one letter a week, four pages of standard writing paper, written in a legible hand and within the prescribed margins. There are some 165 of those letters lying here. Writing them was my greatest joy, it made some sense of my incarceration, and in them I tried — under circumstances so difficult that I can't adequately describe them to you — to develop wider themes, topics which I was often forced to think about in prison like the problem of man's identity and responsibility, of our horizons, and so on. This, too, they forbade for some time, many of my letters weren't allowed through since they were supposed to concern exclusively 'family matters' — but in the end they somehow came to accept it.

I am a writer, writing what I want to write and not what others might like me to, and if I get involved in any other way except by my writing, then it is only because I feel this to be my natural human and civic duty, as well as my duty as a writer. That is, my duty as a public figure on whom it is incumbent, just because he *is* known to the public, to express his views more loudly than those who are not so well known. Not because he is more clever or more important than anyone else but simply because he is, whether he likes it or not, in a different position and possessed of a different responsibility. Even though I naturally do have my own opinions on a variety of issues, I don't hold with any particular ideology, doctrine or, even less, any political party or faction. I serve no one — much less any superpower. If I serve anything, then only my own conscience. I am neither a Communist nor an anti-Communist, and if I criticise my government, then it is not because it happens to be a Communist government, but because it is bad. I am not on the side of any establishment, nor am I a professional campaigner *against* any establishment — I merely take the side of truth against lies, the side of sense against nonsense, the side of justice against injustice.

Nabil Janabi, an Iraqi poet (not a Kurd), was arrested in 1976 for reading a poem to an assembly of Kurds. He was tortured under interrogation, and sentenced to five years' imprisonment. Released in 1981, he refused to support the government in its war against Iran and was forced into exile. He now lives in London. This is the poem he read.

Those words I said

I discovered that the word is a woman who can

Move mountains from their places,
Water from the seas,
Governments from their seats
And repeat the writing of history round the world.

Some rulers find the word their enemy.
Some cut her hair,
Cut off her tongue
Force her to put on
Her veil to cover the truth.
Some of them want the word as
Slave and prostitute.
Want her to love them, not to share
Their rule but live with them
As slave and prostitute.
And if she does, they will be
Generous to her with gold, silver
And jewels.

Some rulers jail the word
In prisons for women.
They chain her feet, they shut her mouth,
Give her no cigarettes to smoke,
No paper to read,
No book, not even a piece of paper
To write her will on
And no pencil to write with.
But despite all the rulers, despite their power,
All the radar and missiles that cover the
Poem's sky,
The word will continue to fly
All over the world.
No power can ban it or stop it
From landing at any airport
For the word is a bird
That needs no entry visa
For freedom
For democracy.

Primo Levi (1919–87) was an Italian industrial chemist
transported to Auschwitz in 1944. His qualifications gained
him employment in the Chemical Kommando, a synthetic

rubber factory. This helped him to survive and to write in later years about his experiences.

Men, not things

If I had not lived the Auschwitz experience, I probably would never have written anything. I would not have had the motivation, the incentive, to write. I had been a mediocre student in Italian and had had bad grades in history. Physics and chemistry interested me most, and I had chosen a profession, that of chemist, which had nothing in common with the world of the written word. It was the experience of the Camp and the long journey home that forced me to write. I did not have to struggle with laziness, problems of style seemed ridiculous to me, and miraculously I found the time to write without taking even one hour away from my daily professional work. It seemed as if those books were all there, ready in my head, and I had only to let them come out and pour onto paper.

Now many years have passed. The two books, above all the first, have had many adventures and have interposed themselves, in a curious way, like an artificial memory, but also like a defensive barrier, between my very normal present and the dramatic past. I say this with some hesitation, because I would not want to pass for a cynic: when I remember the Camp today, I no longer feel any violent or dolorous emotions. On the contrary, onto my brief and tragic experience as a deportee has been overlaid that much longer and complex experience of writer-witness, and the sum total is clearly positive: in its totality, this past has made me richer and surer. A friend of mine, who was deported to the women's Camp of Ravensbrück, says that the camp was her university. I think I can say the same thing, that is, by living and then writing about and pondering those events, I have learned many things about man and about the world.

I must hasten to say, however, that this positive outcome was a kind of good fortune granted to very few. Of the Italian deportees, for example, only about 5 per cent returned, and many of these lost families, friends, property, health, equilibrium, youth. The fact that I survived and returned unharmed is due, in my opinion, chiefly to good luck. Pre-existing factors played only a small part: for instance, my training as a mountaineer and my profession of chemist, which won me some privileges in the last months of imprisonment. Perhaps I was helped too by my interest, which has never flagged, in the human spirit and by the will not only to survive (which was common to many) but to survive with the precise purpose of recounting the things we had witnessed and endured. And, finally, I was also helped by the determination, which I stubbornly preserved, to recognize always, even in the darkest days, in my companions and in myself, men, not things, and thus to avoid that total humiliation and demoralization which led so many to spiritual shipwreck.

A sculptor and member of the Pan-African Congress (PAC), **Pitika Ntuli** (1942–) was living in exile in Swaziland when he was arrested, held for a year and deported. He had established an art workshop for poets, musicians and artists. He now lives in London.

A sculptor survives

I had no recourse to books or visitors. You find yourself dredging up resources from your inner self. Things you knew when you were outside, as well as things you didn't understand, confront you at such a time. You scrape the bottom of your own soul, trying to find answers, and that keeps you occupied. Then you sit down and look at a brick and in your mind you try and carve that brick. At the same time you write poems in your head, poems you cannot commit to paper. To your surprise you discover how quite ordinary verses which you learned at school lubricate your mind and help preserve your sanity. When you're in prison, you are ostracised, cut off from society. When you're placed in solitary confinement, you are being imprisoned within a prison. It is yet another dimension. It was the thought of people in South Africa, my people, who are held in worse conditions than I was, that preserved my sanity. The moment you lose the urge to maintain your sanity, you dive down into despair. It takes you days to get out of the gloom. That's why it is so important that you should always, every moment, consciously struggle, not only to maintain your sanity, but also your temper, because in prison everything is unsettled. You are marked by a kind of permanent impermanence. They scourge you, they irritate you, they want you to lose your temper, to turn you into a caged animal. And if you allow them to do that, you lose your sanity. You have first got to survive mentally, then you will also survive physically.

One day they came to repair a broken window, using a masonite board. When they put that board down I became a thief in jail. I stole that board and hid it under the mattress, and when they left, they simply forgot it. Then I stole a pen from a prison officer and started drawing on the board. I kept my sanity for three weeks working on that thing until they discovered it. It was brown like the bricks, and I used to put it against the wall, where they didn't expect to find it. So that was one material that was available. When they discovered it, their first impulse was to admire the drawing, but then they got angry and threatened to arrest me — in solitary. So actually they couldn't do anything, except confiscate the drawing.

I also had bread, which I would compress and then make into sculptures before eating it. And soap — that I would carve with my finger or a ball-point tip. They knew that they carried some sort of message. They didn't know exactly what that message was, but they felt it was deadly.

I wrote about the human predicament, about the conditions under which we found ourselves behind those grim walls. When you write a piece of poetry, you try to find some order and some sanity. It is also an attempt to maintain contact with your people, as you have been completely removed from society. As you write, you aren't just writing for yourself, you see the people you are writing to, you are communicating with the people who are not there with you, those people you so strongly believe in. In other words, the poems I wrote were conversations, albeit one-sided ones, between me and my people.

Born in London in 1905, the composer **Sir Michael Tippett** was an instinctive pacifist, and in 1940 joined the Peace Pledge Union. In 1942 he was given a conditional registration for war service and was offered several posts concerned with music. He refused them on the grounds that he would be betraying other objectors. In 1943 he was sentenced to three months imprisonment. From Wormwood Scrubs he wrote to Evelyn Maude, a family friend. His First Symphony was first performed in 1945.

The spirit shines clear

It's all very dream-like, as, indeed, freedom often is to me. But here it's stronger. 'I', actually in prison, seems something so natural and yet so like a dream existence. That's enhanced, you see, by not feeling or being a criminal. And there are whole days of impatience — days also of boredom. Wonderful moments like the hundreds of men's voices singing the Old Hundredth — and that brings tears. One is also closer to the spirit here, by the act of cutting off. I've never felt it more strongly though I can't as yet go the violent ascetic way. But I have a sense of cleansing the grossness by means of which the spirit shines clearer through me — it may affect the music, I think, gradually. And

I think the symphony may gain by this enforced rest. I'm pretty certain of it itself, anyhow, and I think I shall pull it off. But I've decided to get the fourth movement done first.

By the time this gets [to] you the thing [prison] will be virtually over — and I have little wish to repeat it — but of course will do so if driven.

2. Defiance

Here I stand, I can do no other.
Martin Luther

Stand firm as an anvil when it is smitten.
St Ignatius

Stand firm, remain steadfast. It may be that obedience to God and loyalty to conscience will cost you or me our lives, our freedom or our home. But let us rather die than sin.
Bishop Graf von Galen *German World War II cleric*

The **Kurds** in Turkey have suffered cultural and political oppression since the 1920s, when they were forbidden to speak Kurdish. One of their number, aged 21, having been forced to move from his home in the eastern provinces, joined a campaigning group and took part in the struggle against the government's policies. He was arrested in the early 1980s when painting slogans in memory of a friend to protest against the regime.

'What is your last wish?'

It was about 1–2 o'clock in the morning. We were caught by the police. We were tortured for a long time after the arrest. As a result of the 'special attention' of the police chief in K., known as '*Baba*' (Father) we were kept for 33 days there. Our hands were tied at the back and we were blindfolded. We were given neither food nor water for 15 days. Had the soldiers, the democrat soldiers, not helped us, we would not have survived. As a result of the resistance we had shown, even some detainees from the right-wing group began to feel sympathy with us. Those detainees were offering us half of their bread rations. We had stood firm against the torture. We did not give each other away.

They applied incredibly hard torture to us. It was so hard that it was a miracle that we survived. They took us to Erolys, a famous mountain. They took our clothes off and buried us in the snow, which was about a man's height as it was winter time. They threatened us and said: 'We are going to execute you. Give us the names of your friends. Tell us about your operations.' As they were not able to get the information they needed, they set up the gallows tree. They put the rope around our neck and asked: 'What is your last wish?' Of course, our attitude was not the one they expected. So they hanged us. When I recovered I found myself in a dark place. I began to wonder whether I was in hell or in heaven. As I recovered a bit more, I discovered that I was in a cell. We were subjected to torture like this several times. Two months later, the trial began.

We were taken to X for the trial. We faced new oppressions there as well. It was a military prison. The military commanders told the soldiers that we were 'Communist traitors'. The soldiers tortured us during the whole period of detention. We were detained for four years. When I was released I was given a two-year sentence of internal exile to a place far away where I would have no friends or family and where

I would not be allowed to work. I have not gone into exile. I am in hiding here.

Born in London and educated at Oxford, **St Edmund Campion** (1540–81) could have continued his career there had he not refused to compromise with Anglicanism. He went abroad to the Catholic College at Douai, and became a Jesuit in 1573. In 1580 Campion became one of the first two Jesuits to return to England to revive Catholicism. After arrest, he was tortured, and became the proto-martyr of English Jesuits when he was hanged, drawn and quartered at Tyburn. At his trial (with seven other priests) he made a spirited speech to the court. He also spoke from the scaffold. He was canonized in 1970 by Pope Paul VI.

Posterity will judge

Lord Chief-Justice: Campion and the rest, what can you say why you should not die?

Campion: It was not our death that ever we feared. But we knew that we were not lords of our own lives, and therefore for want of answer would not be guilty of our own deaths. The only thing that we have now to say is, that if our religion do make us traitors, we are worthy to be condemned; but otherwise are and have been as true subjects as ever the Queen had. In condemning us you condemn all your own ancestors — all the ancient priests, bishops, and kings — all that was once the glory of England, the island of saints, and the most devoted child of the See of Peter. For what have we taught, however you may qualify it with the odious name of treason, that they did not uniformly teach? To be condemned with these old lights — not of England only, but of the world — by their degenerate descendants, is both gladness and glory to us. God lives; posterity will live: their judgment is not so liable to corruption as that of those who are now going to sentence us to death.

[On the scaffold] I am a Catholic man and a priest, in that faith have I lived, and in that faith I intend to die. If you esteem my religion treason, then I am guilty; as for any other treason, I never committed any, God is my judge.

But you have now what you desire.

Georgi Dimitrov (1882–1949) was born in Bulgaria and became a printer and active trade unionist. Imprisoned for anti-militarist activities in 1917, he fled to Germany on his release in 1919. An active communist, he was charged with complicity in the Reichstag fire of 1933. His defiant defence speech, excerpted below, exposed the political nature of the trial and resulted in his unexpected acquittal. He then went to the USSR and subsequently became secretary of the Comintern.

I defend my life

I have decided to defend myself. I want neither the honey nor the poison of a defence which is forced upon me. During the whole course of these proceedings I have defended myself.

I admit that my tone is hard and sharp. The struggle of my life has always been hard and sharp. My tone is frank and open. I seek to call things by their correct names. I am no lawyer appearing before this Court in the mere way of his profession. I am defending myself, an accused Communist; I am defending my political honour, my honour as a revolutionary; I am defending my Communist ideology, my ideals, the content and significance of my whole life. For these reasons every word which I say in this Court is a part of me, each phrase is the expression of my deep indignation against the unjust accusation, against the putting of this anti-Communist crime, the burning of the Reichstag, to the account of the Communists.

I can say with an easy conscience that everything which I have stated to this Court and everything which I have spoken to the public is the truth. I have always spoken with seriousness and from my inner convictions.

I must deny absolutely the suggestion that I have pursued propagandist aims. It may be that my defence before this Court has had a certain propagandist effect. It is also possible that my conduct before this Court may serve as an example for other accused Communists. But those were not the aims of my defence.

I know that no one in Bulgaria believes in our alleged complicity in the fire. I know that everywhere else abroad hardly anyone believes that we had anything to do with it. But in Germany other conditions prevail and in Germany it is not impossible that people might believe such extraordinary things. For this reason I desired to prove that the Communist Party had and has nothing whatever to do with the crime. If the question of propaganda is to be raised, then I may fairly say that many utterances made with this Court were of a propagandist character. The appearance here of Goebbels and Goering had an indirect propagandist effect favourable to Communism, but no one can reproach them on account of their conduct having produced such results.

I should like to point out that not only Communist, but also Social-Democratic and Christian workmen were arrested and their organisations suppressed. I would like to stress the fact that although this decree was directed chiefly against the Communist Party, it was not directed solely against them. This law which was necessary for the proclamation of the state of emergency was directed against all the other political parties and groups. It stands in direct organic connection with the Reichstag fire.

I should like to remind the Court of my application that Schleicher, Bruning, von Papen, Hugenberg and Duesterberg, the Vice-Chairman of the Stahlhelm organisation, should be summoned as witnesses.

President: The Court rejected the application and you have no right to refer to it again.

Dimitrov: I know that, and more, I know why!

The son of a Leicestershire weaver, **George Fox** (1624–91) left home at nineteen to journey round the country on a spiritual pilgrimage. Out of his preaching grew the Society of Friends, or Quakers, with the 'inner light' of God as their central theme. Fox was imprisoned eight times for refusing to conform to the social conventions of his time and for his religious activities. He also refused to bear arms, and in 1651 was in prison at Derby when the Commonwealth army was seeking recruits.

The meaning of virtue

My time being nearly out of being committed six months to the House of Correction, they filled the House of Correction with persons that they had taken up to be soldiers.

Then they would have had me to be captain of them to go forth to Worcester fight and the soldiers cried they would have none but me. So the keeper of the House of Correction was commanded to bring me up before the Commissioners and soldiers in the market place; and there they proffered me that preferment because of my virtue, as they said, with many other compliments, and asked me if I would not take up arms for the Commonwealth against the King. But I told them I lived in the virtue of that life and power that took away the occasion of all wars, and I knew from whence all wars did rise, from the lust according to James's doctrine. Still they courted me to accept of their offer and thought that I did but compliment with them. But I told them I was come into the covenant of peace which was before wars and strifes were. And they said they offered it in love and kindness to me because of my virtue, and such like flattering words they used, and I told them if that were their love and kindness I trampled it under my feet. Then their rage got up and they said, 'Take him away gaoler, and cast him into the dungeon amongst the rogues and felons'; which they then did and put me into the dungeon amongst thirty felons in a lousy, stinking low place in the ground without any bed. Here they kept me a close prisoner, almost a half year, unless it were at times; and sometimes they would let me walk in the garden, for they had a belief of me that I would not go away.

So Worcester fight came on, and Justice Bennet sent the constables to press me for a soldier, seeing I would not accept of a command. I told them I was brought off from outward wars. They came down again to give me press-money but I would take none. Then I was brought up to Sergeant Hole's, kept there awhile, and then taken down again. After a while at night the constables fetched me up again and brought me before the Commissioners, and they said I should go for a soldier, but I told them that I was dead to it. They said I was alive. I told them, 'Where envy and hatred are there is confusion.' They offered me money twice, but I would not take it. Then they were wroth, and I was committed close prisoner.

Now when they had gotten me into Derby dungeon, it was the belief and saying of people that I should never come out: but I had faith in God, and believed I should be delivered in his time; for the Lord had said to me before, that I was not to be removed from that place yet, being set there for a service which he had for me to do.

Petr Grigorenko (1907–87) was a Soviet general, twice wounded and much decorated, who was imprisoned in 1964 for one year, for 'anti-government' propaganda. In 1969 he criticized the Soviet government's failure to return Crimean Tartars to the Crimea after World War II. For this he was arrested, stripped of his rank, and committed to a psycho-prison. He was released in 1974, and emigrated to the USA. He later described the interviews which led to his being 'diagnosed' as suffering from a 'mental illness'.

A general in a psycho-prison

'As long as our country is not provided with a reliable shield against tyranny, it is the duty of every honest man to participate in creating this shield, whatever the threats to him.

'Of course, if it is only those who bow before any arbitrary act of the bureaucracy who are considered normal Soviet people, then I am abnormal. I am not capable of such submissiveness no matter how much I am beaten.

'I have said before and will say again: in 1963 and 1964 I made mistakes, but there was no need for psychiatrists to correct them. I had begun to realise these mistakes before my arrest. I had a great deal of free time in prison, and after I had thoroughly analysed the course taken in the past and read the whole of Lenin once again, I saw what flagrant errors I had made. But these errors on my part were not proof of an unsound mind. It is precisely the normal people who make the most mistakes. This is especially so if they are active, bold and inquiring. I also see mistakes in my activities of the last few years, but again they cannot be corrected by psychiatrists.'

'What are your present mistakes?'

'I do not think that is an appropriate subject for today's discussion. For a practical analysis of recent mistakes, a person who shares my views is needed. I do not think we share the same views. Moreover, I cannot speak about this as if I were making a confession. If I were remorseful about something I would not recant when under the axe. It is unworthy of a man to recant when he is threatened by punishment and death.'

'Treatment could save you from being brought to trial.'

'There is nothing for me to be treated for, and I have no intention of feigning illness in order to be spared responsibility. I am prepared to answer fully for my actions.'

'But if they convict you, you will lose your pension.'

'There is a good Russian proverb: "If they cut off your head, you don't cry over your hair". Whether I am convicted or put in a prison called a special psychiatric hospital, I have still lost my freedom. And a pension cannot take the place of freedom.'

A Christian member of the freedom movement in Kenya, **Josiah Kariuki** (1929–75) was detained by the colonial government from 1953 to 1960. Under detention, he constantly wrote letters of complaint to the British Government and to opposition MPs, smuggling them out of the camps. After Kenya's independence in 1963, he became an MP and was an outspoken dissident. He was assassinated in 1975.

Stop writing letters!

Next morning Marlow took me outside 'C' Camp to a place near the Forest and said that he would shoot me unless I wrote down on a piece of paper that I would not send any more letters to England, that I would co-operate with the Government and that I would help to type in the office. Although the thought of death was still not wholly desirable, I refused. He then took from his car a piece of three-ply wood about three feet by two feet and told me to hold it up above my head at arm's length. He walked five yards away and said that he was going to kill me if I did not agree to write the sentences. Still, not imagining he could be serious, I refused. To my horror he raised his gun and shot at me. I remember a tremendous noise and knowing that I was now dead and then nothing. He had, in fact, shot through the wood and I had fallen down with it. Out of the void I then heard the words *'Simama, simama'* (Swahili for 'Get up') and by a notable piece of deduction in the circumstances I decided that this was unlikely to be the language of heaven or hell and that I was therefore probably alive. As if hypnotized I stood up and faced him and we went through the rigmarole all over again. I refused and he shot again; again I fell into the abyss and knew emptiness and smelt death. Then distantly I heard *'Amka, amka'* (Swahili for 'Wake up, wake up') and for the second time I rose from the dead. My body was now running with sweat and my mind was no longer able to grasp whereabouts we were or what was happening. 'For the third and last time,' he said, 'will you agree to write those sentences?' It was like a scene out of a film and without really knowing what I was being asked I repeated my 'No.' He fired again and this time I felt something sear through the base of the thumb on my right hand. Absolutely certain that I had at least been seriously wounded and was about to die I fell down again. When I saw the blood, which stained all my sweat so that wherever I felt was blood and still more blood, I rushed at him and clasped him round the waist and said, 'Look at this blood, you have killed me, there is blood all over me.' Marlow laughed and said, 'You are very bad hard-core.' He then returned me to the camp and put me in solitary confinement in the small cell. I think now he probably did not mean to kill me, it was merely done to frighten me which it certainly succeeded in doing.

On 1 June I was taken by car from the cell to Compound 13 by Marlow and the Camp Commandant. The detainees had been formed up in a semicircle and those in other compounds were also watching: the crowd was about six thousand. They told me to remove a bench from the car and carry it out into the middle of the detainees. The detainees were all told to stand and the other officers and warders came in to watch. Quite an audience for the performance. The Commandant then shouted in Swahili, 'Here is your leader. He wants to show you he is God. You follow him because he writes letters to the Colonial Office. Do not follow him any more. If you do you will get into the same trouble as he is in today. Mwangi, take off your clothes and lie down on the bench.' I was then given twelve strokes by a Jaluo sergeant-major. He certainly knew how to cane and these were very hard ones. The Commandant then asked me if I would stop writing letters. I replied that I would no longer send out letters when I was convinced that the just complaints of the detainees had been answered. If beatings continued so would my letters. I would never co-operate with the Government or help the Special Branch.

South Korea's most famous poet, **Kim Chi Ha** (1941–) has been a critic of government repression from his student days. He was first arrested in 1964, and has been imprisoned, tortured and held in solitary confinement on several occasions. Following his re-arrest in 1975 he was sentenced to death, but released in 1980. 'From the Darkness' refers to his time in prison in Seoul in 1974.

From the darkness

From the darkness yonder
Someone is calling me
A pair of glaring eyes lurking in the darkness
The blood-red darkness
Of rusty prison bars.
Silence beckons me
And clogged, halting breath.

On a rainy day of grey lowering clouds
Faltering through the calls

Of pigeons cooing in the eaves
It keeps calling and calling me
A tattered blood-stained shirt
Hanging from the window sill
That red soul which thrashed through endless cellar-nights
The congealed cry of a body racked and torn
Beckoning me
Beckoning me.
The silence yonder is calling me
Calling on my blood
To refuse
To refuse all lies.

From the darkness yonder
On a rainy day of grey lowering clouds
From that darkness of blood-red bodies
A pair of glaring eyes.

Sylvia Pankhurst (1882–1958), together with her mother and two sisters, was a leader of the movement for women's suffrage. In the years before World War I, the government tried to discourage acts of civil disobedience by jailing members of the movement. The women responded with hunger strikes to gain public sympathy. The government took to forcible feeding of prisoners. Agitation ceased during the war, and women over 30 years received the vote in 1918. Ten years later full franchise rights were granted to all women over 21.

Forcible feeding

On the third day the two doctors sounded my heart and felt my pulse. The senior told me he had no alternative but to feed me by force. Then they left the cell.

Presently I heard footsteps approaching, collecting outside my cell. I was strangled with fear, cold and stunned, yet alert to every sound. The door opened — not the doctors, but a crowd of wardresses filled the doorway. I struggled, but was overcome. There were six of them, all much bigger and stronger than I. They flung me on my back on the bed, and held me down firmly by shoulders and wrists, hips, knees and ankles. Then the doctors came stealing in. Someone seized me by the head and thrust a sheet under my chin. My eyes were shut. I set my teeth and tightened my lips over them with all my strength. A man's hands were trying to force open my mouth; my breath was coming so fast that I felt as though I should suffocate. His fingers were striving to pull my lips apart — getting inside. I felt them and a steel instrument pressing round my gums, feeling for gaps in my teeth. I was trying to jerk my head away, trying to wrench it free. Two of them were holding it, two of them dragging at my mouth. I was panting and heaving, my breath quicker and quicker, coming now with a low scream which was growing louder. 'Here is a gap,' one of them said. 'No, here is a better one. This long gap here!' A steel instrument pressed my gums, cutting into the flesh. I braced myself to resist that terrible pain. 'No, that won't do' — that voice again. 'Give me the pointed one!' A stab of sharp, intolerable agony. I wrenched my head free. Again they grasped me. Again the struggle. Again the steel cutting its way in, though I strained my force against it. Then something gradually forced my jaws apart as a screw was turned; the pain was like having the teeth drawn. They were trying to get the tube down my throat, I was struggling madly to stiffen my muscles and close my throat. They got it down, I suppose, though I was unconscious of anything save a mad revolt of struggling, for they said at last: 'That's all!' and I vomited as the tube came up. They left me on the bed exhausted, gasping for breath and sobbing convulsively.

Day after day, morning and evening, the same struggle. Sometimes the tube was coughed up three or four times before they finally got it down. Sometimes, but not often — I was generally too much agitated by then — I felt the tube go right down into the stomach; a sickening, terrifying sensation, especially when it reached the breast. My shoulders were bruised, my back ached during the night. I scarcely slept. Often I fainted once or twice after the feeding.

Infinitely worse than the pain was the sense of degradation; the very fight that one made against the outrage was shattering one's nerves and one's self-control. Daily there grew on me more strongly the realization that the other human beings who were torturing me came to the task with loathing and pity and would have refrained from it if they could.

From the moment my door was thrown open at six in the morning I could not cease to think of the doctors' coming, and after I was dressed I could not sit or stand for a moment, but would pace up and down trembling and shivering, with heart beating fast. Often I vomited during the struggle and while the tube was being withdrawn, but at other times I could not. At last I discovered that by thrusting my hand down my throat I could make myself sick. Now, as soon as I could pull myself together after each feeding, I struggled till I had brought up what had been forced into me, choking and straining, the cords of my streaming eyes feeling as though they would snap.

When, with ruthless self-torture, I had brought about the sickness and dragged myself up from it, I sat leaning upon the table, abandoned to tears of despair; my voice, high-pitched and strange, cried out, growing louder and louder, till it filled the place with sound, that it was a scandal four of us should be serving five months in all for one little £3 window; and all because a handful of men stood against us, like a solid wall in their sullen, cruel obstinacy, and would not give way.

St Polycarp (69–155 AD), Bishop of Smyrna from 96 AD, was arrested during the persecution of Christians under Roman Emperor Marcus Aurelius. He could have saved himself by offering a sacrifice to Caesar, but he refused to abjure his faith, and was handed over to the pro-consul for trial. Polycarp remained adamant, and was burned alive.

Do what you will

When he was brought forward the Pro-Consul asked him if he were Polycarp and, when he admitted it, he tried to persuade him to deny, saying: 'Respect your age,' and so forth as they are accustomed to say: 'Swear by the genius of Caesar, repent, say: "Away with the Atheists"'; but Polycarp, with a stern countenance looked on all the crowd of lawless heathen in the arena, and waving his hand at them, he groaned and looked up to heaven and said: 'Away with the Atheists.' But when the Pro-Consul pressed him and said: 'Take the oath and I let you go, revile Christ,' Polycarp said: 'For eighty and six years have I been his servant, and he has done me no wrong, and how can I blaspheme my King who saved me?'

But when he persisted again, and said: 'Swear by the genius of Caesar,' he answered him: 'If you vainly suppose that I will swear by the genius of Caesar, as you say, and pretend that you are ignorant who I am, listen plainly: I am a Christian. And if you wish to learn the doctrine of Christianity fix a day and listen.'

The Pro-Consul said: 'I have wild beasts, I will deliver you to them, unless you repent.' And he said: 'Call for them, for repentance from better to worse is not allowed us; but it is good to change from evil to righteousness.' And he said again to him: 'I will cause you to be consumed by fire, if you despise the beasts, unless you repent.' But Polycarp said: 'You threaten with the fire that burns for a time, and is quickly quenched, for you do not know the fire which awaits the wicked in the judgment to come and in everlasting punishment. But why are you waiting? Come, do what you will.'

Zigan Sha'at (1973–) is a Palestinian youth who lives in the Rafah refugee camp. He was arrested by the Israeli secret police in January 1988 at the age of 14, and spent three days under interrogation, blindfolded and handcuffed. He told his story to Palestinian human rights workers, who stated that parts of his story are confused as he lost all sense of time during interrogation, could not see what was being done to him and was exhausted from lack of sleep and food.

Child interrogation

I was taken to a place near the school. They beat me on my legs and shoulders with sticks and gun butts. Then they put me on a bus. I was on the bus for about four hours, and all the time they beat me, sometimes stopping the bus, and threatened to kill me if I didn't confess. It was very cold. Then they put the handcuffs back on and a bag over my head and took me to be interrogated. There were eight of us and it was in the middle of the night. They brought dogs and the detectives also pretended to be dogs as they beat us. We had to stay standing up.

At last my number, 2040, was called and I was taken into a separate room for interrogation. They told me that I was the son of a dog, the son of a prostitute, a maniac and many other bad things. They told me that I was a leader for the boys in the camp, that I showed them how to throw stones and burn tyres. They said that they had a picture of me doing these things. I asked to see it, but they wouldn't let me. They told me, 'Do you remember how we gassed your mother when she tried to protect you? If you don't confess, we will return to your house and punish your whole family.' I didn't confess.

They took me outside again and ordered a soldier to beat me while they interrogated somebody else. A half or one hour later they took me back into the room and said the same things to me again. This went on for three days: we were forced to stand on the beach, where it was freezing cold. We had to sleep standing up and if we asked to sit down to sleep we were beaten. I couldn't eat, but I did drink a little. Sometimes they took one or two of us to beat us and then two or three times a day we went to be interrogated separately. For these three days

I had the sack over my head. We were always talking to each other, quoting verses we could remember from the Quran.

The questions in the interrogation were always the same, but they used different ways to try and make me confess. Once they strangled me until I nearly died. Each session lasted between half and one hour, and there were usually two secret policemen. They always beat me, usually on my stomach and thighs. Twice they put something on my genitals which made my whole body shake. I was always handcuffed. When we were outside it was the army who beat us. They also poured icy water down our backs every hour or two.

The secret police also threatened me verbally. They said that they would make me have sex with a soldier and photograph it. They asked me to be a spy for them, and said that they would give me a car, money and allow me to travel abroad to study.

I wanted to die. Once I could not stop crying in the interrogation, and they sprayed gas on me until I fainted. I think that I was out for about three hours, and when I got up I felt very dizzy and sick. They told me that if I did not confess they would never allow my brother in Saudi Arabia to come back to Gaza. One of the detectives pretended to be tortured and said that he'd confess, to encourage me to confess, but I didn't. They said that other people had confessed against me, even my brother, and that they have his photograph. They said that if I did confess I would get three or four months in prison, rather than two or three years. I never confessed. I have been back to prison twice since then, but never to interrogation. They thought that because I was young I would talk more easily, but now they know that that is not true.

The Nigerian writer **Wole Soyinka** (1934–) was arrested in 1967 for criticizing the government over the outbreak of civil war. He was imprisoned for 27 months, part of it in solitary confinement. He is now Professor of Literature at Ife University, and holds a Nobel Prize for Literature. The passage below is excerpted from the novel *The Man Died* which deals with Soyinka's period of detention.

A lving death

I summon history to my aid, but more than history, kindred knowledge, kindred findings, kindred rebellions against the lure of tragi-existentialism; for rage is no longer enough to combat the temptations to subside into unproductive, will-sapping wisdoms. I seek only the combative voices and I hunt them down from remotest antiquity to the latest incidental re-encounters on casual forums.

From this pit of anguish, dug by human hands, from this cauldron stoked by human hands, from this deafening clamour of human hate the being that emerges is literally an 'anjonnu' (worshipper of evil spirits). He will return neither understanding nor tolerating as before. He will no longer weigh or measure in mundane terms. Reality for him is for ever tinged in the flames of a terrible passage, his thoughts can no longer be contained by experiences. You, outside of these walls, whose hysteria I confess penetrates my proud defences, I know you sense this menace of a future revenge and must in self-defence redouble your efforts of annihilation — spiritual, psychic, physical and symbolic. And this is why I must dig into my being and understand why at this moment you have the power to affect me. Why, even when I have rationally rejected the tragic snare, I am still overcome by depressive fumes in my capsule of individualist totality.

Said Hermias of Aternias, with his body broken and in a breath that barely held, 'Tell my friends and companions that I have done nothing unworthy of philosophy.' That longing in all human beings that will sooner expend last breath on words of affirmation than conserve it on behalf of life, believing that life is justified if only at the moment of quitting it, the remnant spittle of a parched tongue is launched against the enemy in one defiant gesture of contempt, supplying a final action of hope, of encouragement for the living, validating one's entire being in that last gesture or in a word of affirmation. Overcoming pain, physical degradation and even defeat of ideals to sum up, to send a reprise of faith to the comrades one leaves behind, and make even dying a triumph, an ultimate affirmation.

A young Peking electrician, **Xu Wenli** (1945–), was arrested in 1981 for publishing unsanctioned periodicals, duplicated in his apartment. For a year he was subjected to interrogation in the Chinese style of verbal attack in order to induce a confession. He was, in fact, asked to confess his guilt by the man who was to be his judge at his trial. He did not do so, and was sentenced to 15 years' imprisonment. His account of these events was smuggled out in 1985, one section showing how he questioned the court's authority.

Speaking out

The Court session opened on the morning of 8th June 1982. At the beginning of the proceedings, the presiding judge asked me: 'Do you wish to request the withdrawal of any personnel making up this court?' (No doubt he was thinking to himself that there was no way I would reply 'Yes'.)

'Yes!' I replied affirmatively; Ding was astounded. Taking advantage of his confusion, I hurriedly went on to ask: 'I would ask of the judge whether or not he has called me on several occasions for discussions prior to the opening of this court session.'

'We met for discussions on those occasions, yes,' he replied.

Without letting him go further, I hurriedly went on to enquire: 'And did Your Honour say on each occasion, that I should acknowledge my guilt, in order to secure more lenient treatment?'

'That is so,' he replied, his face relaxing slightly. (No doubt he was thinking: in effect, this man seems to be enumerating my merits, for the leadership and the crowd to hear, but why?)

Feeling that I could no longer continue with this explanation of my legal foundation, but must avail myself of his relaxed frame of mind in order to release my 'bullet' at him, I declared in slow, measured tones: 'For this reason, I request that Your Honour withdraw!'

I fixed him with both eyes, his face instantly turned as white as a sheet, and he directed his stupefied gaze towards the 'string-pullers' sitting in the first row behind me on my right; henceforth, the nervous gaze of this 'puppet judge' never left that direction.

Having evidently received some kind of sign, he announced in a flurry: 'Court adjourned' . . .

Some people may say: 'This is all obvious, everyone knows about it, but there's no point in actually saying it.' No, there is a point. Even though everyone knows about it themselves, there is a world of difference between actually saying it, and not saying it. By saying it, one ensures that those responsible for enforcing the law will find it harder to carry out unlawful acts, and that if they do, it will not be so easy for them to avoid being exposed by others. The law has always been a two-edged blade, and not simply a means of keeping the common folk in line. There is a generation of new people, well-read and conversant with the law, who will no longer be pushed around at will . . .

The court adjourned for about ten minutes, and then reconvened. Naturally, I was overruled.

3. Endurance

In spite of age, insanity, despair,
Grief, or declining powers, we have done
What passes to the living of all men
Beyond our weariness.
William Tyndale

The Man dies in all who keep silent in the
face of tyranny.
Wole Soyinka

To have a quick word with the bee
in its buzzing flight
to tell the ant to hurry
with the bread
for his lady wife
to contemplate the spider
admire the beauty
of its amazing feet
and beg it
to climb more slowly up its web
all these are ways
of resisting.
Unknown Uruguayan prisoner

A Bashkir poet, **Nizametdin Akhmetov** (1947–) was originally sentenced in 1966 on a trumped-up charge of misappropriating state property; his real offence was his association with nationalistically-inspired youth protest movements. From that time he has received repeated further sentences to prison and labour-camps because of his continued protests against the Soviet system. In 1983 he was transferred to a special psychiatric hospital and released in 1987.

A human being

I am afraid to write to you, my friend. I fear that you may read my letter like a letter from a madhouse (from where else, you will shrug). But I have no one I could write to, whom I could ask for what is ultimately most deeply human. But I fear even more that they will use the extra strong drugs on me, turning me into an idiot, who will not see even his end with a sane mind. So listen to the friend.

Circumstances force me to write to you in a way I have never written to anyone. That is a letter, not a last will, a necessary explanation and not a posthumous note — keep that in mind and don't panic.

I am in a very bad way. Never have I suffered so much, never was my situation so hopeless. I have dropped out of society, from the scope of its laws, I am absolutely without rights, depersonalised, even dehumanised. Can you understand the situation, that of a 'socially dangerous mentally-ill person' in our country — and all the more my situation, that of an 'especially dangerous state criminal' and of an 'especially dangerous recidivist'? There is only one way to escape all these torments (except torments of conscience), only one way of crawling out of here — that is to betray oneself and leave, but no longer as Nizametdin Akhmetov. This is a way prohibited for me, but that means that they will grind Nizametdin Akhmetov to nothingness on the millstone of 'state security'. Of course, I am not ill. Yet I am in an institution with the means of making me a patient. That is no exaggeration: psychiatry has now reached the limit reached by physics when it split the uranium nucleus. It is not just this one man with the white coat over his MVO [Secret Police] uniform who is against me — behind his back is the entire state. There is no doubt I am being ground to pieces. It is horrible — an unbearable different torment, this so-called treatment. The 'medicines' they feed and prick me with would be bought with pleasure by Satan for his hell, the medieval inquisitors would have given a lot for them. Such suffering I have never known. And I am afraid of not bearing up; my will-power is not unlimited. But how should I live after that — despising myself?

I know that they talk about me as of a person who slanders his country. This is not so. I love my homeland, because I love my mother, my house, my country, my people. They try to interpret my conflict with the 'powers that be' as a conflict with my mother country. But these are not synonymous. One's mother country remains one's mother country, regardless of the type of government, and the real patriot is often persecuted and dishonoured. I am more Russian than many Russians. However, as far as nationality is concerned, I think in a different language. I am for the genuine and free equality of nations and peoples.

If I am in any way guilty before my mother country then I want to be judged by it to the highest degree (and by my conscience). But who is my judge now? What kind of great patriotic act is performed by their keeping me in jail since I was 18 and tormenting me, tormenting me every hour! I have nothing further to say to my mother country than 'Let me stay as I am to the very end'.

The last thing that can happen to a person may happen to me. In any case, whether I die or whether they drive me mad — that will be the end, the end of a human being. Even if that does not happen in a human way, as with human beings, it will happen to a human being — I wanted to stress that. And I would like to be spoken of, and to be remembered, as a human being.

This poem was written by an **unknown prisoner** in Libertad Prison, Montevideo, Uruguay, an institution built in the 1970s to house political prisoners. It used a harsh programme of physical deprivation and psychological harassment to break the resistance of recalcitrant political prisoners. Prisoners were only allowed to refer to each other by numbers, smiling and laughter were forbidden, and rules changed arbitrarily to create disorientation. The poem was written on cigarette paper.

Hay dias en que me pasa esto

Some days this is what happens to me
I look for the word
and can't find it
there must be one

for sure
the Spanish language
they say
is so rich
scrupulously I go over
the length of my cell
there are fourteen tiles
but it's not there
I can't see it
I've got the concept clear
for what I want to say
what I want to say to you
I look under the blanket
just in case
the bastard's gone and hidden itself
but it's not there
it's no use
I can't find the word
And I'd like to say
to say to you
that I know
that we know we're prisoners
we've been arrested
there's no question it's tough
not to walk along avenues
streets
back streets
that we miss
the kick of each day
and how we miss
I mean how we long to hear
the laughter of a kid
a child
a youngster playing in the street
do you know anything more catching
more healthy
more convincing
than the laughter of a child?
We know all that
which before
perhaps
we didn't value so highly
and yet
If I could find the word

if I could unearth it
I'm sure
you would be pleased

Help look for it
compañeros.

An Austrian, **Bruno Bettelheim** (1903–90) spent nearly two years in the Dachau and Buchenwald concentration camps following the Nazi occupation of Austria in 1938. He then went to the USA where he became a renowned academic and recognized expert in the treatment of child psychosis.

The last human freedom

Even those prisoners who somehow managed to remain in control of some small aspect of their lives, eventually had to come to longer range terms with their new environment. The mere fact of survival meant that in the matter of Caesar's dues, it was no longer a question of whether to render them or not, nor even, with rare exceptions, of how much to render. But to survive as a man not a walking corpse, as a debased and degraded but still human being, one had first and foremost to remain informed and aware of what made up one's personal point of no return, the point beyond which one would never, under any circumstances, give in to the oppressor, even if it meant risking and losing one's life. It meant being aware that if one survived at the price of overreaching this point one would be holding on to a life that had lost all its meaning. It would mean surviving — not with a lowered self respect, but without any.

This point of no return was different from person to person, and changed for each person as time passed. At the beginning of their imprisonment, most inmates would have felt it beyond their point of no return to serve the SS as foreman or block chief, or to like wearing a uniform that made them look like the SS. Later, after years in the camp, such relatively external matters gave way to much more essential convictions which then became the core of their resistance. But those convictions one had to hold on to with utter tenacity. About them, one had to keep oneself informed at all times, because only then could they serve as the mainstay of a radically reduced but still present humanity. Much of the tenacity and relentlessness of political prisoners in their factional warfare is thus explainable; for them, political loyalty to party was their point of no return.

Second in importance was keeping oneself informed of how one felt about complying when the ultimate decision as to where to stand firm was not called into question. While less radical, it was no less essential, because an awareness of one's attitude toward compliance was called for almost constantly. One had to comply with debasing and amoral commands if one wished to survive; but one had to remain cognizant that one's reason for complying was 'to remain alive and unchanged as a person.' Therefore, one had to decide, for any given action, whether it was truly necessary for one's safety or that of others, and whether committing it was good, neutral or bad. This keeping informed and aware of one's actions — though it could not alter the required act, save in extremities — this minimal distance from one's own behavior, and the freedom to feel differently about it depending on its character, this too was what permitted the prisoner to remain a human being. It was the giving up of all feelings, all inner reservations about one's actions, the letting go of a point at which one would hold fast no matter what, that changed [the] prisoner.

Those prisoners who blocked out neither heart nor reason, neither feelings nor perception, but kept informed of their inner attitudes even when they could hardly ever afford to act on them, those prisoners survived and came to understand the conditions they lived under. They also came to realize what they had not perceived before; that they still retained the last, if not the greatest, of the human freedoms: to choose their own attitude in any given circumstance. Prisoners who understood this fully, came to know that this, and only this, formed the crucial difference between retaining one's humanity (and often life itself) and accepting death as a human being (or perhaps physical death).

A medical doctor, **Edith Bone** (1889–1975) was born in Hungary but became a British subject in the 1930s when she was living in England. She returned to Hungary after World War II and was arrested by the communist government in 1949 and falsely accused of being an English spy. She was sentenced to 15 years imprisonment, but was released during the 1956 uprising. For the entire seven years of her incarceration, she was held in solitary confinement and for five months in total darkness. She was not given her spectacles, books or a newspaper for three years.

Breadcrumbs and a spy-hole

I was deprived of books and writing materials. But I had continued to make up doggerels, which I repeated carefully three times a day, so as not to forget them. They were growing so numerous, however, that repeating them daily began to take up too much time.

It was the bread that again helped me. By this time, being an accomplished breadcrumb technologist, I decided to make myself a printing set out of bread. It must be admitted that, however little I thought of the quality of my verses, I did feel I should like to see them with my bodily eyes and not only carry them in my memory.

I began to shape letters out of long very thin rolls of breadcrumb specially processed for the purpose. When a letter was formed I gave it a little bang with my fist so that it was flattened and all the joints pressed together.

The hardest part was to make letters of the same size. This was difficult because, of course, I could not make them all at the same time; I had to wait until no one was about.

In the end I had four thousand letters and a compositor's case with twenty-six separate little pigeon-holes, and could lay out on my table not less than sixteen lines of verse, doggerel or poetry, at a time. This was great fun.

One of the things the staff made every effort to enforce was preventing me from knowing what was going on outside my cell. Why this should have been so is still a mystery to me, but they were certainly very much concerned about it. The natural result was that although I was only very mildly interested in what was going on outside my cell, I made up my mind to beat them at this game if possible. One of the main amusements in prison is to make fools of the screws.

I decided I would try to contrive a spy-hole in my door through which I could look out, just as they could look in through the regulation spy-hole which is a feature of every prison door. The door was made of two-inch solid oak, but of course its surface was not flush. It was built up of several beams and there were points where three of these joined; obviously these joints were weak spots, which could be attacked.

I had noticed long before that a nail, or rather the large head of a nail, projected from the door close to the floor. It stood to reason that it must be a large nail. I decided that the first thing to do was to pull it out and see whether it could be made into a bradawl. It only projected about an eighth of an inch, but that was enough to get a purchase on it with a cord, and then pull. This is not, of course, the most efficient way of pulling out nails, but I had no other. From this a second problem arose; I needed a cord, a strong cord. Where could I get one? The jailers were sensitive about the smallest piece of string, presumably because of their inexplicable, unreasonable and inconsistent fear of suicides among the prisoners.

I decided that the best possible cord could be made of threads pulled out of the coarse linen towels which we were given. These linen threads were thick and strong. Of course, I could not tear strips from my towel — that would have been noticed and my cell would have been searched and my precious cord discovered. But the towel had some lengthwise red stripes in it, two on each side, and I decided to draw threads on each side of these red stripes, since the absence of thread would be much less noticeable there. This I did, with precautions; and it was not at all easy, because the guard looked in every now and then through the spy-hole, and one never knew when he was peeping in. One had to be very careful not to be caught in the act of pulling threads out of the towel. These were only changed once a fortnight and so it took me about two months to get the required thirty-two threads from which to plait my cord.

Fortunately for myself, I had always been a fanatical lover of knots, and possessed that most remarkable publication, *The Ashley Book of Knots*, which I had studied assiduously and which, in addition to knots, also contained a number of sinnets. I plaited a beautiful sinnet — a round one, the sort known as coach-whipping — out of thirty-two threads in groups of eight.

This cord was strong enough to carry even my own weight, so there was no fear of its breaking. I put a strangler knot (this, too, out of the Ashley book) round the nail head, and, with my foot against the door, pulled for all I was worth; but the nail still resisted all my efforts. I realized that mere pulling was not enough. The nail would have to be loosened by joggling it up and down and right and left. For a long time I seemed to be making no headway, but I persevered until I felt a slight wobble. I loosened and pulled day after day, for many weeks, whenever I could be sure that none of the guards was loitering near my door, and in the end I got that nail out. This was triumph.

The nail was about an eighth of an inch thick and three inches long. I put an edge on the end of it instead of the existing point by the simple expedient of rubbing it on the concrete floor, which was exactly like a carborundum whetstone, especially noticeable in its effects on the soles of one's shoes or boots. The result was a bradawl. With it I succeeded in boring a hole in my door at a point where three members of solid oak met. It was only a pinhole, of course, and it had to be very carefully concealed. It would not have done, for instance, for any wood-dust to have fallen outside, so I used my mouth as a pump and sucked out the little splinters of wood as my bradawl removed them.

By a dispensation of providence, the oak had been so blackened by age that it was exactly the colour of my black convict bread. Thus, the little hole could be stopped up by a tiny plug which matched the wood so perfectly that my spy-hole was never discovered. The plug was a necessity, as otherwise my little pin-point spy-hole would have showed up like a bright star whenever there was a light in the cell and none outside. I never took out the plug without taking care to block the light.

Until I was transferred to another prison I had the constant use of this spy-hole and it gave me more information on the routine of the prison than my jailers intended.

Fenner Brockway (1888–1988) was a leader of the No Conscription Fellowship in World War I, and spent three years in prison or army detention cells. Released in 1919, he became a prominent Labour Party activist and worker for peace organizations. He was made a life peer in 1964.

The sun on the wall

We COs had the same treatment as all other hard labour prisoners (that is, the harshest treatment meted out in English prisons), but we had the strengthening sense of comradeship and of standing out for our convictions. Yet even for most of us imprisonment sometimes became unbearable. We were locked in our cells for eighteen out of twenty-four hours each day. We could not speak to each other without the risk of bread and water punishment. We received and wrote one censored letter a month and had one half-hour visit, always in the presence of a warder. We were treated like caged animals, without minds or personality, and were starved of all beauty. The strain of this month after month was disastrous to self-control, and the long hours of solitary confinement drove one to the verge of mental and nervous breakdown, which could be conquered only by a great effort of discipline.

At eleven o'clock on November 11 German acceptance or rejection of British terms would be made known. This must have happened while I was still on punishment diet, because I remember sitting on the shelf-table in the denuded cell, my feet on the stool, watching the sun creep along the wall towards eleven o'clock. I cannot reproduce the chaos and intensity of my thoughts.

Was the slaughter of four years to end? Was all the anxiety to be over? Was our long imprisonment to end? Was I to see my family and children? Was this strain of solitary confinement and punishment diet to pass? Was I to see the fields and woods and hills and sea?

The line of the sun on the wall approached eleven. I watched it, fascinated. The warder had so far forgotten official reticence as to tell me that the hooters in the town would sound if the armistice were signed. I listened for them, body and mind tense. The sun crept on. It reached the crack in the wall which I estimated would be eleven. Still silence. I lost my head. I leaped across the cell and dug my fingers into the wall and tried to hold the sun back. Then in a great blare came the sound of the hooters. I broke down . . .

Educated in Australia, **Sheila Cassidy** qualified as a medical doctor in England. She went to Chile in 1971 to gain experience before returning to England and completing her qualifications as a surgeon. Working in Santiago, she was asked by a priest to treat a patient with a bullet wound in his leg. As a doctor, she considered it her duty not to judge but to treat him. For this she was detained and tortured by the security forces. Released after two months, she was expelled from Chile.

A doctor's prayers

They secured me to the bottom half of the bunk, tying my wrists and ankles and upper arms and placing a wide band around my chest and abdomen. Then it began. I felt an electric shock pass through me and then another and another.

I made to scream, but found there was a gag in my mouth.

Then the questions began.

The hope of release was a very important factor in my initial ability to withstand pain, for it did not occur to me that this could go on for long and it seemed a matter of hanging on till help came. I was taught in medical school that pain had three components: the actual pain experienced, the memory of past pain and the fear of future pain. Thus at the very beginning, with no knowledge of how severe the pain could become, and believing that it would be of short duration, I was able to act more bravely than I did later. At the beginning too, I believed that the lives of two of my friends depended upon my silence and this is also very important, for resistance to torture is closely related to motivation for not talking.

I embarked, therefore, upon a fabrication which was to have many unexpected repercussions. If it seems that to lie under such circumstances is difficult I can assure you that it was not, for all their questions were direct and their belief in my answers coupled with the repeated painful stimuli made my imagination extremely active . . .

After breakfast I sat on my bunk and gave myself seriously to thinking. God was very real to me, and I asked myself and Him just what it was He had in mind. There was no blinding light or voice from behind the mountains (in my experience there never is!) but it seemed to me that if I was going to spend all day alone I must spend a great deal of it in prayer. There was absolutely nothing else that I could do to be of any use to anybody, so apart from doing everything within my power to maintain my health and sanity I must pray.

I was not unused to spending several hours in prayer, for I had often spent four or five hours on my mountain top, leaning against the wall of the Benedictine monastery and giving myself to the love and praise of God. It was not easy, however, in a prison cell, and I soon realized that this was going to be very hard work for it was much easier to read or lie on my back on the bunk and think. Not by nature an orderly person, I knew by some instinct that if I was to survive being alone twenty-four hours a day I must keep myself busy. I therefore mentally divided the day up and made myself a sort of timetable so that I had periods of prayer, of reading, of exercise and of rest.

When I tried to pray I found that it was very difficult to be quiet before God, for I was filled with fear and anxiety for the future. Unable to be at peace, I presented Him with my anguish and with that of all the other prisoners, with whom I felt an enormous bond. Although I was so alone and so far from my friends and family, I felt curiously united with many people.

I thought of my friends the Benedictines. I could see them gathered in choir praying, and I added my voice to theirs and found that we were joined by all the other monks and nuns all round the world in a great river of prayer. It is difficult to explain just how this was: it wasn't an emotionally comforting experience and I didn't 'feel' the prayers of others for me, but I knew that I was not alone in my worship, that I was part of the Body of Christ.

Born of a wealthy Jewish family, **Alfred Dreyfus** (1859–1935) became a French army officer in 1890. He was assigned to the élite general staff and seemed destined for a successful career. But in 1894, against a background of anti-semitism, he was accused of passing secret information to the German Embassy, court-martialled and found guilty of treason. He was formally degraded in public and sentenced to life imprisonment on Devil's Island off the coast of French Guinea, where he was held for a time in solitary confinement and chained to his bed at night. He had, in fact, been sentenced on forged evidence, and was granted a presidential pardon in 1899, though he was not finally cleared until 1906.

A duty to endure

7 September 1896

Yesterday evening I was put in irons.

Why, I know not.

Since I have been here, I have always scrupulously observed the orders given me.

How is it I did not go crazy during the long, dreadful night? What wonderful strength a clear conscience and the feeling of duty toward one's children gives one! As an innocent man, my imperative duty is to go on to the end of my strength. So long as they do not kill me, I shall ever and simply perform my duty.

As to those who thus constitute themselves my executioners, ah! I leave them to the judgment of their own consciences in the day when the truth shall be revealed. Sooner or later in life everything is bound to come out. What I suffer is horrible, yet I no longer feel anger against those who thus torture an innocent man; I feel only a great pity toward them.

8 September 1896

These nights in irons! I do not even speak of the physical suffering, but what moral ignominy, and without any explanation, without knowing why or for what cause! What an atrocious nightmare is this in which I have lived for nearly two years!

In any case, my duty is to endure to the limit of my strength; my whole will shall be bent to that.

Same day, 2 o'clock, evening

Nearly two years of this have worn me out. I can do no more. The very instinct of life falters.

Some time later

Dating from the 6th of September, when my feet were inserted in the two rings, it was no longer possible for me to move about. I was fastened in an unchangeable position to my bed. The torture was hardly bearable during those tropical nights. Soon also the rings, which were very tight, lacerated my ankles.

Up to the 4th of September, 1896, I had occupied my hut only at night and during the hottest hours of the day. Except in the hours which I gave to my little walks about the two thousand square feet of the island which was reserved to me, I often sat in the shade of the hut, facing the sea; and though my thoughts were sad and preoccupied, and though I often shook with fever, I at least had the consolation of looking upon the sea and letting my eyes wander over its waves, often feeling my soul in the days of storm rise up with its furious waters. But from the 4th of September, 1896, the sight of the sea and of all the other world was shut off, and I stifled in a hut where there was no longer air or light.

In the course of the month of June, 1896, I had had violent attacks of fever, followed by congestion of the brain. During one of these nights of pain and fever I tried to get up, but fell helpless to the floor and lay there unconscious. The guard on duty had to lift me up, limp and covered with blood. During the days which followed, my stomach refused all food. I grew much thinner, and my health was grievously shaken. I was still extremely weak when the arbitrary and inhuman measures of the month of September 1896, were taken; and as a result I had a relapse. It was under such conditions that I thought I should not be able to go further; for whatever the will and energy of a man may be, human strength has a limit, and this limit had been reached. So I stopped my diary with the request that it should be given to my wife. It was just as well, for a few days afterwards all my papers were seized.

But on one of these nights of torture, when riveted to my bed with sleep far from my eyes, I sought my guiding star, my guide in moments of supreme resolve. I saw all at once the light before me illuminating for me my duty: 'Today less than ever have you the right to desert your post, less than ever have you the right to shorten even by a single hour your wretched life. Whatever the torments they inflict on you, you must march forward until they throw you into your grave, you must stand up before your executioners so long as you have a shadow of strength, a living wreck to be kept before their eyes by the unassailable sovereignty of the soul which they cannot reach.'

Karl Gaspar (1947–) was born in Davao City, Philippines. After obtaining an MA in economics, he became a teacher and then, as a Catholic layworker, he became interested in development work and social action for the poor. In March 1983 he became executive secretary of the Resources Development Foundation. That same month he was arrested and charged with conspiracy to rebel. He was acquitted and released in February 1985.

The offering of life

What is essential is that we understand imprisonment as an integral part of commitment. Without this the detainee just becomes angry and bitter and is not able to grasp the meaning of his present tribulation. This meaning lies in his love for God, for country and for the people. On the one hand, no sacrifice is too small or insignificant and on the other hand, the offering of life itself is not too great.

As long as the detainee asserts his rights and deepens his commitment to serve the people, he remains free. The powers-that-be can only physically imprison the body. They can never imprison a person's total being, especially that part of him that dreams. He can remain free within prison walls if he can still raise his mind and heart to the infinite space above. There he can hope and dream for the day when the boundary of his life will no longer be the barbed wire that encircles the detention center but the very spheres of the earth. He can claim to be as free as the birds because he can still look up to the heavens and pray even as he seeks to resign himself to God's will.

As long as the detainee can sing a haunting song to break the stillness of the nights, a song of deliverance that lifts the hearts of his companions, the bell of freedom rings. As long as a detainee can bring his hands to embroider the image of a bird that dares to break free from a cage, he expresses his indomitable will to struggle. As long as he can plant a seed that will one day be a flower, he knows that captivity will never hold him.

What is the secret? Is it *grace*? Perhaps it is. The grace that has led us to a deepened solidarity with the poor, those poor whose wisdom and courage have continually humbled us.

It is never easy to keep on trusting God. In the earlier stage of my detention, I would nag him every day to get me released. And when night came and I was still in prison, I used to feel so rejected. Slowly, painfully, I realized that I had never fully trusted God. The crisis came at the height of our hunger strike, when I was so weak I thought I'd be rushed to a hospital. It was in the dead of night, the pain was very intense and I felt I was slipping into unconsciousness. Only then did I come to trust him absolutely and to find the courage to say, 'It's all up to you now. Your will be done.' Of course the struggle remains to keep that trust alive and I know it will never be easy!

Somehow, though, with a greater trust in his goodness and love, we become more at home in whatever situation we find ourselves, no matter how hard the circumstances.

John Gerard (1564–1637) was a Roman Catholic priest and

member of the Society of Jesus. He was born of a Roman Catholic family in Derbyshire, and educated at Oxford. He attended seminaries in France, and returned secretly to England in 1588, when to be a Roman Catholic priest was accounted high treason, punishable by death. He was betrayed and arrested by pursuivants (priest-catchers) in 1594. After being held in different prisons until April 1597, he was taken to the Tower of London and tortured, in a futile attempt to make him reveal the whereabouts of other Roman Catholics. He escaped in October 1597, and continued his work under constant danger of arrest until 1606, when he returned to France. He wrote his autobiography at the request of his Jesuit superiors.

An amazing providence

As we were preparing everything for Mass before daybreak we heard, suddenly, a great noise of galloping hooves. The next moment, to prevent any attempt at escape, the house was encircled by a whole troop of men. At once we realised what was afoot. We barred the doors: the altar was stripped, the hiding-places opened and all my books and papers thrown in. It was most important to pack me away first with all my belongings.

I was hardly tucked away when the pursuivants broke down the door and burst in. They fanned out through the house, making a great racket. The first thing they did was to shut up the mistress of the house in her own room with her daughters, then they locked up the Catholic servants in different places in the same part of the house. This done, they took possession of the place (it was a large house) and began to search everywhere, even lifting up the tiles of the roof to examine underneath them and using candles in the dark corners. When they found nothing, they started knocking down suspicious-looking places. They measured the walls with long rods and if the measurements did not tally they pulled down the section that they could not account for. They tapped every wall and floor for hollow spots; and on sounding anything hollow they smashed it in.

I had made up my mind to die in this way between the two walls rather than come out and save my life at the sacrifice of others. Indeed, during those four days of hiding, all I had to eat was a biscuit or two and a little quince jelly which my hostess happened to have by her and had handed to me as I was going in. As she had not expected the search to last more than a day she had looked for nothing else.

During the whole of the third day they found nothing at all. They decided, therefore, to spend the next day tearing off the plaster.

Meanwhile they set guards that night to watch any attempt I might make to escape. From where I was hidden I heard the password which the head of the party gave his men, and if I could have come out of my hiding-place without being seen I would have used it and tried to get away. But there were two men watching in the chapel where the entrance to my hiding-place was, and there were several others in the plastered room, which they had been told about.

But an amazing Providence protected me. Here I was in my hiding-place. I had got into it by raising part of the floor under the grate. It was made of wood and brick and constructed in such a way that a fire could not be lit in it without damaging the house. But wood was kept there as though it were meant for a fire.

That night the men on guard decided to light a fire in the grate and they sat down by it for a gossip. In a few moments the bricks, which were not laid on other bricks but on wood, came loose and almost fell out of position as the woodwork subsided. The men noticed this and poked the hearth with a stick and found the bottom made of wood. I heard them remark what a curious thing it was, and thought that there and then they would smash open the hiding-place and peer in. However, they decided to put off their investigations until the next day.

Escape was out of the question now. I began to pray earnestly that, if it was for God's greater glory, I might not be captured in that house and bring retribution on my host, nor in any other house whatsoever where others would suffer for it. My prayer was heard and in a most wonderful manner. God kept me safe in that house.

The next day the search was resumed with great thoroughness. But they left alone the top room which had served as a chapel and in which the two guards had made the fire above my head and had commented on the strange structure of the grate. God had wiped all memory of it from their mind. During all that day not a single pursuivant entered the room, and it was, not without reason, the most suspected room in the house. If they had entered they would have found me without any search at all; rather, they would have seen me, for the fire had burned a hole in my hiding-place, and I had to move a little to one side to avoid the hot embers falling on my head.

But they kept to their plan of stripping off all the plaster from the other large room and with the help of a carpenter they began their work close to the ceiling not far from where I was. (The lower parts of the walls were covered with tapestries.) Going right round the room they ripped off the plaster until they were in front of the exact spot where I was hiding. There, despairing of finding me, they gave up. My hiding-place was in a thick wall of the chimney behind a finely inlaid and carved mantel shelf, which they could not remove without risk of breaking. Yet if they had had the slightest suspicion that I was behind they would have smashed it to pieces. They knew that there were two flues and thought it would be impossible for a man to hide there.

Earlier, on the second day of the search, they had been in the room above and had examined the fireplace through which I had got into my hole. With the help of a ladder they had climbed into the flue and sounded it with a hammer and I had heard one of them saying to another: 'There might conceivably be room for a person to get down here into the wall of the chimney below if this grate was raised.' 'Hardly,' said the other, whose voice I recognized, 'there is no entrance down that way into the other chimney. But there might easily be an entrance at the back of the chimney.'

As soon as he had said this he gave the place a kick. I was afraid he would notice the hollow sound of the hole in which I was hiding. But God, who set limits to the sea, said to these determined men: 'You have come as far as this, but you go no farther,' and He spared his sorely stricken children and would not give them up into the hands of their persecutors. Nor would He allow anything worse to come upon them for their great charity to me.

As their search was a failure they thought that I had managed to escape somehow or other and they went off at the end of the fourth day. The doors of the house were then barred and the mistress came to call me out. Like Lazarus, who was buried four days, I came forth from what would indeed have been my tomb if the search had continued a little longer. I was very wasted and weak with hunger and lack of sleep. All that time I had been squatting in a very confined space.

Kitty Hart (1927–) was a Jewish schoolgirl in Poland when she and her mother were arrested by the Gestapo in 1942 and sent to Auschwitz. She became a nurse, and worked on the *Kanada Kommando* which was located in the actual gas chamber area. One of her tasks was to sort the clothes and possessions of the victims. She was freed by US forces in 1945.

I had grown up

Only sheer faith and will power could keep one alive. Death seemed an easy way out. All that was necessary was a slight touch of the electrified fence which held us prisoners — and finish. Every day girls were found dead near the fence. I so often toyed with this idea, and why I really clung to my life so desperately I don't know. Probably because I was a coward and lacked the courage to take it.

It was generally believed that our situation was hopeless. There was the constant fear that our *Kommando*, like the *Sonderkommando*, would be exchanged, burned. Everyone was convinced that the Germans would never let us out alive, for we knew too much, being direct witnesses of mass murders. There could not possibly be a return. The very fact that we had been moved out here and altogether isolated meant only one thing. Here we were surrounded by nothing but bodies, flames, chimneys, machine-guns, fences and the SS. Only a miracle could save us, but no one really believed in miracles. I do not know if at that time anyone believed in God. If there was a God, we argued, how was it then that He could not hear the terrible cries of the innocent, suffering, burning people. Here we lived always in the present for no one knew whether there would be tomorrow.

All this time twenty thousand people were going to their funerals daily. Was there no end to it? Inside the gas chambers they were forever improving on their already efficient methods. They were certainly gaining experience. Previously people's belongings had all been mixed up and the sorting took a long time. Now notices were displayed for all shoes, stockings and other clothing to be tied together, so that they should not get lost or mixed up in the 'dressing and disinfecting' rooms. Even numbered tickets were issued to be placed on the clothes. Sometimes soap and towels were distributed, particularly if there was any evidence of uneasiness among the crowds. Everything was done to avoid panic which appeared to frighten the German cowards. The next minute when people expected water to come from the 'showers', the gas came on . . .

I turned round to have a last look at that terrible place. I had arrived during the night, and now I was leaving it in the night. It seemed just like a lifetime since that night of arrival although it was in fact just under two years.

I think I had learned a lot in that time. I had grown up, and grown old in experience, and I knew how to fight for my life in any circumstances. In a way it had been a good schooling. Only here one could get to know the true character of a person, not like in civilization where people tend to hide behind masks, disguising their real selves. Here was no need for disguise and all one's points, good or bad, were exposed. Only here could one encounter such real friendships, where one friend would literally give up the last crumb of bread, or drop of water to save another, or even risk destruction in order to help others. Here, too, one came across the other extreme — the utterly selfish who only thought about their own survival at the expense of their own people.

And so on this bleak November night I took one last look at Auschwitz.

Dr Eugen Kogon (1903–87), a German, was incarcerated in Buchenwald from 1939 to 1945 as an anti-Nazi journalist. He had been gaoled several times in the 1930s. He was a Christian writer of distinction and in 1949 became the first chairman of the European Union Movement.

Their lives shed radiance

Admission to a concentration camp constituted the shock that immediately hurled the newcomer in one direction or the other. The indignation or desperation that followed the initial terror decided whether he would gradually gain inward perspective and thus a chance for individual adaptation to the new life, or whether he would swiftly succumb. In the former case there followed a process of habituation, of transformation of individual character. During this second stage the ease and speed with which a way was found toward 'normalcy amid the abnormal' depended on the pluck and determination with which the new goal was envisioned.

This period of initial adaptation was full of dangers. Not only the hands, the soul had to grow calluses. The change in mentality was by no means a simple matter of good or evil, conceived as standards of value. Both aspects pervaded it. Its main characteristic was a process of regression to a more primitive state. The range of sensations was almost automatically reduced. The mind developed a protective crust, a kind of defensive armor that no longer transmitted every strong stimulus to the sensitive membranes. Pain, pity, grief, horror, revulsion and approval, if admitted in their normal immediacy, would have burst the receptive capacities of the human heart. Terror alone, lurking everywhere, would have effortlessly brought it to a stop. Men grew hard and many of them had their sensibilities dulled.

Behind this protective armor of the mind, however, there developed in not a few cases a refinement of conscience that sometimes rose to extraordinary heights. In some cases the tension between regressive emotional primitivism and growing sensitivity of conscience found its only possible release in a heightened religious faith. Provided a man had any trace of moral sense and true religious devotion, these qualities, at the very core of personality, were, if anything, promoted by the powerful appeal emanating from the humanity and inhumanity of the concentration camp. In keeping with camp conditions their presence and their effect could be but rarely manifested in the open, especially since the outwardly predominant groups in the camps acted at best on political, never on religious motivations and applied the highest standards of ethical conscience only in exceptional circumstances.

There can be no question but that the merest rudiments of spiritual care, especially among the Poles, could have prevented much moral disintegration, much brutality, much unhappiness. It might have reassured thousands, succoured hundreds in their last minutes, given countless sick and maimed new inner strength and the will to recover. But instead, these blessings remained confined to an infinitesimally small circle of men who were unusually courageous and already endowed with strength of character.

It was the pure in heart who suffered the least damage, those men of shining integrity who strove to give their all, who never took umbrage no matter what they faced, who steadfastly put evil to one side. There were such men in the camps, and to them the words of the gospel may be applied: *pertransierunt benefaciendo* — their lives shed radiance and beneficence on the rest of us.

William Tyndale (1484–1536) was a religious reformer who made an influential translation of the Bible into English, his New Testament being printed in Cologne in 1525 after he had been forced to leave England. Although some copies were burned, it later became the first volume of the scriptures to be printed in England. His translation aided the rapid spread of Lutheran doctrines, and was not popular with the Catholic hierarchy. In 1535 he was seized at the instigation of Henry VIII, whose divorce he condemned, and imprisoned in the castle at Vilvorde, near Brussels, from whence he wrote to the prison governor. He refused to recant, and in 1536 he was first strangled and then burnt at the stake.

A candle in the dark

I believe that you are not ignorant of what has been determined concerning me [by the Council of Brabant]; therefore I entreat your Lordship, and that by the Lord Jesus, if I am to remain here during the winter, you will request the Procureur to be kind enough to send me from my goods which he has in his possession, a warmer cap, for I suffer extremely from cold in the head, being afflicted with a perpetual catarrh, which is considerably increased in the cell. A warmer coat also, for that which I have is thin; also a piece of cloth to patch my leggings: my overcoat has been worn out. He has a woollen shirt of mine, if he will be kind enough to send it. I have also with him leggings of thicker cloth for putting on above; he also has warmer caps for wearing at night.

I wish also his permission to have a candle in the evening, for it is wearisome to sit alone in the dark. But above all, I entreat and beseech your clemency to be urgent with the Procureur that he may kindly permit me to have my Hebrew Bible, Hebrew Grammar, and Hebrew Dictionary, that I may spend my time with that study. And in return may you obtain your dearest wish, provided always it be consistent with the salvation of your soul. But if any other resolution has been come to concerning me, before the conclusion of the winter, I shall be patient, abiding the will of God to the glory of the grace of my Lord Jesus Christ, whose spirit, I pray, may ever direct your heart. Amen.

4. Facing Death

Dead men meet on the lips of the living.
Samuel Butler

Mummy! But I've been good! It's dark!
A child being shut in a gas chamber, 1942

I believe in the sun even when it is not
   shining
I believe in love where feeling is not
I believe in God even if he is silent.
Written on the wall of a cellar in which a Jewish
victim of Hitler's persecution hid and died

Soraya Abolfathi was a woman member of the Iranian resistance group, the Mojahedin, which opposed the Khomeini regime. In the early 1980s, while pregnant, she was imprisoned and executed. She refused to ask for mercy so that her execution could be delayed until after the birth of her baby. She wrote a last letter to her husband.

I stare at your star

Alas our living together was very short-lived. During this period my inexperience and the occasional mental strain did not allow me to be a good and ideal wife for you. I wish I had an opportunity to make up for those days, but God's wish has proved to be otherwise. Although we spent no more than a few months together, nonetheless I have retained great memories and love in my heart. During these days of separation, I stare at your star before going to sleep every evening. Most nights you come to my dreams and it is at such times that one really recognises the depth of one's love and affection. Nowadays I have a lot of time to think; to remember the past and the severed ties with the world and the beloved ones. This separation is at times extremely agonising, but when one thinks of the splendour of this path and the causes of such a separation, then one perceives the importance and significance of what one is doing.

Unfortunately lack of facilities does not allow me to write much more, even though my heart is overflowing with emotions and words for you. Whatever I do and whenever I write, your image comes before my eyes. But there is nothing we can do about this.

My will and my last words are that you keep up the struggle even more unwaveringly and that you comply with organisational principles and criteria down to the letter. It may actually be pointless to remind you of such matters, for you know them far better than I do. My other request is that you take care of 'X' and remember him, for he badly needs you.

I sacrifice our sacred love for the sake of a greater love; the love of God, of people and of struggle. I expect you, too, to take the same step. Pray to God, so that He may include me among the martyrs. Send my salutes to all the Sisters and Brothers. Tell them that in my will, I have asked them to follow the organisational regulations precisely. I shan't take up any more of your time. I am sending you the last thing I wrote here and a poem entitled 'Embrace Me'.

I love you my dear.

Steve Biko (1946–77) was born in Cape Province, South Africa. He became a student leader at the University of Natal, and formed the South African Students Organisation in 1968. In 1976 he was detained for three months. The ideological 'father' of the Black Consciousness Movement, he was detained on several occasions in the 1970s, the last being in August 1977; as a result of police torture, he died of brain damage the following month. In 1977, shortly before his arrest, he gave an interview setting out some thoughts on detention.

Proud or dead

You are either alive and proud or you are dead, and when you are dead, you can't care anyway. And your method of death can itself be a politicizing thing. So you die in the riots. For a hell of a lot of them, in fact, there's really nothing to lose — almost literally, given the kind of situations that they come from. So if you can overcome the personal fear for death, which is a highly irrational thing, you know, then you're on the way.

And in interrogation the same sort of thing applies. I was talking to this policeman, and I told him, 'If you want us to make any progress, the best thing is for us to talk. Don't try any form of rough stuff, because it just won't work.' And this is absolutely true also. For I just couldn't see what they could do to me which would make me all of a sudden soften to them. If they talk to me, well I'm bound to be affected by them as human beings. But the moment they adopt rough stuff, they are imprinting in my mind that they are police. And I only understand one form of dealing with police, and that's to be as unhelpful as possible. So I button up. And I told them this: 'It's up to you.' We had a boxing match the first day I was arrested. Some guy tried to clout me with a club. I went into him like a bull. I think he was under instructions to take it so far and no further, and using open hands so that he doesn't leave any marks on the face. And of course he said exactly what you were saying just now: 'I will kill you.' He meant to intimidate. And my answer was: 'How long is it going to take you?' Now of course they were observing my reaction. And they could see that I was completely unbothered. If they beat me up, it's to my advantage. I can use it. They just killed somebody in jail — a friend of mine — about ten days before I was arrested. Now it would have been bloody useful evidence for them to assault me. At least it would indicate what kind of possibilities were there, leading to this guy's death. So, I wanted them to go ahead and do what they could do, so that I could use it. I wasn't really afraid that their violence might lead me to make revelations I didn't want to make, because I had nothing to reveal on this particular issue. I was operating from a very good position, and they were in a very weak position. My attitude is, I'm not going to allow them to carry out their programme faithfully. So if they had meant to give me so much of a beating, and not more, my idea is to make them go beyond what they wanted to give me and to give back as much as I can give so that it becomes an uncontrollable thing. You see the one problem this guy had with me: he couldn't really fight with me because it means he must hit back, like a man. But he was given instructions, you see, on how to hit, and now these instructions were no longer applying because it was a fight. So he had to withdraw and get more instructions. So I said to them, 'Listen, if you guys want to do this your way, you have got to handcuff me and bind my feet together, so that I can't respond. If you allow me to respond, I'm certainly going to respond. And I'm afraid you may have to kill me in the process even if it's not your intention.'

Edith Cavell (1865–1915) was an English nurse who became matron of a training school for nurses in Belgium in 1907, and remained there after the country was occupied by German forces in 1914. She sheltered escaping British and allied soldiers in the training school as part of an escape-line to Holland. When the Germans found the escape organization, she was tried and shot by a firing squad. From her cell she wrote to her nurses.

Face to face with death

This is a sad moment for me as I write to say good-bye. To my sorrow I have not always been able to talk to you each privately. You know that I had my share of burdens. But I hope that you will not forget our evening chats.

I told you that devotion would bring you true happiness and the thought that, before God and in your own eyes, you have done your duty well and with a good heart, will sustain you in trouble and face to face with death. There are two or three of you who will recall the little talks we had together. Do not forget them. As I had already gone so far along life's road, I was perhaps able to see more clearly than you, and show you the straight path.

One word more. Never speak evil. May I tell you, who love your country with all my heart, that this has been the great fault here. During these last eight years I have seen so many sorrows which could have been avoided or lessened if a little word had not been breathed here and there, perhaps without evil intention, and thus destroyed the happiness or even the life of someone. Nurses all need to think of this, and to cultivate a loyalty and team spirit among themselves.

If any of you has a grievance against me, I beg you to forgive me; I have perhaps been unjust sometimes, but I have loved you much more than you think.

I send my good wishes for the happiness of all my girls, as much for those who left the School as those who are still there. Thank you for the kindness you have always shown me.

Etienne-Pierre Gorneau (1773–93) was a notary's clerk in the French Ministry of the Interior. His correspondence with friends was critical of the Republic and of its deputies in the National Assembly, and he was arrested after one of his letters was intercepted. He was guillotined for counter-revolutionary correspondence, and on 4 October 1793 wrote a last letter to his family. It was appropriated by the court, placed in the files of the director of public prosecutions, and found there nearly two hundred years later.

In vitam morte datus

I send you my last farewells. My only regret in leaving life is that I cannot embrace you. No other attachment holds me here: he who has never committed a crime, who has done no wrong to anyone, who was a good human being, sensitive and generous, that man dies at peace. I hoped by my work to serve a more securely based Republic. I have always desired the good of my country. I have always abhorred despotism and worshipped liberty. Today, I am the victim of some inconsequential matter, a mere imprudence committed at the age of twenty, and I die without fear.

I hoped, together with my elder brother, to become the support of the latter days of my good parents, who have brought me up with the greatest care, who showed us the most loving kindness during our childhood. All such hopes are now dashed.

And you, true brother, sincere friend, be, in my stead, the intrepid defender of the rights of man. When you have served your country, take care of our young brother, look to his keep and take care of our only sister and shed tears for our friendship only as long as needs be to erase the memory of a brother who worshipped you and who will, in a few hours, be happier than you.

Sooner or later, by some event or another, one must necessarily come to this pass. May *maman* above all try to be consoled for my loss; let her know that I am at peace, as I go towards death and shall no longer be unhappy. I thought the approach of death would be more terrible, but I am experiencing the opposite.

I am leaving a prison that is a true preparation for this eternal act. I was thrown there, on the straw, with some forty other poor devils, all of whom are awaiting the same fate. I don't know whether I should believe in presentiments, but for several days I thought about my affair and the fate that awaited me. When I saw that I was suddenly transferred to Sainte-Pelagie, I said, 'I'm done for.'

Tell my cousin, Dupuy, to make sure that he collects from Sainte-Pelagie the following objects that he lent me. Here are the instructions that I have given to the citizen keeper:

I beg Citizen Boucherot, keeper of the house of Sainte-Pelagie, to hand over or to have handed over by a chamber comrade to the bearer, my cousin, the following effects that belong to him: 1. one trestle bed; 2. one mattress; 3. *Crebillon*, in three volumes; 4. *My Mathematics*, by Saurin in five octavo volumes; 5. one telescope.

I have sold to my chamber companion the rest of my books, in exchange for money lent me.

I take my sincere farewell of all my friends and relations; I embrace them for the last time. I want my father to keep this letter for his descendants, to remind them that I existed and perished on the scaffold, a victim of my opinions, on 14 Fremaire [4 December 1793 old style] Year II of the French Republic, between noon and one o'clock, or eleven o'clock, on the Place de la Revolution.

In vitam morte datus [given by death into life].

Married with two children, **William Hockett** was a farmer in North Carolina when he was conscripted into the Confederate Army in June 1863. He was then 36 years old. He refused to bear arms and refused to purchase exemption, although he could have afforded to do so. He travelled with the wagon-train of his unit and maintained a journal, until taken prisoner by Union cavalry in July 1863 in the confusion after Gettysburg. This selection is from his journal.

American Civil War objector

13 June 1863

This evening I was before Colonel Kirkland. He said the authorities of North Carolina had sent me out there as a man capable of making a soldier, and that I would have to comply with orders or he would order me shot, and said I might take a gun and go into the ranks, or he would order me shot that evening or the next morning, and I might take my choice. I told him that I would not take a gun nor march in the drill, so he said: 'Which will you choose, to be shot evening or morning?' I told him I should choose neither, but if my God whom I served permitted him to take my life I would submit to it; I would die a martyr for Christ's sake. He said he had full power, without permission, to kill me if I did not comply. I told him I did not deny that he had, so far as the power of man extended, but there was a power above man's, and he could not remove a hair of my head without my Heavenly Father's notice. He wanted to know if I was a good workman. I told him that I was counted a passable hand. He said I was the very man for him and he had the very place to put me; it was to go to the wagon-yard and work there. I told him that I would receive no appointment to work at anything that was to carry on war. He ordered me to say no more but to go to the wagons, and sent a man to take me to Captain Vogler of the wagon-train. He told me to go and mow grass for the horses, but I refused on conscientious grounds. They said that I should be shot. I said that my God told me not to do so, and that I feared Him more than what they could do. So when they found that I would not comply they sent me back to camp, saying that they had no use for such a fellow. They then reported me to the colonel, who said that he would have me shot that night or the next morning.

The eve of 23 June 1863

'O Lord, my Heavenly Father, my prayer is that Thy name be glorified and not my will be done. But if it be Thy will that I should lay down my life, be Thou pleased to pardon all my sins, for Thy dear Son's sake, and take away the fear of man, and leave me not in the hour of trial, but support me by Thy arm of power; for my hope is in Thee, that Thou wilt control the raging of men.

'Be pleased to be near and comfort and protect my dear wife and children in their lonely condition, that they may be enabled to press forward and not faint by the way, but put their trust in Thee, who alone can save. O Lord, comfort my aged father, whose heart yearns for his dear son.

'O God, here am I. My heart is resigned. Come life, come death, Thy will be done, not mine.'

I requested my tent-mate that if my life was taken from me he would let my dear wife know what had become of me. He agreed to do so.

24 June

I was ordered out and required to fall in line with the company and drill, but I refused. They tried to make me, and I sat down on the ground. They reminded me of the orders to shoot me, but I told them my God said to fear not them that kill the body, but are not able to kill the soul; but rather to fear Him that is able to destroy both soul and body in Hell. The company was then ordered to fall back eight paces, leaving me in front of them. They were then ordered by Colonel Kirkland to 'Load; Present arms; Aim,' and their guns were pointed directly at my breast. I raised my arms and prayed: 'Father, forgive them; they know not what they do.' Not a gun was fired. They lowered them without orders, and some of the men were heard to say that they 'could not shoot such a man.' The order was then given, 'Ground arms.'

Geeti-os-Sadat Jowzi was a young member of the Iranian Mojahedin movement. In 1981, shortly before her execution, she wrote a last letter to her parents.

No more time

My greetings to you come from every single cell in my body. I kiss you all from this far-away place, particularly my extremely affectionate and caring mother who, throughout her life, burnt like a candle to light up our lives. My father, too, has always been considerate and warm-hearted towards me. He has devoted all his life and time to our happiness and the spring of his life has so quickly turned into autumn, without even seeing summer. I pray to God for patience and perseverance. You cannot imagine how much I am missing the dear Mansoor and that naughty menace, Nasser. The same is also true of all the children in the family.

Mother, please tell everyone that I went along this path with utmost pride and honour, in the hope that my humble life may be a sacrifice to the freedom of all the deprived people throughout the world. I hope the day will come when you, at least, can see the sort of society which I had longed for.

For God's sake, mother, please do not cry for me. Whenever you want to cry, just think that it will agonise me. For once, do not listen to others but think for yourself. You know, I wanted to talk to you about a few things, because I am missing you very much and I want you to believe what I have to say. I have seen things happening here and crimes being committed which no one has ever seen or even heard of before.

Give all my possessions to the Mojahedin. Send my regards to those friends of mine you know, both my school friends and the warm-hearted kids in the hostel, and ask them to forgive the wrongs they may have seen in me.

Mother, I just wanted to write something to you in these final moments. God knows how much I have missed you all, particularly yourself and father, since I was separated from you. I missed you even more greatly than before when they brought in a mother and her 14-year-old daughter together. Another girl, who had neither a mother nor a father, kept asking us: 'Don't you miss your parents?' And then I would just eat my heart out . . .

Well mother, I have nothing else to say. Actually I mean I have no more time, otherwise I could go on talking to you for years. I kiss you all from this far-away prison. God be with you all.

Arthur Koestler (1905–83) was born in Hungary, but was working as a special correspondent for an English news-paper during the Spanish Civil War. In 1937 he came under suspicion by General Franco's forces, who thought he was a Russian. He was arrested, placed in solitary confinement and sentenced to death. He was released after three months following diplomatic pressure.

Nature sees to it

Every man needs a different pill to help him to arrive at a *modus vivendi* with his misery. Job cursed God when his sores festered; the prisoners in Malaga sang the 'International'. I, too, had my pills, a whole collection of various sorts of them, from the equation of a hyperbola to every kind of synthetic product of the spiritual pharmacy.

One of my magic remedies was a certain quotation from a certain work of Thomas Mann's; its efficacy never failed. Sometimes, during an attack of fear, I repeated the same verse thirty or forty times, for almost an hour, until a mild state of trance came on and the attack passed. I knew it was the method of the prayer-mill, of the African tom-tom, of the age-old magic of sounds. Yet in spite of my knowing it, it worked.

A similar effect to that of these anaesthetising exercises I could obtain by the opposite method, that is, by sharp abstract speculation.

I would start a train of thought deliberately at some given point, such as Freud's theories about death and the nostalgia for death; after a few minutes a state of feverish exaltation was evoked, a kind of running amok in the realm of reasoning, which usually ended in a day-dream. After a while I became sober again and the attack had passed.

The healing power of both methods was derived from the same device: that of merging that stark image of the firing-squad with the general problem of life and death, of merging my individual misery with the biological misery of the universe; just as the vibrations and tensions of a wireless-receiver are conducted to earth, where they disperse; I had 'earthed' my distress.

In other words I had found out that the human spirit is able to call upon certain aids of which, in normal circumstances, it has no knowledge, and the existence of which it only discovers in itself in abnormal circumstances. They act, according to the particular case, either as merciful narcotics or ecstatic stimulants. The technique which I developed under the pressure of the death-sentence consisted in the skilful exploitation of these aids. I knew, by the way, that at the decisive moment when I should have to face the wall, these mental devices would act automatically, without any conscious effort on my part. Thus I had actually no fear of the moment of execution; I only feared the fear which would precede that moment. But I relied on the feeling I had experienced while waiting for Bolín's shot; that dream-like feeling of having one's consciousness split in two, so that with one half of it one observes oneself with comparative coolness and aloofness, as though observing a stranger. The consciousness sees to it that its complete annihilation is never experienced. It does not divulge the secret of its existence and its decay. No one is allowed to look into the darkness with his eyes open; he is blindfolded beforehand.

This is why situations lived through are never so bad in reality as in imagination. Nature sees to it that trees do not grow beyond a certain height, not even the trees of suffering.

Christian Langedul was sentenced to death and burnt at the stake in August 1567 for receiving a second baptism as an adult. This marked him out as an Anabaptist, a sect widespread in Europe but which was persecuted by both Catholic and Protestant authorities. He was tortured under interrogation but refused to declare the whereabouts of fellow members. He wrote to his wife about his experiences under torture.

You can but kill me

It was next my turn. You may conceive how I felt. As I approached the rack I was ordered to strip or to say where I lived. I therefore undressed, and gave myself up to the gentlemen, fully prepared to die. They now cruelly racked me. I think two cords fastened on my thighs and legs broke. They also drenched me with water, pouring it into my mouth and nose. After releasing me they inquired if I would now speak. They entreated me, then menaced me; but I did not open my mouth. God had shut it. They then said, 'Give him another taste of it.' This they did, calling out, 'Away, away; stretch him another foot.' I thought. 'You can but kill me.' While thus lying stretched out, drawn by cords on my head and chin, and on my thighs and legs, they said, 'Speak, speak.' I kept my mouth closed. They said, 'Say where you live, and where your wife and children are.' But I said not a word, for the Lord kept the door of my lips. After they had long tried to make me speak, they at last released me. Two of them, the executioner and his servant, then carried me between them from the rack. You can imagine how they had dealt with us and what we must have felt, and still feel. Holding me by my arms they dragged me out of the torture chamber into the porter's room above. I slept well, but am not yet able to stand, for my feet from the tension are still insensible. But I trust, through God's mercy, all will be well.

Our God is mighty. He did not suffer me to be tempted above that I was able to bear. My confidence in him is strong that he will continue to afford me his grace, for I am sure that there is no other way or truth to be found.

Matthew was tortured after me. He named his own house and the street where we live. He also said that we lived in a gateway, and I think there is no other gateway in the street but ours. You had better therefore immediately remove if you have not left, for I think the magistrates will go there. Let no one go to the house who is in danger of apprehension. I have yet much to say, but the time is short.

Of you and the children I dare scarcely think; it grieves me much to part with you.

I am not much recovered from the torture, as you may suppose; but I hope all will be well, and that you will not fret too much about it.

Howard Marten (1884–1961), an English bank cashier, was one of a party of 41 conscientious objectors whom the army sent secretly to France in 1916. This step was taken because France was an active-service zone where those deemed to be soldiers could be shot for disobeying orders. Thirty-four of the party were sentenced to death. The sentence was afterwards commuted to ten years penal servitude.

Trial by court martial

One good fellow brought me some bread, cheese and onion, contributions from different men, and when dinner-time arrived I had no lack of friends. Under such circumstances to win the confidence of these men gave one a tremendous sense of uplift. Most of them, while sympathetic, strongly urged me to give up the struggle, expressing genuine concern at the punishments which they prophesied would surely be visited upon me if I persisted in my refusal to obey orders.

We were placed in handcuffs and locked in the cells, and tied up for two hours in the afternoon. We were tied up by the wrists to horizontal ropes about 5 feet from the ground, with our arms outstretched and feet tied together. Our cells were roughly constructed from planks of wood, the wall of the prison forming the back. Then we were confined to cells for three days on 'punishment diet' (four biscuits a day and water). We were also handcuffed with our arms behind us and then placed in the cells, to the recesses of which little daylight penetrated. Being now confined to cells, we were exempted from the nightly tying up, but during the whole of the first of the three days we remained in handcuffs (except during the short time we were being interviewed by the officers), although on retiring for the night the handcuffs were fastened with our hands in front instead of behind us.

During the week-end I was alone in the first of the three cells, the remaining eleven being next door, and they naturally found their quarters rather cramped. By means of a small aperture in the partition of rough planks, we were able to speak to one another and also to exchange books. On the Sunday morning we were allowed out to do some washing, and after dinner all the prisoners, including ourselves, were drawn up in the courtyard to hear the promulgation of the death sentence passed a few days earlier on a soldier who had been found guilty of disobedience. Later in the day we held a Friends' Meeting, in which I participated, assisted by the chink in the cell partition.

We heard it rumoured that four of us would be tried at an early date by Field General Court Martial, so that our trial was apparently to be made a test case.

On the morning of June 2nd I and my three comrades, together with two other prisoners, were marched away under escort with rifles and fixed bayonets. During the time I was reading my defence the court was very still and I was given an attentive hearing. During the hearing of my case it seemed to me that some of those participating appeared to feel their position uncomfortable. While waiting outside the court, one of our number overheard an officer remark to a companion that 'it would be monstrous to shoot these men.'

On the evening of Thursday, June 15th, the four of us who had been court martialled were taken by an escort of military police to the Henriville Camp in order to hear our sentences read out. It was evidently intended to be an impressive function, as a large square consisting of the NCC and labour battalions was drawn up on the parade ground. These men occupied three sides of the square, with a miscellaneous collection of spectators in the background, while we, with our escort, were placed on the remaining side. After a hum of conversation and comment had been suppressed by the NCOs, I was marched out a few paces in advance of my companions towards the centre of the square. An officer, who, by the way, had been a member of the first court martial to try my case, read a long statement of my crimes, and then announced the sentence of the court:

'To suffer death by being shot.'

I have often been asked what my sensations were at that moment and have found it difficult to recollect very clearly. I think I may say that for the time being I had lost the sense of 'personality', and, standing there on the parade ground, I had a sense of representing something outside my own self, supported by a stronger strength than frail humanity. However, in a few moments it was evident that the whole had not been said, and the officer went on to tell (after a pause) that 'this sentence had been confirmed by the Commander-in-Chief (another long pause), but afterwards commuted by him to one of penal servitude for ten years.'

A descendant of a famous German field-marshal of the nineteenth century, **Count Helmuth von Moltke** (1907–45) practised as an international lawyer in Germany in the 1930s. He was a devout Christian, an intellectual idealist and a strong opponent of Nazism from its beginnings. In the early years of World War II, he formed a discussion group which met at his estate in Kreisau, Silesia, to plan a new Germany after the hoped-for downfall of Hitler. Although they took no part in it, the members of the group were arrested after the July 1944 plot against Hitler. Von Moltke was sentenced to death on 10 January 1945, and wrote the same day to his wife. He was executed 13 days later. He had two sons, then aged three and seven.

I wept a little

I must first say, quite decidedly, that the closing hours of a man's life are no different from any others. I had always imagined that one would have no feeling beyond shock, and that one would keep saying to oneself, 'This is the last time you'll see the sun go down, this is the last time you'll go to bed, you've only twice more to hear the clock strike twelve'. But there is no question of any of that. Perhaps I'm a little above myself, I don't know, but I cannot deny that I feel in the best of spirits at the moment. Of course I do not know whether I shall be put to death to-morrow. It may be that there will be a further hearing; perhaps I shall be beaten or put in store. Try to get in touch with me, for that may perhaps preserve me from too fierce a beating. I know after to-day's experience that God can turn to naught this beating too — even if I have no whole bone in my body before I am hanged. At the moment I do not fear it; yet I should prefer to avoid it.

I am quite certain that you will never lose me on this earth — no, not for a moment. And this fact it was given us to symbolize finally through our common participation in the Holy Communion, that celebration which was my last. I wept a little, not that I was sad, not that I was dispirited, not that I wanted to turn back — no, I wept for gratitude, because I was overwhelmed by this proof of the presence of God. True, we cannot see him face to face, but we cannot but be overmastered when we suddenly realize that a whole life-time through he has gone before us as a cloud by day and as fire by night. Now nothing further can happen.

Since God has the unbelievable goodness to be in me, I can take with me not only you and the boys but all those whom I love and numberless others who are not so near to me.

My dear, my life draws to its close, and I can truthfully say of myself, 'He died in fullness of years and of life's experience'. That does not imply that I would not gladly go on living, that I would not gladly walk further at your side on this earth. But for that I should need a new commission from God, since the one for which he created me stands completed.

Born a Catholic near Norwich, **Robert Southwell** (1561–95) became a Jesuit priest after studying in Rome. He became a member of the mission to England when Roman Catholic priests were liable to be arrested for treason. He was seized in 1592, tortured unsuccessfully to gain evidence of other priests, then hanged, drawn and quartered in 1595. He was a religious poet who wrote much of his work in prison.

My feast is done

O life! what lets thee from a quick decease?
O death! what draws thee from a present prey?
My feast is done, my soul would be at ease,
My grace is said: O death! come take away . . .

Thus still I die, yet still I do revive,
My living death by dying life is fed;
Grace more than nature keeps my heart alive,
Whose idle hopes and vain desires are dead.

Sith my life from life is parted,
Death, come take thy portion;
Who survives when life is murdered,
Lives by mere extortion.

Come, cruel death, why lingerest thou so long?
What doth withhold thy dint from fatal stroke?
Now pressed I am, alas, thou dost me wrong,
To let me live, more anger to provoke . . .

Born of an ardent Catholic family in Hampshire, **Chidiock Tichborne** (1558–86) was thrown into the Tower of London, disembowelled and executed for alleged complicity in a plot against Queen Elizabeth I. He was condemned on information extracted from others by torture. In his last speech he said: 'A dear friend told me the whole matter, and I denied to be a dealer in it. But I was silent and so consented.' This poem was written three days before his execution.

The untimely end

My prime of youth is but a frost of cares,
   my feast of joy is but a dish of pain;
My crop of corn is but a field of tares,
   and all my good is but vain hope of gain.
The day is past, and yet I saw no sun,
And now I live, and now my life is done.

My tale was heard, and yet it was not told,
   my fruit is fallen, and yet my leaves are green;

My youth is spent, and yet I am not old,
    I saw the world, and yet I was not seen.
My thread is cut, and yet it is not spun,
And now I live, and now my life is done.

I sought my death, and found it in my womb,
    I looked for life, and saw it was a shade;
I trod the earth, and knew it was my tomb,
    and now I die, and now I was but made.
My glass is full, and now my glass is run,
And now I live, and now my life is done.

5. Faith

I have finished the course, I have kept faith.
St Paul

If nothing will do unless I make a continual
butchery of my conscience I have
determined to suffer, if frail life might
continue so long, even till the moss shall
grow on mine eyebrows rather than thus to
violate my faith and principles.
John Bunyan

Father **Daniel Berrigan** (1921–) is an American Jesuit priest who has been imprisoned several times for anti-war activities. In September 1980, he and seven others entered a General Electric nuclear plant in Pennsylvania and poured their own blood over components of nuclear warheads. They were arrested, tried and found guilty of criminal mischief. During the trial Daniel Berrigan was asked why he had made the incursion.

The push of conscience

The question takes me back to those years when my conscience was being formed, back to a family that was poor, and to a father and mother who taught, quite simply, by living what they taught. In a thousand ways they showed that you do what is right because it is right, that your conscience is a matter between you and God, that nobody owns you. In the life of a young child, the first steps of conscience are as important as the first steps of one's feet. And I feel that there is a direct line between the way my parents turned our steps and this action. That is no crooked line.

Dear friends of the jury, you have been called the conscience of the community. Each of us eight comes from a community. Every one of us has brothers and sisters with whom we pray, with whom we offer the Eucharist, with whom we share income and, in some cases, the care of children. Our conscience, in other words, comes from somewhere. We have not come from outer space or from chaos or from madhouses to King of Prussia [town in Pennsylvania].

We have come from years of prayers, years of life together, years of testing. We would like to speak to you about our communities, because it is our conviction that nobody in the world can form his or her conscience alone. We come as a community of conscience before your community of conscience to ask you: are our consciences to act differently than yours in regard to the lives and deaths of children? I could not *not* do this. I mean that with every cowardly bone in my body I wished I hadn't had to enter the GE plant. I wish I hadn't had to do it. And that has been true of every time I have been arrested, all those years. My stomach turns over. I feel sick. I feel afraid. I don't want to go through this again. I hate jail. I don't do well there physically. But I cannot *not* go on, because I have learned that we must not kill if we are Christians. I have read that Christ underwent death rather than inflict it. And I am supposed to be a disciple. The push of conscience is a terrible thing.

So at some point your cowardly bones get moving, and you say, 'Here it goes again', and you do it. And you have a certain peace because you did it, as I do this morning in speaking with you.

One remains honest because one has a sense, 'Well, if I cheat, I'm really giving over my humanity, my conscience.' Then we think of these horrible Mark 12A missiles and something in us says, 'We cannot live with such crimes.'

In time we drew closer. We were able to say: 'Yes. We can do this. We can take the consequences. We can undergo whatever is required.'

I talked openly with Jesuit friends and superiors. They respected my conscience and said, 'Do what you are called to do.'

And what issued was a sense that, with great peacefulness, with calm of spirit, even though with a butterfly in our being, we could go ahead. And so we did.

A Lutheran pastor and a one-time lecturer in theology at Berlin University, **Dietrich Bonhoeffer** (1906–45) was a strong opponent of the Nazis. At the outbreak of World War II, he was in the USA on a lecture tour and could have remained there. But he chose to return, though aware of the danger to a known opponent of Nazi ideology. He was imprisoned in April 1943 on suspicion of participation in a resistance group. Though never tried, he was hanged at Flossenburg in April 1945, when Hitler knew the war was all but over. His theological views grew during his imprisonment into a new interpretation of Christianity which has made a great impact on modern theology. In 1943 he wrote to his fiancée, Maria von Wedemeyer-Weller.

Where faith belongs

You cannot know what it means in my present situation to have you. I am certain of God's special guidance here. The way in which we found each other and the time, so shortly before my imprisonment, are a clear sign for this. Again, it was a case of *hominum confusione et dei providentia*. Everyday I am overcome anew at how undeservedly I received this happiness, and each day I am deeply moved at what a hard school God has led you through during the last year. And now it appears to be his will that I have to bring you sorrow and suffering . . . so that our love for each other may achieve the right foundation and the right endurance. When I also think about the situation of the world, the complete darkness over our personal fate and my present imprisonment, then I believe that our union can only be a sign of God's grace and kindness, which calls us to faith. We would be blind if we did not see it. Jeremiah says at the moment of his people's great need 'still one shall buy houses and acres in this land' as a sign of trust in the future. This is where faith belongs. May God give it to us daily. And I do not mean the faith which flees the world, but the one that endures the world and which loves and remains true to the world in spite of all the suffering which it contains for us. Our marriage shall be a yes to God's earth; it shall strengthen our courage to act and accomplish something on the earth. I fear that Christians who stand with only one leg upon earth also stand with only one leg in heaven.

Corder Catchpool (1883–1952) was a Quaker who served in France in World War I with the Friends Ambulance Unit and was awarded the Mons Star. In 1916 conscription was introduced, and he decided he could not serve a military machine. He spoke of 'a call I have heard above the roar of the guns'. He therefore returned home, becoming an absolutist conscientious objector, i.e. he refused to undertake alternative service, or any service, which would aid the war. He also considered it right that he should share the sufferings of those other absolutists who had not sought the exemption which he could have gained by his service in the Ambulance Unit. He was imprisoned for over two years. After the war he took up relief work in Germany.

The absolutist and the Carmelite

I once brought a nun in my Ambulance car to refuge at Abeele out of a shelled village, a nun of the strait order of Carmelites, who live wholly separate from the world, almost from each other. I had to tease her a little on the misfortune of speaking to a man, strictly forbidden to her Order, which she took in good part, solemnly assuring me that she had absolution for the exigencies of war, though this was the first time she had needed to use it! We soon came to something deeper. I was putting my ideal before her — a life of happy usefulness in service for one's kind. 'Yes,' she said, 'right and best for all except the few who are called to serve by a life of prayer for the sinful world.' I can see her now, coarse brown habit, earnest face, lighting up with a beautiful smile as she spoke of eleven *happy* years of that awful self-discipline and hardship, incomparably more severe than prison conditions — pleading for my recognition of *her* call, *her* wrestling, as true service to

God. I could not deny it; but to-day I can enter into a fellowship and understanding that was not possible then. The inexplicable Absolutist is a man to whom the sinfulness of war seems so appalling that he *must* struggle against it, wrestle to deliver a world bound by it; might and main; struggle as never before for anything in his life; hears a call to it; feels that anything less would be to him drifting with the tide — not stemming it. *He has to breast it.* Exhausting, apparently so useless; ceaseless temptation to give up in weariness and drift into some quiet backwater of Alternative Service — good, useful, interesting, obvious service — victims to be pulled ashore — but yet, for him, something less than the utmost struggle against the flood. And, as all *effective* opposition to war — everything that the Authorities do not construe as virtual acquiescence in passive compliance with the war — brings a man to-day inevitably into prison, he becomes a sort of involuntary, let us hope only temporary, Carmelite. 'Tis the only way for the moment in which he can struggle — he *has* to do it. Isolation is not the path of service he would choose, far from it; but his solitude is sanctified by the belief that he *is* helping to free the world from war, to make life amongst men now and forever sweeter in all the human relationships of those who will survive. A glad service, in which he is prepared for any risks; precisely the same aim and devotion, I believe, as that of the 'conscientious soldier'. And so, I am helped to face a long sentence by thinking of that woman, her call to a desperate spiritual adventure, her prayer-life for the sinful world, victorious through faith in one whose strength is made perfect in human weakness.

I have now been in prison just as long as at the Front, viz. nineteen months. I wish the Government would see the reasonableness of releasing me at this point of the proceedings — on principles of symmetry!

Born in Johannesburg, **Frank Chikane** (1951–) was an active member of the Student Christian Movement. He was ordained in 1980 and took up a ministry in Krugersdorp, during which time he was arrested several times and tortured. In 1985 he was charged with treason because of his involvement in the United Democratic Front. Released after three months, he went into hiding and then to Europe, but returned to South Africa in 1987 voluntarily in spite of the risk of further detention. In the same year he was appointed general secretary of the South African Council of Churches.

Going through the pain

The torture involved being forced to remain in certain contorted positions for many hours until the body gave in. When I could not keep the prescribed positions any longer, I was assaulted with fists and various other objects like a broomstick. At times I was chained against other objects in a crouching position, handcuffed to my feet, and left in that position for a very long time. Once I was hung head-down with my hands and feet over a wooden stick, and assaulted in that position. I do not remember much of the details of the latter experience as it looks like I lost consciousness.

Afterwards I was confused with my whole body completely unstable. Walking was a struggle, and when I arrived at the prison where I was kept, I could not stand steadily as the warders checked me into the prison. I remember the prison warders making a laughing-stock of me, saying I had gone through some good 'music' and that I was continuing to 'dance'. The last ordeal of my six weeks of torture had involved being kept standing in one spot for fifty hours continuously without sleep. I was chained against the bars of the heating system, underfed, interrogated and assaulted continuously by teams of interrogators who changed shifts every eight hours, twenty-four hours around the clock.

It was during this ordeal when I tried to make sense of the Gospel and the sermons I preached about 'loving your enemies'. I began to ask questions about God's power and concern. But one thing that kept me strong and made me survive was the experience of the Lord Jesus Christ; that for the salvation of the world it did not seem like Jesus could have let the cup pass.

The experience of the apostles also kept me strong. For it does not seem as if the Gospel we have today could have been passed over to us without them going through the persecution they suffered even unto death. But as I went through the pain I began to understand that, in fact, Christians have an enormous responsibility in the world, far more than they are aware of. I felt it was a matter of life and death for me to suffer for the sake of others; the weak in our society, the brutalized, for the sake of Christ's body, that is, his Church. I felt more empowered to say to my torturers during my fifty-hour ordeal, men who had told me I was going to die 'slowly but sure' that 'Christ will be honoured in my body whether by life or by death'.

My torturers asked me in the course of this ordeal to make a choice between dying slowly in a painful way and co-operating by collaborating with them against those I am called to minister to. I told them that collaboration and co-operation with the evil racist system in South Africa was out for me. It was a call for me to abandon the very fundamentals of my faith and calling. I told them that instead they had to decide whether to let me die or live, being conscious of the consequences of both options. But I did not have to make the choice; it lay in their hands. Through pain they made me feel at one stage that if I was to die, then the faster the better.

At one stage they suggested that I should commit suicide to speed up my death. My response was that Frank Chikane did not have the right to take his own life, and, anyway, I was not going to let them off the hook by terminating my own life, and make them feel less guilty after what they had done.

By the forty-eighth hour I no longer felt normal enough to be able to continue intelligently answering their questions, and I decided to keep quiet after telling them about my position. I announced that I was not going to answer questions any more. For two hours they tried every method to force me to talk, but in vain. On the fiftieth hour I was loosened and driven from Krugersdorp to Rustenburg prison. Throughout my time at Rustenburg I was kept in solitary confinement.

It took me about three months arguing with the magistrates who visited me once in three weeks according to the regulations before I got a copy of the Bible. The security police's argument was that they would not give me a Bible because '*dit maak jou'n terrorist*' (it makes you a terrorist). They felt that the Bible did not seem to help me. It is clear that for them, like all oppressive regimes, the Bible helps you only if it makes you submissive to the dictates of the oppressor. When, at last, they did give me a copy of the Bible, they gave me an Afrikaans one, maybe to force me to read their language. But nevertheless it was a blessing to have a Bible, whatever the language.

Born in June 1912, **William Douglas-Home** was commissioned into an armoured regiment in World War II and sent to France soon after D-Day. His regiment was ordered to take part in an attack on Le Havre, which contained a large civilian population. The German general asked permission to evacuate all civilians before the attack, but was refused.

As a culmination of his existing doubts as to the government's conduct of the war, Douglas-Home refused to obey an order to take part in the attack, was court-martialled and given 12 months imprisonment with hard labour.

A soldier refuses an order

8 Sept. 1944

Dear Pa and Ma,

I am afraid I have got myself into trouble. I have refused an order to go and attack Le Havre. I spent the whole of last night thinking about it, and decided to do so.

I do hope you won't be upset. Probably there will be no trouble about it — on the other hand I might be court-martialled and dismissed from the Service.

You have always been very tolerant about my point of view and, after all, it's the only consistent end to my useless army career. It's entirely their own fault for keeping me in it. I've made repeated requests to Waddell to let me go and he wouldn't. I applied to resign my commission when I saw how the 'unconditional surrender' racket was causing unnecessary casualties, and he held up the application.

However he's very friendly — as is everybody.

It's quite unnecessary to attack the foul place. It's purely to allow some politician to say all France is liberated. As a port it will be useless for some time. The German Commander offered to send out all civilians, if he was given three days. It was refused. That was four days ago and the battle hasn't started yet. The thousands of casualties there'll be could have been utilised to keep the Germans in there till the end of the war — not that they have the least desire to get out.

Don't worry about this letter. I've been blowing up for it for years and it's a certain relief to let out the gas.

You will probably think I have made a great mistake. On the other hand you may think it was inevitable.

It may well be that nothing will come of it all.

Wormwood Scrubs (1944)

It makes me laugh sardonically to think that I, who have run wild and unhindered, and broken most of the commandments, should be imprisoned for refusing to break the sixth. Tell Alec to abandon the tribunal idea. My position is clear. I have gone against my conscience in the past if I thought it the most intelligent thing to do. It is not so spotless that I can use it for a shield. Far from it. It has one or two particularly nasty dents in it, and to hide behind its dented armour would be laughable. It so happens that what I did at Le Havre my conscience agrees with, but that is not the point. The point is that I am a political objector, that I say, and shall continue to say, that this war has exceeded its playing time. I don't put Mr Churchill's conscience in the witness box. I assume he's doing his best and I think he's wrong. I ask the same treatment in return, and refuse to be labelled and put aside as what the world wrongly regards as a crank. I could be just as good a soldier as the Duke of Marlborough (past or present) but I am not a soldier, and I entirely disapprove of the modern D. of Marlborough's war. It is my object to teach people, however inadequately, that soldiers have minds of their own. Consciences are private affairs, and I will not have mine vetted by some seedy old knight who sold the troops marmalade in the Crimean War. Sorry, that's used up all the paper.

Franz Jägerstätter (1907–43) was an Austrian farmer who refused to serve in the army under Hitler. The penalty for refusal was death. He was a sexton in his village church and received only village school education. He wrote to his wife before his sentence (of execution by beheading) was announced.

Our joy to continue

Dearest wife, today it is seven years since we spoke our vows of love and fidelity before God and the priest, and I believe we have faithfully kept these vows to this day. I also believe that, even though we must now live apart, God will continue to give us the grace to keep them until the end of our lives. When I look back upon all this joy and the many graces that have been mine for these seven years, it seems at times almost to border on the miraculous. If someone were to tell me that there is no God or that God does not love us — and if I were to believe him — I would not be able to explain how all this has come to me. Dearest wife, this is why, no matter how we may dread the future, He who has upheld us and given us joy till now will not abandon us then either. If only we do not forget to give thanks and do not hold ourselves back in our striving for heaven, God will permit our joy to continue on for all eternity.

Though I sit behind prison walls, I still believe I can build further on your love and devotion in the days to come. And should I have to leave this life, I will still [rest easy in] my grave, for you know that I am not here as a criminal. It makes me very happy that you have had a Mass read for today, for I know you have given special thought to me while participating in it.

Howard Moore (born 1889) refused to serve in the US armed forces in World War I. As a conscientious objector, he was an 'absolutist' in that he refused to co-operate with the war machine in any way. In November 1918, he was sentenced to 25 years hard labour and held for a lengthy period after the war ended.

If he can stand that, he'll win

On Armistice Day, November 11, 1918, I arrived with a number of other COs at the Fort Leavenworth Disciplinary Barracks. Many of us had seen this forbidding mass of steel and concrete when we first came west from Camp Upton; but now we entered the military prison for the first time, and immediately came to grips with its realities. For refusing to work in the prison I was placed in solitary confinement, shackled to the bars of my cell in a standing position for nine hours each day, on a bread and water diet. 'The hole', as solitary confinement is called in prison, meant a cell nine by five feet, with a barred door, and usually a heavy wooden door in addition so that the only light came through small ventilation slits at top and bottom.

I had a cell without the wooden door, so at least I saw the light of day. There was no bed or blanket, nothing but a toilet at the back of the cell. Here I was to stay until I agreed to work and otherwise conform to regulations.

I soon learned that I was not alone. The cell was alive with bedbugs, which furnished an uneasy diversion as I watched them crawling up my manacled arms and dropping into my hair from the ceiling. By twisting and pressing my body against the bars I could crush some, but not all. Standing nine hours in one spot is exhausting; to sit or lie becomes a pressing need. At the end of the day when the shackles were unlocked, even the concrete floor seemed a haven of rest. But soon it felt cold and unbearably hard. At night the bedbugs were more numerous and more active and were joined by rats, which kept pouncing on my chest as they played around the cell. Since no attempt was ever made by prison authorities to rid the place of vermin, I had to conclude that they were part of my punishment.

When the officer of the day with his guards made rounds to count the prisoners, a guard would shout 'Attention!' and all prisoners were expected to stand with folded arms near their cell doors. But he found me lying on the floor — such an affront to his dignity that he lost count and bellowed that I had better be standing when he came around again. Finding me in the same position on his second round, he became apoplectic and ordered the guards to lash me upright to the cell-door. This was done, but apparently their heart was not in their work, for I easily loosened the ropes and slipped to the floor again. On his third time around the officer turned livid with rage and ordered the guards to enter my cell and teach me a lesson. They proceeded to beat me with their clubs. When I regained consciousness my head was in the lap of the regular guard on the wing. He was soaking up the blood from my hair and face with a handkerchief and saying as though to himself, 'Jesus, if he can stand that, he'll win.'

I relate this incident not boastfully. I knew from past experience that once you conform in any way it will be used against you. It was hard to know just where to draw the line to avoid mere pettiness, but I was determined that I would never work in prison or willingly cooperate to keep myself there. I had to make sure there was no question as to where I stood in my absolute refusal to accept the status of soldier. After this episode I was not again singled out for extra punishment.

One day, standing chained to the bars, resting my head on my arms and lost in daydreams, I felt a sudden burning pain in my hand. A trusty was holding his lighted cigarette against my fingers. Trying to smile, I asked him if he enjoyed hurting me. Had I cursed him, I am sure he would have continued with sadistic delight to torture me. But some color appeared in his pasty face; I don't know whether he felt ashamed or was merely taken aback by my reaction, but he turned and sauntered down the corridor. Later I learned that this man, known as Red, was the terror of the prison.

But Red came peacefully to my cell many times after this. He would bring letters from his sweetheart to share with me. Several times he came with pencil and paper and asked for help in writing to the girl. I imagine that the letters I dictated affected him more than her, for I always presented him as a kind and understanding person. I hoped to influence Red in this way if it were possible. It was a satisfaction when he told me one day that he had never before known anyone whom he could regard as a friend.

It is to men like Red that prison authorities turn to carry out petty torments. He was just another link in the chain of terror forged to reduce the inmates to meek obedience.

From the utter monotony of the day, the nights offered little relief. When the lights went out the bugs became more ravenous and the rats more active. There was no way to shut out the prison noises. Men talked in the corridors, their conversation mostly obscene and profane. Sharp cries came from the wing that held the sexual deviants. And day and night I heard a cry of 'Fight! Fight! Fight!' as regular as the ticking of a clock — the litany of some demented soldier, perhaps a once healthy but sensitive young man whose mind had cracked under military pressures and like a broken phonograph record continued to repeat the same note. Were the thousands of other inmates conscious of any more purpose in their lives?

At last the morning light, like a gray mist, filtered through the barred windows. Bugs disappeared into crevices; where the rats hid by day I did not know. There was a clang of bells, and the officer of the day made his rounds. The chains of the handcuffs rasped against the bars as they were applied to our wrists, and another day of standing in shackles began.

Now, half dozing on my manacled arms, I heard the voice of Arthur Dunham, a religious objector who had shared our tent at Fort Riley during my hunger strike, asking, 'If you don't believe in God, what sustains you?' and I answered him again, 'My own sense of moral responsibility. To accept an authority outside oneself is to deny oneself the right to make an ultimate decision. Understanding that and the consequences likely to follow is to know freedom in the deepest sense.'

Sir Thomas More (1478–1535) was Lord Chancellor of England under Henry VIII. A deeply religious person, he was a humanist and accomplished writer. He refused the Oath of Supremacy which stated that Henry was supreme head of the church, although ordered by the king to do so. He was imprisoned in the Tower of London in 1534 and from there wrote to his daughter Margaret with 'coals' from the fire, being deprived of pen and ink in the last months before his execution.

Look first upon God

Surely, Meg, a fainter heart than thy frail father hath, canst thou not have. And yet I verily trust in the great mercy of God, that he shall of his goodness so stay me with his holy hand, that he shall not finally suffer me to fall wretchedly from his favour. And the like trust, dear daughter, I verily conceive of you. And so much the more in that if we call his benefits to mind and often give him thanks for them, we may find many tokens to give us good hope, in spite of all our manifold offences towards him, that, if we will heartily call for it, his great mercy will not be withdrawn from us.

And truly my dear daughter, in this is my great comfort, that albeit I am of nature so shrinking from pain, that I am almost afraid of a fillip, with a heavy fearful heart forecasting all such perils and painful deaths as by any manner of possibility might later befall me, and in such thought often lying long restless and wakeful while my wife thought I had slept; yet any such fear and heavy pensiveness — I thank the mighty mercy of God — I never in my mind intended to consent to do anything, even though it mean enduring the uttermost, that in mine own conscience would damnably cast me in the displeasure of God.

And whereas it might haply seem to be but small cause for comfort because I might take harm here first in the meanwhile, I thanked God that my case was such in this matter through the clearness of mine own conscience, that though I might have pain I could not have harm, for a man may in such a case lose his head and have no harm. For I was very sure that I had always from the beginning truly accustomed myself to look first upon God and next upon the King.

A German U-boat commander in World War I, **Martin Niemoller** (1892–1984) became a Lutheran pastor, and spoke out against Nazism in the 1930s. He ignored a ban on his preaching, and was imprisoned or in concentration camps from 1937 to 1945. He later became actively involved in the peace movement.

In December 1937 he wrote to his wife, Else, from Moabit prison. Hansjochen is one of his sons.

When the powerful are silent

It is good too that God imprisons someone who can endure it physically and bear it mentally, and someone with whom he still has a few things to work in peace and quiet, so that the time is not wasted on him! And whose wife can endure thanks to a congregation which spoils her — even if somewhat turbulently! Yes, it is almost frightening to think of all the love that one can not only not repay but that one can spiritually hardly grasp and take in! I receive greetings from the boys and girls in confirmation class that are full of an unconscious, pastoral energy. I stand before it as if beholding a miracle, considering that I give decidedly impartial and sober lessons. Then there are the theology students who write a sermon on a postcard to which one can only respond and bow. Then Hansjochen with all his fifteen years brings one — thank God, unknowingly — to one's senses. When the *powerful* are silent out of fear or cleverness, the children proclaim God's praise and his power, because otherwise 'the stones' would have to cry out.

So it may be that we can celebrate Christmas this year with new confidence that 'the great joy' will occur once again *to all* people! So, love, now you know the general course that I am following.

Nicola Sacco and Bartolomeo Vanzetti were poor Italian immigrants to the United States, landing in 1908 when Sacco was 17 and Vanzetti 20 years old. Sacco became a shoemaker and Vanzetti a labourer. Both were involved in trade union work during and after World War I. In 1920 they were charged with murder in a payroll robbery but consistently proclaimed their innocence. Amidst a wave of public anti-radical hysteria, they were convicted on the basis of what was widely held to be fabricated evidence. Later another man confessed to the crime.

They were executed by electrocution on 23 August 1927. Vanzetti, who was unmarried, wrote this last letter to Sacco's son, Dante, then 13 years old.

Deadly against us

I still hope, and we will fight until the last moment, to revindicate our right to live and to be free, but all the forces of the State and of the money and reaction are deadly against us because we are libertarians or anarchists.

I write little of this because you are now and yet too young to understand these things and other things of which I would like to reason with you.

But, if you do well, you will grow and understand your father's and my case and your father's and my principles, for which we will soon be put to death.

I tell you now that all that I know of your father, he is not a criminal, but one of the bravest men I ever knew. Some day you will understand what I am about to tell you. That your father has sacrificed everything dear and sacred to the human heart and soul for his fate in liberty and justice for all. That day you will be proud of your father, and if you come brave enough, you will take his place in the struggle between tyranny and liberty and you will vindicate his (our) names and our blood.

If we have to die now, you shall know, when you will be able to understand this tragedy in its fullest, how good and brave your father has been with you, your father and I, during these eight years of struggle, sorrow, passion, anguish and agony.

I assure you that neither have I been a criminal, that I have committed no robbery and no murder, but only fought modestly to abolish crimes from among mankind and for the liberty of all.

Remember Dante, each one who will say otherwise of your father and I, is a liar, insulting innocent dead men who have been brave in their life. Remember and know also, Dante, that if your father and I would have been cowards and hypocrits and rinnegetors of our faith, we would not have been put to death. They would not even have convicted a lebbrous dog; not even executed a deadly poisoned scorpion on such evidence as that they framed against us. They would have given a new trial to a matricide and abitual felon on the evidence we presented for a new trial.

Remember, Dante, remember always these things; we are not criminals; they convicted us on a frame-up; they denied us a new trial; and if we will be executed after seven years, four months and seventeen days of unspeakable tortures and wrong, it is for what I have already told you; because we were for the poor and against the exploitation and oppression of the man by the man.

The day will come when you will understand the atrocious cause of the above written words, in all its fullness. Then you will honor us.

Now Dante, be brave and good always. I embrace you.

PS. I left the copy of *An American Bible* to your mother now, for she will like to read it, and she will give it to you when you will be bigger and able to understand it. Keep it for remembrance.

6. Family

Just ask my contemporaries
Camp women, prison women, martyrs
And we will tell you of the numb terror
Of raising children for execution
At the block, or back to the wall,
Of raising children for the prisons . . .

Anna Akhmatova *whose son was kept in gaol
by Stalin as hostage for her good behaviour*

I gave the boy
a pair of pigeons
born and bred
in my harsh prison.
They had taped wings . . .
But the tape from his pigeons
he removed one day,
and set them free.
. . . I guess we're of one mind.
Why cage pigeons
who prefer free flight
in the vaster, bluer skies?

Mila Aguila *a Filipina poet whose only son was
12 when she was arrested in 1984*

The letter below was written to her father in the mid-1970s by an anonymous **Filipina woman** active in that country's political struggles. At the time she was pregnant, in solitary confinement and had recently witnessed the murder of her husband by security forces.

I inherited your obstinacy

I tried to postpone this dreadful moment of truth. For it pains me deeply to acknowledge that you have chosen to place insurmountable obstacles along the path of rekindling our past intimacy. I was and still am determined to preserve and develop our relationship, not only out of deep parental affection but also a firm belief, as I had told you earlier, that you are actually a friend in the present struggle of our people for national freedom and democracy.

Papa, please help me to understand your seeming callousness over my situation, I am seven months pregnant, a grieving widow and detained in solitary confinement in a small windowless room in this army camp. Yet, you refuse to visit me even just to commiserate with my harsh plight. You should have taken into consideration the fact that I was in a state of shock, having witnessed the martyrdom of my husband, Noel, whom you had refused to acknowledge because of his worker origin. When you saw me two days after his death, I was still wearing the same dress which I used to drench the blood off his face while softly calling his name and embracing and begging him to answer. I treasure this unwashed dress for it bears the blood of a man who had died in the service of his fellowmen.

You neglected to respond to my great need to be comforted in my gravest hour of bereavement. Did your friend tell you that his men peppered our hut with bullets? That it was truly a miracle that I survived without a scratch, no thanks to his brave soldiers? Did he also tell you that his men had forced me to walk for hours without rest and with my hands tied behind my back over tortuous mountain trails? That I collapsed and nearly had an abortion? Did he finally tell you that his men did not allow me to clear Noel's body before it was unceremoniously thrown into a makeshift grave?

Papa, you, more than anyone else, ought to know that I do stand firmly on my principles. You have often complained that I had inherited your obstinacy on questions of principles. Thus, your present attitude of pitting our political differences, on the one hand, against our personal relationship, on the other, as mutually exclusive opposites, is liable to leave me with no alternative except to resolutely abide by my principles irrespective of what this may do to our relationship later. That you are willing to forget your pregnant daughter in prison, as long as she remains steadfast in her commitment to the revolutionary movement of our people, is a choice you have to make or have made.

But why should we insist on giving each other a choice when we can live in mutual respect and deep affection despite our differences? We have a basic unity for we do not belong objectively in the ranks of the oppressors. Our differences should be threshed out through persuasion, in recognition of our respective rights and not on the basis of a parent-daughter relationship. I am, after all, a full grown woman now and about to become a mother.

You should understand, Papa, that I owe much of what I have become from you. I was reared strictly on the Christian ethic of service to one's fellowmen. You also taught me about honesty, integrity and incorruptibility. It was a must for me then to keep repeating the golden rule everytime I was caught taking advantage of my playmates or brothers. Are you surprised then that I abhor the exploitation of man by man? Should you wonder why I insist on equality and the right of every man to the same opportunity as the others?

In two months' time, I shall be giving birth. I hope it will be a boy so that I can name him Noel Roberto, in honour of the two men who have affected me most. When he is old enough, I shall tell him often about his martyred father and his Christian grandfather. I promise to give him what each of you has given me: the loftiness of ideals and the necessity to practise them.

St Margaret Clitherow (1556–86) was born in York, England. Shortly after her marriage she became a Catholic, and was imprisoned three times. She set up rooms in her and her neighbour's houses for hearing Mass and for educating Catholic children. She was arrested and brought before a court, but refused to plead so that no witnesses could be called, thereby protecting her neighbour. This means that she was punished by '*peine, forte et dure*', i.e., she was slowly pressed to death by heavy stones being placed on her supine body. She was canonized in 1970 by Pope Paul VI.

Flesh is frail

You charge me wrong. I do not desperately or willingly procure mine own death, for, not being guilty of such crimes as were laid against me, and yet condemned to die, I could not but rejoice, my cause being also God's quarrel. Neither did I fear the terror of the sentence of death, but was ashamed on their behalf to hear such shameful words uttered in that audience as to strip me naked, and press me to death amongst men, which methought for womanhood they might have concealed.

As for my husband, know you that I love him next unto God in this world, and I have a care over my children as a mother ought to have. I trust I have done my duty to them to bring them up in the fear of God, and so I trust I am discharged of them. And for this cause I am willing to offer them freely to God that lent them to me, rather than I will yield one jot from my faith.

I confess death is fearful, and flesh is frail. Yet I am minded by God's grace and assistance to spend my blood in this cause as willingly as ever I gave my child the breast, and desire not to have my death deferred.

Since the Iranian revolution or 1978, the **Bahai** religion, which was founded in Iran, has been subject to severe persecution. Many adherents have been imprisoned, and many executed. **Suhrab Habibi** was executed in June 1981. In his final hours he wrote to his wife and children.

Be steadfast like a high mountain

My dear and affectionate Parvin, my dear children, apples of my eye.

It is five minutes to 11 p.m. on 13 June 1981. We have been summoned by the revolutionary court and called to the field of martyrdom. My wish is that you may share the tranquillity of conscience and confidence of heart that I feel in these last moments before my physical separation from you. It is stated in our Sacred Writings that we Bahais should always observe calmness, dignity and moderation.

Farewell, farewell to all of you. I wish you all success.

You, dear Ilham, and Ru'ya, are very fortunate girls to have a mother like mama who is not only your mother but your friend and confidant. I have not much to tell you now. All that I might wish to tell you is already recorded in the Sacred Words of God. Remember me in your devotions; I shall feel close to you in spirit. Always try to serve under the Bahai administration.

As for worldly belongings, I have only an uncompleted house and some unpaid debts. You are welcome to dispose of the house or use it in any way you deem fit.

My dear Parvin, take good care of the children. My children, take good care of mama. May your father be sacrificed for you. I hope that you will not cry and mourn, for this is against the wish of God.

Before I finish, I remind you again that whenever you feel moved to converse with me, read the Words of God. Whatever is in the true essence of my heart is recorded in the Books and Tablets.

I have [made] two bracelets which are in the pocket of my short-sleeved shirt in prison. There is a ring in the pocket of the jacket which I am wearing.

My dear wife Parvin, I wish you happiness and success during your life. The will of God is that we should be physically separated, but spiritually we are always together. Do not grieve and have no sorrow because of what has happened to me. Be steadfast like a high mountain. My dearest children, Ilham and Ru'ya, will be under your care.

Ask forgiveness from all my friends and family.

Eugene Heimler (1922–1990) was a young writer in Budapest, Hungary, when, in 1944, he was sent to Auschwitz. All his family died there. After liberation he was, for a period, Director of Social Work for the London County Council, and then Professor of Human Social Functioning in Calgary, Canada. He later ran a clinic in North London, using his psycho-therapeutic knowledge to help concentration camp survivors.

A miracle happened. A smile . . .

It was only some hours later that I began to understand why these prematurely aged children clung to me.

Experience and materialist ideology alike had taught these children to look for a self-interested motive behind every human act. A person who was kind to them must, therefore, be either a homosexual with designs on their bodies, or a Nazi spy wanting to use them as informers. The idea that the human soul has a thousand shades of feeling, that at times all logical reasoning is submerged in the depths of the soul, the idea that someone might wish to stretch out a hand towards them simply because they were helpless and weak, would have been completely unacceptable and confusing to these children, and would have roused profound suspicion. So I became a 'commissar' in their eyes; they believed that I was 'organizing' them on the express instructions of the Buchenwald Communists. The perverse wickedness of the Nazi machinery had managed to paralyse their youthful souls, transforming them into cold little human machines. The ten-year-olds could still cry, but not those of fourteen, who were impudent, bullying and dangerous.

Next morning, at the Appel, sixteen children crowded around me. The *Lageraltester* — a German Communist — growled at me, saying that I should have lined the children up in a separate group. He, too, believed that I was the special agent of Buchenwald. Thus the seventeen of us stood in a separate group. Then in came the SS *Hauptsturmfuehrer*, a man of middle age, with the infamous skull and cross-bones adorning his uniform cap. Without a word he passed by the two thousand men until he reached our little group. And then a miracle happened. A smile stole on to the face of the SS officer. He even smiled like a human being. He stroked the children's heads, and turned to me.

'You must take good care of these children. Is that understood?'

'Yes, *Herr Hauptsturmfuehrer*.'

'Not a hair of their heads must be touched while I am here.'

'Yes, sir.'

'Take them to the kitchen to peel potatoes. You go with them and look after them.'

'Yes, sir.'

And I marched the youngsters off towards the kitchen.

The eyes were popping out of the head of Hans Kapo, the prisoner in charge of the kitchen, as we entered in a body.

'Since when do they put Jews in charge at Buchenwald?'

There was no answer. Kapo paced up and down. After five minutes he pulled up in front of me.

'You aren't a Jew. Right?'

'I am a Jew!'

'You can't be a Jew!'

By now I had had enough.

'Listen, Kapo,' I said, 'I am a Jew whether you like it or not. Furthermore, whether you like it or not, I am going to stay here with the children. Furthermore, you're going to get a bigger kick in your arse from me, and from the kids, and from Buchenwald than you've ever had in your life — unless you shut that filthy big mouth of yours.'

For the first time, he glanced at me as if I were a human being. Then he scratched his head.

'You haven't got a sense of humour,' he said. 'I was only joking.'

'I was joking, too,' I said, with a straight face.

After that we started peeling the potatoes.

I would often pray to God. I thanked Him for my good fortune in having weathered the past months, and that now, fortified in body and soul, I had charge of sixteen young lives for whom I felt responsible. I felt these days that, in my own small way, I was part of creation: and I sensed within myself something of that vast power that was responsible for me. I felt that God frequently works out His plans through human beings, and that if only we listen to human words and voice, we can often hear Him speak. And whenever I succeeded in bringing curiosity, interest, a smile, or sometimes tears into the eyes of these wretched children and felt proud of myself for it, I also thought that in my very self-praise I was praising that Infinite power which had granted me the opportunity of playing a positive role in this inferno. I felt that I had strength only because He was present in my blood and in my senses, and that so long as I realized this force within me, the Germans would be unable to touch me.

During the Cultural Revolution in China, many urban intellectuals were sent to forced labour camps in remote country areas. In 1969 **Yang Jiang**, then aged 58, a writer and lecturer, was sent to such a camp while her husband, Mo-cun, was placed in a neighbouring camp. They were 'rehabilitated' after two years. Here she describes a clandestine visit to her husband.

A watery journey

I felt a sudden desire to go see Mo-cun. I knew that it was against regulations to go see him without first getting permission, but at that time they wouldn't blow the bugle, line us up in formation, or take roll. I decided to sneak around the kitchen and take the western road.

The fields around me were all laid out with irrigation ditches; normally dry, they turned into rivers of water following the rains. As I crossed a small bridge I was faced with a pathway that was completely flooded, the water mixing with that in the irrigation ditches to form a small river. But it was only a matter of a few steps before I could be on the road itself, and since I wasn't about to turn back then, I very gingerly stepped into the shallow water on the bank. There were a few spots on the uneven ground where the water was relatively deep, but I somehow managed to cross to the crest of the bank without incident. Taking a look behind me, I was relieved to find that I was not being pursued, so I stepped onto the road and headed west, making a mental note to take a different route on my return trip.

The mud on the road forced me to go slowly, one cautious step at a time. More than once I nearly walked right out of my boots when they stuck in the mud. Not only that, several mud clods somehow worked their way into the boots themselves. It was a wide road, level and straight for all but the last twenty or thirty feet before the brick kiln, where it was all caved in. Since it had rained for several days, this spot had now turned into a swamp, looking for all the world like a shallow pond, with two embankments running right down the middle. I stepped up onto one of the embankments and promptly sank into the water; it had only been a ridge formed by passing carts, and once it was saturated with water it crumbled as soon as it was touched. The water only lacked a couple of inches of completely covering my rainboots. I pressed on, one tentative step after another, using my walking stick for added support, until, to my own amazement, I forded the pond without incident.

Once I had reached the brick kiln at the top of the little hill, I had to turn and head north. After a heavy rainfall, the water rose until the spot became an island in the midst of rapidly flowing water.

I walked along the northern bank, watching the expanse of water grow broader and broader. Mo-cun's dormitory was located on the other side, where he lived in the last of several rows of grey, tiled buildings. By the time his dormitory was in sight, the river was at least three metres across. A small bridge had been washed away and was now floating in a heap downstream. In the torrential downpour, the sky and the ground seemed to have fused together. But the three-metre wide river in front of me had cut the road off completely.

Now if I went all the way to the foot of the hill beneath the brick kiln and hopped over into the little island, then jumped across to the other side, wouldn't that put me where I wanted to be? As I looked over at the other side I saw nothing but rock-strewn ground, with no road in sight; but at least over there I could count on an open stretch of ground, unbroken by any river. However, the footing was very slippery on the riverbank, and I couldn't be sure of my footing in rainboots as I would in cloth shoes. Another question mark had to do with the firmness of the mud on the little island. I tested the ground with my walking stick, and it seemed firm enough so I stuck the end of the walking stick deeply in the ground and vaulted over onto the island, then repeated the procedure to jump over to the opposite bank. The road back was full of bumps and hollows, and if I wasn't stepping into mud I was sloshing through water; but after more hardships and obstacles than I could count, I somehow managed to make it to the front door of Mo-cun's dormitory.

I opened the door and walked in, much to his surprise.

'What are you doing here?'

'I came to see you,' I said with a smile.

Anka Kowalska is a Polish writer who was detained when
martial law was declared in 1981. She had been editing
unofficial publications. All her notes and diary were
confiscated so she wrote on scraps of paper the size of
postage stamps. Whilst in detention she wrote the poem
from which extracts are taken here. '19-500 Goldap' is the
postal address of her detention centre from which she was
released in 1982 on grounds of ill-health.

19-500 Goldap

Those concussed are at last taken to hospital
those lamed during the last transport can now walk
and that one who's been lying facing the wall these last three days
is just a hysteric
isn't the Children's Home looking after her child?

Several women had letters from home
which said that seven weeks
ago
the husband was arrested
granny was well
father had a heart attack but wasn't too bad

A Red Cross commission arrived
'Have you any problems? Are you ladies hungry?
Are you in touch with home?'
'They threatened executions, they threatened Siberia'
'But now you are all right? We see you have baths'
'Our families took a long time to find us'
'Well, it's wartime post — and now?'
'Now I've received a letter two months old'
'That's excellent' 'There's a woman here with tubercular kidneys'
'Make a note of this, we must somehow'
'Security are forcing her to collaborate'
'That, madam, is not our business
We are the Red Cross'

In 1970 **Adriana de Laborde** graduated in physics at La Plata University, Argentina, and then worked there as a teacher and researcher. In February 1977 she was abducted when seven months pregnant and taken to a police interrogation centre. She later testified before a Commission of Inquiry.

A prison birth

On 15 April I began to go into labour. After three or four hours of being on the floor with contractions that were coming faster and faster, and thanks to the shouts of the other women, I was taken away in an army patrol car with two men in front and one woman behind (the woman was called 'Lucrecia' — she used to take part in the torture sessions).

We drove in the direction of Buenos Aires, but my child wouldn't wait and at the crossroads of Alpargatas the woman shrieked that they should stop the car on the verge, and there Teresa was born. Thanks to the forces of nature, the birth was normal. The only assistance I received was when 'Lucrecia' tied the umbilical cord which was still linking me with the child as there was nothing to cut it with. No more than five minutes later we drove on, supposedly in the direction of a hospital. I was still blindfolded and my child was on the seat. After many twists and turns we arrived at what I later learnt was the building of the Detective Squad of Banfield. There I saw the doctor. He cut the umbilical cord in the car and took me up two or three floors to a place where they removed the placenta. He made me undress in front of an officer on duty. I had to wash the bed, the floor, and my dress, and clear away the placenta. Then, finally they left me to wash my baby, while they continued with their insults and threats. On entering the building they took off my blindfold saying, 'It's not necessary now', so that for the rest of the time I could see their faces.

In Banfield the rules were much stricter. We left our cells to eat only once every two days. In each cell there were three or more women, and for a lavatory there was a bottle of bleach with the top cut off. I managed to arrange for Patricia Huchansky de Simon to be put into the same cell as me and my baby, and she helped me a great deal in the first few days when I was racked with post-natal pains.

Finally, on 25 April I was dropped off four blocks away from my parents' house, with my baby in my arms; I was in a nightdress and slippers, without any identification and the two of us were covered in fleas. At practically the same time my husband was released from La Plata.

Roman Mirga and his parents were playing as a gypsy trio in a Warsaw cafe in November 1942 when they heard that the Nazis were about to round up all gypsies and put them in concentration camps. Roman was seventeen. The family and other gypsies decided to try to get to Hungary, travelling secretly by horse-drawn gypsy caravan, disguised as Polish peasants. Roman was married by gypsy rites on the journey. The group was discovered on the Austrian border and transported to Auschwitz. Roman's father was allocated to the camp orchestra, which played to allay the victims' fears as they entered the extermination buildings. Roman became a translator for Dr Mengele. The whole family apart from Roman died in the camp. Roman escaped in 1944, was hidden by a Polish peasant woman for several months until liberated by the Russians. He made notes while in hiding, and later told his story to a fellow Pole, writer Alexander Ramati.

Taking a bath

The Gypsies in the camp, those outside the hospital, had a childlike mentality. They believed that they would get through the war. A Gypsy can cry for himself, but he will never lose hope, never lose his song. This has helped us survive through thousands of years. Our Aryan origin was our insurance — no crematorium for us; starvation, yes, but even this did not deter our people from playing, singing and dancing in Auschwitz.

I ran to the hospital past armed soldiers, orderlies carrying the sick or dead in addition to white-aproned doctors and nurses moving in and out of the barracks — and bolted into the *Noma-Abteilung*, my eyes darting towards Zoya's bunk. My heart froze. It was empty! She must have been moved to another place. I refused to believe the worst. But I could not find her, methodically though I scanned the room, bunk after bunk, all three tiers.

I rushed over to the wooden partition which was Professor Epstein's cabinet. He was sitting at his desk studying an X-ray against a lamp. 'My wife!' I cried out.

He lowered his eyes. I let out a scream like a wounded animal, then ran all the way back to the bed I had come to twice daily for the past weeks. But no miracle occurred. The bunk was still empty. I slumped down, my fingertips caressing the crumpled blanket left behind. I sat there motionless for some time, stricken with pain, yet unable to weep and find some relief in tears, for in Auschwitz I had forgotten how to cry. I barely heard the approaching footsteps, the consoling words of Professor Epstein, or his receding footsteps. Then someone brusquely touched my arm.

'Will you move, please,' I heard a Polish nurse say. I turned. Behind her stood two orderlies carrying a stretcher with a new *noma* patient, a five-year-old boy.

'We need the bed,' the nurse said. 'And you'd better hurry to the *Appellplatz* or you'll miss roll-call.'

During the night of 1 August 1944, the night of the Auschwitz massacre of 4,000 Gypsies, I was glued to the window, never having closed my eyes, listening to the orchestra, knowing that my father's music had accompanied my mother on her last journey, yet assured that, as long as I could hear the sounds of his violin, he at least was still alive.

In the first pale light of the breaking day, I saw SS men fanning through the camp, seeking out the few people still hiding in latrines or clinging to roofs, and shooting them on the spot. Then the guns fell silent, the soldiers left, and complete quiet enveloped the camp. Tongues of flame were still rising to the sky from the crematoria, but not a sound was breaking the stillness of the fading night. My hands grabbed at the window-sill. There was no music anymore. The violins had stopped playing.

I screamed, for I knew at that moment from the depth of my soul that I would never see my father again. It was the orchestra's turn to take a bath.

Her husband having already been burnt as an Anabaptist, **Janneken Muntsdorp**'s similar fate was delayed to allow her to give birth to her daughter whilst in prison in Antwerp, Belgium. Before going to the stake, she wrote a letter to her infant daughter for her to read in later life. It is dated 10 August 1573.

I must leave you here alone

My dearest child, the true love of God and wisdom of the Father strengthen you in virtue, you who are yet so young, and whom I must leave here in this wicked, evil, perverse world.

Since the Lord has so ordered and foreordained that I must leave you here, and you are deprived of father and mother, I will commend you to the Lord. I can help you in no other way; I had to leave your father for the Lord's sake, and could keep him only half a year, after which we were apprehended because we sought the salvation of our souls. They took him from me, not knowing my condition, and I had to remain in prison and see him go before me. And now that I have abided the time and borne you under my heart with great sorrow for nine months, and given birth to you here in prison, they have taken you from me. Here I lie, expecting death every morning, and shall soon follow your dear father. And I, your dear mother, write you, my dearest child, something for a remembrance.

Since I am now delivered up to death, and must leave you here alone, I must through these lines cause you to remember, that when you have attained your understanding, you endeavour to fear God, and see and examine why and for whose name we both died; for you must know that it is not for the sake of any evil. For when we sought here in quietness and gentleness to practise our faith, then they did not leave us in peace; then our blood was sought.

My dear child, I pray you, that wherever you live when you are grown up, and begin to have understanding, you conduct yourself well and honestly, so that no one need have cause to complain of you. And always be faithful, taking good heed not to wrong any one. Do not accustom your mouth to filthy talk, nor to ugly words that are not proper, nor to lies; and run not in the street as other bad children do; rather take up a book, and learn to seek there that which concerns your salvation.

And where you have your home, obey those whose bread you eat. If they speak evil, do you speak well. And learn always to love to be doing something; and do not think yourself too good for anything, nor exalt yourself.

Oh, that it had pleased the Lord, that I might have brought you up; I should so gladly have done my best with respect to it; but it seems that it is not the Lord's will. Your father and myself were so well joined that we would not have forsaken each other for the whole world, and yet we had to leave each other for the Lord's sake. So I must also leave you here, my dearest lamb; the Lord that created and made you now takes me from you.

Your dear father demonstrated with his blood the genuine truth, and I also hope to attest the same, though flesh and blood must remain on the posts and on the stake, well knowing that we shall meet hereafter.

Hence, my dear child, be content. Always be honourable and courteous toward all men, and let your modesty be manifest to all men when you have attained to your understanding.

And now, Janneken, my dear lamb, who are yet very little and young, I leave you this letter, together with a gold *real*, which I had with me in prison, and this I leave you for a perpetual adieu, and for a testament; that you may remember me by it, as also by this letter. Read it, when you have understanding, and keep it as long as you live in remembrance of me and of your father. I kiss you heartily, my dear lamb, with a perpetual kiss of peace. Follow me and your father, and be not ashamed to confess us before the world, for we were not ashamed to confess our faith before the world.

Remember thereby your dear father, and me, your dear mother, who have written this with my own hand, for your edification. I herewith bid you adieu and farewell; I hope to seal this letter with my blood at the stake.

This is the testament which I wrote in prison for my daughter Janneken, whom I bore and gave birth to here in my bonds.

A well-known Egyptian writer and journalist, **Farida al-Naqqash** was arrested together with her husband in 1972 for participating in student opposition to the Egyptian administration. She was held in solitary confinement for a month and a half, and wrote to her husband from prison.

Return to the children

I spoke to you at length yesterday evening during the power-cut, and was at that time sure that you were still in Tora prison. I opened my window to release my secret silent message; and also to hear the sound of the cockroaches as they moved about in circles, squares, and straight lines, creating a true Kafkaesque atmosphere. I deliberately listened and watched in order to share with you and with the dear residents of Tora the experience of filth, rats, cockroaches and sickly smells. Or is this simply a masochist tendency? or a fantasy? better that one of us avoid pain, I think. I turned to gaze on the neglected gardens — but found they had done some cleaning up yesterday. They had pruned my tree, and watered the lawn profusely. The area super-intendent was paying us a visit, and bricks were laid, and badly whitewashed, around the lawn. The month-old piles of rubbish were cleared, and the management requested all residents in both polite and impolite terms to clean up their areas. However, I now realize that the silent celebration which I shared from my window was for your release in the evening. But I am truly happy, my dear, that my guess proved wrong, with regard to yesterday, that day full of excitement. I dozed a little at about 4 o'clock. After less than five minutes I suddenly jumped at the sound of a loud scream from Gassir.

He was crying in pain, and I was about to faint. Yet I managed to stay calm and call your name. Now I know how anxiety can affect the imagination, and fill the mind with delusions.

Now you are there, and the 'language of absence' which children practise so well has receded. I call it the language of absence: it occurs when children awake suddenly, calling for someone other than their parents; someone who is dear to them, whom they refer to in the third person. I don't know whether this is a melodrama but it is painful in any case.

You are now free to embrace Rasha and Gassir, and to think of me. Your horizons are wider. This is splendid, my kind and brave dear. My heart is now assured, and for this there is a price that you will pay. You will become anxious on my account, and worry as I used to, alone and under pressure. You will go to the Party Office to face the backlog of work and the numerous tasks. Yet believe me, if I swear by that small world which binds the three of you, I am now happy, and I don't care how long this imprisonment lasts.

Yet, I am full of joy for your return. This will be your happiest return since we met. I love you because you returned to the children, and continue to love you even if you are returned to prison, as you no doubt shall be. What shall I say?

There are many trees here by the wall, with leaves that grow quickly and secretly in the night to hide us from secret informants and blind jailers. Our world will be born in spite of everything, and our flag flies over many places in the world because of the sacrifices of the best individuals. Our sorrows will not hold us back, for they belong with the burdens of the people who command our loyalty and faith, and whose wisdom is our teacher. This conclusion pleases me, to a letter which turns out to be a sad one in spite of all my efforts.

St Perpetua was under instruction as a potential member of the Christian church in Carthage, Africa, when, in 203 AD, she was arrested and thrown to the beasts. She was about 22 years old and with a baby at the breast.

My prison a palace

While we were still under arrest I was baptized, and I was inspired by the Spirit not to ask for any other favour after the water but simply the perseverance of the flesh. A few days later we were lodged in the prison; and I was terrified, as I had never before been in such a dark hole. What a difficult time it was! With the crowd the heat was stifling;

then there was the extortion of the soldiers; and to crown all, I was tortured with worry for my baby there.

Then Tertius and Pomponius, those blessed deacons who tried to take care of us, bribed the soldiers to allow us to go to a better part of the prison to refresh ourselves for a few hours. Everyone then left that dungeon and shifted for himself. I nursed my baby, who was faint from hunger. In my anxiety I spoke to my mother about the child, I tried to comfort my brother, and I gave the child in their charge. I was in pain because I saw them suffering out of pity for me. These were the trials I had to endure for many days. Then I got permission for my baby to stay with me in prison. At once I recovered my health, relieved as I was of my worry and anxiety over the child. My prison had suddenly become a palace, so that I wanted to be there rather than anywhere else.

One day while we were eating breakfast we were suddenly hurried off for a hearing. We arrived at the forum, and a huge crowd gathered. We walked up to the prisoners' dock. All the others when questioned admitted their guilt. Then, when it came to my turn, my father dragged me from the step, and said: 'Perform the sacrifice — have pity on your baby!'

Hilarianus the governor said to me: 'Have pity on your father's grey head; have pity on your infant son. Offer the sacrifice for the welfare of the emperors.'

'I will not,' I retorted.

'Are you a Christian?' said Hilarianus.

And I said: 'Yes, I am.'

Then Hilarianus passed sentence on all of us: we were condemned to the beasts, and we returned to prison in high spirits. But my baby had got used to being nursed at the breast and to staying with me in prison. So I sent the deacon Pomponius straight away to my father to ask for the baby. But my father refused to give him over. But as God willed, the baby had no further desire for the breast, nor did I suffer any inflammation; and so I was relieved of any anxiety for my child and of any discomfort in my breasts.

7. Forgiveness

In spite of everything I still believe that people
are really good at heart.

Anne Frank

O Lord,
remember not only the men and women of
good will
but also those of evil will.
But do not remember all the suffering
they have inflicted upon us;
remember the fruits we have borne
thanks to this suffering —
our comradeship, our loyalty, our humility,
our courage, our generosity,
the greatness of heart
which has grown out of all this;
and when they come to the judgement,
let all the fruits that we have borne
be their forgiveness.

Prayer found scribbled on a piece of
wrapping paper near the body of a child at
Ravensbrück concentration camp

Members of the Dutch Reformed Church, **Corrie** and **Betsie Ten Boom** were sisters living in Holland during the Nazi occupation of 1940–44. They built a secret hiding-place in their house in old Haarlem for Jews, but were arrested and spent five years in Ravensbrück concentration camp. Corrie survived to write of her experiences.

Forgiving the SS guard

It was at a church service in Munich that I saw him, the former SS man who had stood guard at the shower room door in the processing centre at Ravensbruck. He was the first of our actual jailers that I had seen since that time. And suddenly it was all there — the roomful of mocking men, the heaps of clothing, Betsie's pain-blanched face.

He came up to me as the church was emptying, beaming and bowing. 'How grateful I am for your message, Fraulein,' he said. 'To think that, as you say, He has washed my sins away!'

His hand was thrust out to shake mine. And I, who had preached so often the need to forgive me, kept my hand at my side.

Even as the angry, vengeful thoughts boiled through me, I saw the sin of them. Jesus Christ had died for this man; was I going to ask for more? Lord Jesus, I prayed, forgive me and help me to forgive him.

I tried to smile, I struggled to raise my hand. I could not. I felt nothing, not the slightest spark of warmth or charity. And so again I breathed a silent prayer. Jesus, I cannot forgive him. Give me Your forgiveness.

As I took his hand the most incredible thing happened. From my shoulder along my arm and through my hand a current seemed to pass from me to him, while into my heart sprang a love for this stranger that almost overwhelmed me.

And so I discovered that it is not on our forgiveness any more than on our goodness that the world's healing hinges, but on His. When He tells us to love our enemies, He gives, along with the command, the love itself.

Adolfo Perez Esquivel, an Argentinian, is a leading member of the non-violent liberation movement in Latin America. In Argentina in 1977 he was arrested, tortured and spent 15 months in prison. Following his release, he returned to his work with *Servicio Paz y Justicia*, an organization for peace

workers in Latin America. He was awarded the Nobel Peace
Prize in 1980.

Discovered hope

I was in a torture centre, imprisoned in a small narrow cell without
light or sanitary facilities. When they opened the door letting in the
light, I could see many inscriptions on the walls. One day they left the
door open a little longer than usual, and when I looked more closely
around the cell I saw, on one wall, a big blood stain. Below it, written
by a finger dipped in the blood, it said: '*Dios no mata*' — 'God does not
kill.' This is something that is burned into my memory and will be
with me the rest of my life.

We weren't allowed any type of manual labour. The Bible, the
gospels, and all spiritual books were prohibited. But I meditated a lot
on the time Jesus spent wandering in the desert. For me this silence of
God was to make a desert within myself and to discover how, while my
body was in prison, my spirit was free. This was a slow and very
painful process.

In prison you are naked, destitute. You are only a number. Then
the question is: what is there for us to redeem ourselves as persons? For
me, prayer was important — learning more profoundly what it is to
pray and discovering what is continual prayer. Meditation. Feeling
the permanent presence of God and especially listening to the silence
of God. What does God want to say to us through the signs of our
times? This was most important for me.

As for mental health, it is the same as with prayer. In prison you
have to do a complete job of resisting mentally and spiritually in the
face of oppression. For me, it was a difficult but rich experience to
understand the meaning of the gospel and its nonviolent power,
especially under torture, to see and discover how these persons who
were torturing us are also our brothers, to look for a Christian response
in the face of being tortured.

There is something very strong in the gospel, which I believe is the
root of the whole gospel: the power of love. When you experience this
extreme situation of being between life and death, you try to
understand what Christ said on the cross: 'Father, forgive them, for
they don't know what they are doing.' But I thought that, yes, these
people *did* know what they were doing. This was very contradictory
for me, and I tried to understand more deeply through prayer and
meditation, what was it that Christ was trying to say to us in this
supreme moment? It is this experience of the forgiveness of Christ that
we have to accept and carry on.

Another thing I discovered was hope. I had never before thought so deeply about hope. In prison, I discovered the force of concrete hope, which was our force of resistance. There was also a shared hope with my fellow prisoners. I saw that many others, through pain, were discovering themselves as persons and were discovering faith. I believe it is in these critical moments that you discover your true identity, because you are completely empty, and there is nothing to meet but yourself and God.

Michael Etkind was born in Lodz, Poland in 1925. He and his family were forced to move into the Lodz ghetto after the German occupation of Poland in 1939. Having endured life in the ghetto until 1944, he was forcibly transported to Czestochowa concentration camp, then via Buchenwald to Sonneburg camp. In 1945 he and the other inmates were sent on a death march to the east to avoid Allied armies advancing from the west. But they were met by the Soviet army, though not before half of the initial 600 had died or been shot by their guards. After three days he found himself in a Soviet military hospital, starved and emaciated.

An act of kindness

A nurse came in, and told me to follow her. She took away my striped uniform and took me to the shower room. I got a new pair of yellow pyjamas and a pair of sandals and followed her to an upstairs ward. The lights were switched off, except for a small table lamp on the nurse's table. I fell asleep late.

We all got up for breakfast, and queued for food in another room. My appetite was good. The weather was beautiful. I sat down on the wide flight of steps outside the main entrance. A group of men were advancing towards me on the other side of the road. I recognised the guards. They were the same men who two days earlier were leading me and the others. They stopped to rest on the grass verge. Their prisoners were all older Germans in civilian clothes. I crossed the road and stood beside them in my yellow pyjamas. 'Water, please,' they beseeched me, touching my feet. Without a moment's hesitation, I picked up their flasks, recrossed the road and found a well. A young Czech girl was pumping water into a bucket. When she had finished I tried to push the long arm of the pump up and down, but could not manage it. The girl laughed and offered her help. She was pumping and laughing while I was holding the flasks underneath the spout. I made three or four trips until all the flasks were filled. The Germans thanked me profusely and began to quench their thirst.

The guards, who were looking away while this was going on, now turned towards me. Each of them embraced me and shook my hand. They had tears in their eyes — not a word passed our lips. I recrossed the road and walked away. I walked for about half an hour, but time ceased to exist for me and I felt weightless, as if my feet were not touching the ground. There are no other words I can find to describe that feeling. I climbed a grassy hill just off the road, and lay on my back, amongst a clump of trees and looked at the blue sky above the gently swaying leaves. I heard the singing of the birds and felt at peace. No thoughts entered my mind and there was no awareness of my body. I do not know how long this trance lasted — perhaps an hour or two. Suddenly I heard a motorcycle engine 'revving up'. This sound brought me down to earth. I went back to the hospital in time for supper. No one had missed me. Nobody said a word.

Rabbi **Hugo Gryn** (1930–) was a 14-year-old boy when in 1944 he arrived at Birkenau concentration camp from his birthplace in Czechoslovakia. He is now the senior rabbi of a synagogue in London.

You cannot wreak vengeance

In May 1945 I was just liberated from the concentration camp of Gunskirchen, which was part of the Mauthausen network of camps, and some of my friends, who were in better physical shape than I, found a most sadistic Nazi sergeant and strung him up. There was a catharsis going on and I was at that point all of 15 years old and there was that bit of me which felt that there was something right about it. And there was that bit of me, and it has not left me, which scared me. Because I knew that this was really responding in kind, and that if you want to consider yourself a civilised human being you cannot go up and down the world wreaking vengeance. That was what this was. But I can understand the enormously strong power that would give me something to pay back the suffering, the humiliation.

Eugenia Ginzberg was a Communist Party member, a teacher and journalist who was arrested in 1937 in one of Stalin's purges. She had worked for an historian who had been accused of Trotskyism, and this was enough for her to be sent to the labour camps in Siberia. She was released in 1955. At one time during her detention she was put to work in the kitchen of a prisoners' transit camp, where she became friendly with Helmut, a German who also worked in the kitchen. (The NKVD was the State Security organization which preceded the KGB.)

Bread for the enemy

A few days later an incident took place which restored an acute sense of life and indignation to me, both of which had been blunted by camp life and the struggle for existence.

One morning a party arrived at the camp made up of men who had been worked to exhaustion in the mines and were no longer any good for underground operations. On their march back they had died — I was going to say like flies — but at Kolyma it was truer to say that the flies died like people.

As usual on such occasions, there was a great bustle in our kitchen, preparing extra quantities of skilly and white bread, and washing piles of extra bowls.

As I bent over the sink a man poked his head with a dirty towel wound round it through the hatch.

'Which of you's from Kazan?' he asked in a hoarse voice.

I started, racked by conjectures. Might my husband be one of these dying men? Could it be a message from one of my friends, and if so, from whom?

'One of the chaps here is from Kazan. He's at the end. He won't see the night through. He heard there was a Kazan woman here and asked me if there was a chance of his getting a decent bite for his last meal? Could you spare a ration for a fellow townsman, since you're working where the food is?'

His voice shook from a mixture of acute envy and humble admiration for anyone who occupied such an exalted position as to be 'where the food is'. 'He promised me half,' he went on, rubbing his forehead and cheeks with his grubby sleeves, for he was sweating from the proximity of the sink.

'Here you are,' I said, holding out the ration. 'Give him my good wishes. But before you go, what's his name?'

'He's a Major Elshin. He worked in the Kazan NKVD.'

I dropped the piece of bread. As if in a close-up I saw the comfortable office, the big window that looked on to Black Lake Boulevard. I heard the velvety tones of the major's voice: 'Make a clean breast of it . . . an emotional nature like yours . . . taken in by that depraved crowd.' He it was that decided that my crime fell under the deadly section 8, that I was a terrorist, liable at worst to be shot, at best to be kept in solitary confinement. No doubt if he had set me free he would himself 'have been ground to powder by the wheel of history', but it was well within his power to have sentenced me to five years instead of ten, to have spared me the brand of terrorism, to have condemned me instead for 'anti-soviet agitation', which would have given me a chance of staying alive. And those sandwiches! Could I ever forget those halved French rolls covered with slices of tender, sweet-smelling pink ham, and how he had set the plate before me, a hungry prisoner brought up from the cellars, and tempted me with the words: 'Just sign and you can eat as much as you like.'

'What's the matter? Did you know him? He doesn't seem to have been too bad a chap. A lot of the NKVD men who were sent to the mines were done in by the other prisoners, but no one seems to have had it in for this one. Anyway, what's the odds now? He's going to kick the bucket, I've seen enough of them. Once their gums recede and their teeth begin to fall out . . .'

A shadow of fear crossed the man's sunken eyes; fear that the promised half-ration was going to slip from his grasp at the last moment.

Those teeth, protruding, falling out of their sockets. That was scurvy. I'd seen Tanya's when she was dying in the transit camp. The teeth decided me.

'Here's the bread. Give it to him. But just tell him who has sent it to him. Remember my name and repeat it to him.'

Suddenly my legs gave way and I collapsed on to the box we used as a table.

'What's happened?' asked Helmut anxiously.

'The man who's asking for bread was my interrogator.'

During the next few days I was very unhappy. The convoy had gone on and I didn't know whether the elegant major, whose task had been to offer the carrot while others plied the stick, had died or not. What upset me was my own behaviour. How had I been capable of descending to such petty revenge as to insist on his knowing my name so as to poison the last mouthful of bread he would eat in this world? In this inferno we had all paid our debts, even the major, by his death — and such a death.

While I was tormented by these thoughts, Helmut was lyrical about the incident of the bread ration. As we were working together, he whispered to me: 'Because you have given bread to your enemy, you'll live, you'll know what it is to be free.'

A young white South African, **Anita Kromberg** became involved in the End Conscription Campaign and is an active member of the International Fellowship of Reconciliation (IFOR). She was arrested in September 1985 and held in solitary confinement for 13 days. She was then released under a court order obtained by her lawyers.

Enemies don't give each other presents

When I opened the door the one in charge, Captain Taylor, flashed his identification card at us. I asked the other officers to introduce themselves saying, 'This is my home and if you are going to spend some time in it I would like to know your names.' Captain Taylor looked a bit taken aback but he introduced them. They spent the next two hours searching the flat and picking up papers and then told me I was being detained.

My cell was five paces by six paces. I was allowed out for an hour or two in the morning to exercise in the courtyard. A while later breakfast was brought in and after that the cell was unlocked. I was able to shower, wash my clothes, do ballet exercises (I got quite supple!) and do walking meditation. I also read my Bible and sang hymns. A co-worker was in the cell next door and we could hear each other singing, which was very encouraging.

Most mornings a security officer came for me and I would be interrogated for most of the day — altogether about 59 hours! My investigating officers asked questions about my whole life — where I worked, where I studied, why I worked with conscientious objectors, about IFOR, about my travels, everything. Basically I have lived my life openly and have nothing to be ashamed of, so I felt OK about talking. In the first few days I was actually strengthened by talking about my belief and my actions.

There were a number of things which helped me during the detention. One was to treat the police officers well — ask their names, greet them, smile and treat them as friends. I explained to them what I was doing and trusted that they would respond to me as a human being, and on the whole they did. The questioning became like a long conversation, with me asking as many questions as they did. We talked a lot about other things — wine, whales, perfume, seafood — you name it. It was good for me to relax and laugh. Of course it was all part of a strategy to keep me relaxed, but I certainly didn't mind because I knew there were no deep, dark secrets which could be spilled out if I got too comfortable. But at times the questioning became harsher. The army is crucial to the existence of apartheid. Any critique of it is labelled 'unpatriotic' or 'subversive'. It is difficult to know how much they know. Often they are guessing and even more often just plain lying. I was often lied to in detention, though at the time it is hard to sort fact from fiction because you have no reference points in prison. But I was able to hang on to the truth, as I understand it, so their lies and tricks didn't really worry me.

When I was returned to my cell in the later afternoon I would do some Bible reading. Much of the Gospel message became clearer to me, and confirmed me in my commitment to peace and justice. I began to work my way through from the beginning, and every day there were verses which said I was being persecuted because of my faith and that I would not be tested beyond my endurance.

The only 'hangover' I still have is a tendency to have headaches which come any time day or night, apparently because solitary confinement and continuous artificial light interfere with your biological clock. Inside prison I lost my appetite and after a week couldn't keep any food down. I saw the doctor and his first question was, 'Have you been assaulted?' He gave me medicine to calm my stomach and said he could not treat the cause, detention, but only the symptoms.

We were (and are) so fortunate to be free. There are thousands still locked up, and many are very badly treated. We were well treated — partly because we are white and partly because of the vast amount of support we have, both inside and outside South Africa.

Being 'inside' helped me to know that if detention is a consequence of my work, then it is all right for me to be in prison. I accepted that prison was my home, and lived fully in that reality. It didn't matter that I had no news of the 'outside' world because my work of loving people and building relationships and making peace could continue inside. Everyday I looked for 'joys', good things to celebrate and hold on to, and there are many: hot water in the showers, a friendly warder, the hymnbook . . . One thing that kept me strong was knowing that I still had choices to make and could do so whatever the consequences. My choice was to treat the people around me with love and justice. I hope that this attitude reached the police officers I saw every day. I feel close to them now and also sorry for them, for they are trapped in the web of fear which traps white South Africans. When I left, the Lieutenant gave me a bottle of wine — a precious gift, for I believe it was given in friendship. Enemies don't give each other presents.

A radical polemicist, **Thomas Paine** (1737–1809) was born at Thetford, England, but emigrated to the (then) British colonies in North America. His writings had a great influence on the American Revolution. In 1792 he went to France, where he voted with the Girondists and against the execution of the King. This aroused Robespierre's enmity, and Paine was imprisoned during the Terror of 1794. He was released after 11 months following representations by the American ambassador.

A fortunate illness

Towards the later end of December of that year, a motion was made and carried, to exclude foreigners from the Convention. Conceiving, after this, that I had but a few days of liberty, I sat down, and brought the work [*The Age of Reason*, Part I] to a close as speedily as possible; and I had not finished it more than six hours, in the state that it has since appeared, before a guard came about three in the morning, with an order, signed by the two Committees of Public Safety and Surety General, for putting me in arrestation as a foreigner, and conveying me to the prison of the Luxembourg. I contrived, in my way there, to call on Joel Barlow, and I put the Manuscript of the work into his hands, as more safe than in my possession in prison; and not knowing what might be the fate in France, either of the writer or the work, I addressed it to the protection of the citizens of the United States.

About two months before, I was seized with a fever, that in its progress had every symptom of becoming mortal, and from the effects of which I am not recovered. It was then that I remembered with renewed satisfaction, and congratulated myself most sincerely, on having written the former part of *The Age of Reason*. I had then but little expectation of surviving, and those about me had less. I know therefore, by experience, the conscientious trial of my own principles.

I have some reason to believe, because I cannot discover any other, that this illness preserved me in existence. Among the papers of Robespierre . . . is a note in the handwriting of Robespierre, in the following words: 'Demand that Thomas Paine be decreed of accusation, for the interest of America as well as France.' From what cause it was that the intention was not put in execution, I know not, and cannot inform myself; and therefore I ascribe it to impossibility on account of that illness.

The Convention, to repair as much as lay in their power the injustice which I had sustained, invited me publicly and unanimously to return to the Convention, and which I accepted, to shew them I could bear an injury without permitting it to injure my principles, or my disposition. It is not because right principles have been violated, that they are to be abandoned.

Richard Sellar was a Quaker and fisherman in Scarborough, England, who was 'pressed' (forcibly conscripted) into the Navy in 1665 during a war against the Dutch. He refused to serve, and was severely beaten, put in irons for a fortnight and then brought before a Council of War.

At peace with adversaries

The Commander asked me if I would go on board of an hoy that had six guns? I refused, and desired to stay on board, and bear the punishment that I had to abide. Then he bid the Council of War go on with their business; so they did proceed, and I being set on a bulk-head, being so lame with the irons that I could not stand, heard them pass sentence of condemnation upon me. The Judge said I should be put into a barrel or cask driven full of nails, with their points inwards, and so roll'd to death. But the Council of War, taking it into consideration, thought it too terrible a death, and too much unchristian-like, so they agreed to hang me.

With sweat running down, and tears trickling from my eyes, I told them, the hearts of Kings were in the Hand of the Lord, and so are both yours and mine; I do not value what you can do to this body, for I am at peace with God and all men, and you my adversaries; for if I might live an hundred years longer, I can never die in a better condition.

The next morning, it being the second day of the week on which I was to be executed, about eight of the clock, the Rope being reeved upon the Mizen-Yard's arm, and the boy ready to turn me off, and Boats having come on board with the Captains of the other ships that were of the Council of War, I was thereupon called to come to the Execution place. The Commander first asked the Council, 'How their judgment did now stand?' Most of them did consent, and some of them were silent. Then he desired me freely to speak my mind, if I had anything to say before I was executed. I told him, I had little at present to speak. There came a man, and bid me go forward to be executed, so I stepped up upon the Gunnel to go towards the rope; but the Commander bid me stop there. Then said the Commander unto me, 'Come down again, I will not hurt an hair of thine Head, for I cannot make one hair grow.' Then he cried, 'Silence all Men,' and proclaimed three times over, 'that if any Man or Men on board of the Ship, would come and give evidence, that I had done anything that I deserved death for, I should have it, provided they were credible persons.' But nobody came, neither opened a mouth against me. So he cried again, 'Silence all Men, and hear me speak.' Then he proclaimed, 'that the Quaker was as free a man as any on board the Ship.' So the Men heaved their hats and with a loud voice cried, 'God bless Sir Edward, he is a merciful Man.' The shrouds and tops, and decks being full of men, several of their hats flew over board, and were lost.

Eight days after, we were engaged with the Hollanders; we lost about two Hundred Men. The Lieutenant meeting me asked me if I had received any wounds? I told him I had received none, but was well. He asked me how came I to be so bloody? Then I told him it was with carrying down wounded men. So he took me in his Arms and kissed me; and that was the same Lieutenant that persecuted me so with the irons at first. The Commander being there, and several Captains with him, he came from his Company to me, and laid his hand upon my head and said, 'Thou has done well, and very well too.' Then I told him, There was one thing I requested of him yet, that he would be pleased to give me a certificate under his hand, to certify that I had not run away. He said, 'Thou shalt have one to keep thee clear at home, and also in thy fishing,' for he knew I was a fisherman.

Edicio de la Torre (1943–) is a Filipino who was ordained a Roman Catholic priest in 1968, and became a professor of social ethics. In the early 1970s he helped to found the Federation of Free Farmers, an association of rural activists. First arrested in 1974, he spent a total of nine years in prison until his final release in 1986 after President Aquino came to power.

Fear leaves me

Prison is like a novitiate. You learn a spirituality, a spirituality for struggle. It's a time to gather yourself together as a human being. You're not worried about skills or assignments — just as in a religious novitiate — but about what you are and what is your total commitment. In prison I made my decision to be with the poor forever.

I'm not bitter. If I were it would mean the last five years were senseless and without meaning, useless. I learned so many lessons in prison and formed deep friendship. I grew, I think. It needn't have been in prison but that's where it happened. If I had been tortured badly or been kept in isolation, I'd probably feel differently.

The president of the Tondo squatters organization was arrested and tortured and then put in with us. She had given the military some information. She was in a state of shock. The prisoners who met her put her in a circle and began to sing songs of welcome.

She said, 'I resign from all my involvements. I'll turn my back on you.' She did as she said and she wouldn't eat or talk afterwards.

She felt a deep sense of guilt for giving the information, she told me later, and had nightmares that the people of Tondo were lynching her. I was called to talk to her and tried to explain forgiveness.

There are two ways to look at forgiveness, I told her. We can wait for the person to repent and then forgive. But if we recognize the worth of a person we forgive beforehand, then the person gets the grace of repentance.

I told her a story about a man in the movement who under torture had given information and afterwards felt guilty and worried. One night in prison he heard someone moving by his bed and thought he was going to be killed. A voice spoke close to his ear: 'We are more angry at the army than you. You're still one of us. Later we'll worry about the damage you did. Now, sleep, knowing you are one with us.'

We have to forgive. We are all weak. In prison you know this very well. You've heard the expression 'wounded healer'. That's what we are in prison. You have to know weakness in order to forgive and restore a person. In prison we know human limitations. In prison we're more tolerant and human. Don't crush the bruised reed.

Ben Weir (1923–) is a Presbyterian Church minister in the US who had lived in Lebanon for 31 years when, in 1984, he was abducted by a Shi'ite Muslim group. Held as a hostage, part of the time 'hog-tied and blindfolded', he was released after 16 months, and returned to the US, where he became Moderator of the 198th General Assembly of the Presbyterian Church. He and his wife Carol have four children, among whom are Chris and John.

A difficult dilemma

One of my guards was replaced by a younger man. He was very gentle and often asked if there was anything I wanted. Each time he took me to the bathroom and brought me back to be chained in my room once more, he would say as he attached the padlock, 'I regret that I have to do this. You remind me of my father, and I want you to know that I respect you. I hope that before long you will be able to go home.'

My response was always, 'I know that you have instructions and that you are not free to do what you want. I understand.'

Sometimes one of the men would be curious about me and my attitude and would ask what I was thinking. 'If you were released and had the opportunity someday to recognize me, what would you do? Would you try to capture me?'

I would reply, 'No, I don't want to turn you in. Rather I want you to know that I forgive you and I hope you will find a more profitable and self-fulfilling line of work. My faith teaches me to forgive.'

There was a variety of attitudes among the guards. One would be belligerent but later try to make up for it. The one who was mocking and silly didn't seem to know how to relate to me at all. Two or three of the younger men were sympathetic and tried to show it, extending little kindnesses or encouraging me by saying, 'You will be going home soon.'

This remark was no help because I believed they did not know and were only trying to cheer me up. Officially, the more responsible guards distinguished between me as a person they respected, in contrast to the actions and policies of my government, which they regarded as oppressive and hurtful.

I often wished I could meet these men under the different circumstances of freedom and openness. Then I could get to know them as they were in a normal situation. However, the truth was that I was a captive and they were the captors. Our relationship inevitably was mostly distant and untrusting. This posed a dilemma: how to try to understand them, love them, and pray for their welfare.

I had to learn that God knows their inmost hearts as he knows mine. He wants to be merciful to us all. We are all human beings, wanting to live lives of peace and joy. I believed then, as I pray now, that in spite of the ambiguity of our relationship, God wishes fulfillment for their lives. How he will lead them into peace and self-fulfillment I don't know, but I continue to pray that their lives may be filled with his blessing.

On October 4, 1984, I celebrated Christine's birthday. Ten days later I celebrated John's. It hurt not being able to express my love for them directly.

To make a birthday cake for Chris, I took a little cheese carton and poked holes in it. I rolled pieces of foil from the cheese into small candlelike shapes.

I sang 'Happy Birthday' several times during the day; I thought about her and wept; I made prayer wishes for her and felt the emptiness and the deprivation of my life. Ten days later I made a cake for John. These imaginary moments with my family stimulated my will to survive. A month earlier I had hoped to be with Carol for our thirty-fifth wedding anniversary. Now I inwardly promised myself, 'I will come through this and be with them to celebrate their future birthdays!'

8. Freedom

Under a government which imprisons any unjustly, the true place for any just man is also in prison.

Henry Thoreau

First they came for the Jews
and I did not speak out —
because I was not a Jew.

Then they came for the communists
and I did not speak out —
because I was not a communist.

Then they came for the trade
unionists and I did not speak out —
because I was not a trade unionist.

Then they came for me —
and there was no one left
to speak out for me.

Pastor Martin Niemöller

An **anonymous Turkish prisoner** smuggled letters out of prison during the 1980s. He had been involved in anti-nuclear protests, and had received a sentence of several years.

Snow is freedom

It's snowing!

A while ago one of the young ones came over as I was sitting on my bed. 'It's snowing!' he said. 'It's beautiful outside. Come, have a look!'

He opened the window and from behind the iron grille we watched the flakes dance in the beam of the searchlights.

It felt like flying. It always does when I watch the snow fall — as if the flakes are stationary and I'm going up. But here I now had more of that feeling. The sharp contrast between the deep amber glow of the light — they use sodium lamps — and the night blue of the sky enhances the mystery of the flickering things in the air that obey no dimensions. They defy the gross difference in size between themselves and the earth so as to levitate, rebelling against the pull of gravity. Snow is freedom.

One of the kids asked: 'Who has the morning shift in the yard — us or the ward across?'

'Why?'

'If it's us we get to play snowballs. By the time *they*'re through, it'll all be slush!''

'Don't worry,' I said. 'No smuggler is going to go out in the yard at eight o'clock in the morning to play snowballs. It's only the politicals who are that romantic!'

And there we stood in awe, quietly whispering in respect to the silence snow commands, inhaling the cold air. It's just as cold inside, actually. The central heating is out of order and will be throughout this winter, so when I look around I see people sitting in their beds with their overcoats and woollen caps. I myself am like a gypsy: I'm wearing everything I own.

It's 1:30 am. Lights out upstairs. I wanted to go on so I'm at a table downstairs. There's me writing and two chronic insomniacs deep in discussion — in whispers: the rest are trying to sleep.

I do not believe we're in iron cages. For freedom is not an absolute concept we try to realize and suffer as we, perforce, fail, but the perception of our human condition in relation to the world and the conscious struggle for self-realization. If there was no restraint, nothing to change, nothing to be changed, 'absolute' freedom, the concept of freedom would have no meaning. Man can only enjoy freedom in his choice to change. So, at this particular moment, I am figuratively or philosophically free while someone else who feels himself ineffective and irresponsible *vis-à-vis* the world is not, though he may roam across it all his life! Freedom is not a spatial category. As a poet said: 'There are those whose bodies are imprisoned and whose minds travel; and those whose minds are imprisoned and whose bodies travel.'

Adriana Borquez (1936–) is a Chilean who was educated at the University of Chile and trained as a teacher. She became involved in community work among shanty-town dwellers, and took up adult literacy work. As a devout Christian she wished to share their experiences. In 1975 she was abducted and became a '*disparu*' (disappeared one). She was first tortured in a Santiago prison, the *Colonia Dignidad,* and then held in a large house which had been converted into a detention centre. She escaped by a subterfuge after being held for three months, and fled the country clandestinely.

The choice

Sometimes I ask myself, for whom is this situation worst: for me or for those who are ordered to 'look after' me — because this is the reality. Here they are looking after me for something. I know they are not allowed to ill-treat me or obviously abuse me (I caught a furtive glimpse of the entry-book as I passed through the hall one day, and next to my name it said 'White glove' — after being here for so long I'm doing well at understanding the technical vocabulary!) and neither are they allowed to communicate with me. The people higher up are trying for something more than vengeance or extracting information. This is the dangerous bit, because I don't know exactly what I have to fight against and against what I must defend myself. For now, I must try to preserve my 'self'. I feel this is the most important thing and it is to this end that I shall make each gesture and direct my thoughts — continue 'being' because this way I can escape from them, because this way I shall continue to be free.

To be free is to have the ability and the opportunity of choosing at decisive moments in your life. I know that very well. I realized it with intensity for the first time in my life at the *Colonia Dignidad.* It was when I was tied to the grid and received the first electric shocks which shook my body. During those moments I chose and that made me feel free forever. I could have talked, and so betrayed my friends, fellows and the organization to which I belong and by doing so deny my struggle and my principles. Or I could have assumed the responsibility of my convictions, my values, my actions and my words and confronted torture without denunciation, without accusation, without escaping behind the shield of someone else's orders. At this moment I chose to be faithful to the direction of my life, not to drag others into the hell that I was suffering, not to put them on the tracks which would have led to the destruction of the organization. I chose to die there if it were necessary. I freed myself then because I felt bound to my principles of honour and decency, and because I felt afraid of the idea of having to assume the shame of treachery. On the other hand, I also realized that never again would I be able to give myself completely, unreservedly to people, because this act of freedom of mine has put a barrier between the others — as I can't know how they will choose at any given time — and me, who chose the way of freedom (and loneliness). We, the 'disappeared ones' are exactly that, 'disappeared'. Without any known existence, without even the right to be able to do anything because to do something is a way of recapturing your own identity. The reality is that in some way we are nothing. We have no reference, we are not here, and yet we do exist, with great intensity, and we are here.

Michael Davitt (1846–1906) was an Irish nationalist who became the father of the Land League, an agrarian reform organization founded in 1879 in the interests of Irish tenant farmers. It achieved an advantageous settlement, in effect a social revolution by non-violent means. Davitt was four times imprisoned; during his incarceration in 1881–2 he wrote a series of 'lectures to a solitary audience' — a pet blackbird which shared his cell. In the 1890s, be became an MP.

Irish freedom

It was a lovely morning in the autumn of 1881, and the infirmary garden in Portland Prison was aglow with the bloom of the late summer flowers which the governor had kindly permitted me to sow in the early portion of the year. The English Channel, which often lulls the weary Portland prisoner to sleep by the storm-chorus of its waves as they dash against the rocks underneath the walls, lay in unruffled calm. From the headland upon which the great convict establishment stands could be seen the picturesque shadows which the Dorsetshire cliffs fling out upon the bosom of the sea. Away beyond the coast-line appeared harvest-fields and homesteads, melting into the distance, and so sadly suggestive of what imprisonment was not — liberty, home, and friends — conjuring up that contrast between the manacled and the free which constitutes the keenest mental pain in the punishment of penal servitude.

It was a day which would fill one's whole being with a yearning to be liberated — a day of sunshine and warmth and beauty, and the moment had arrived when my resolution to give freedom to my little feathered 'chum' could no longer be selfishly postponed. I opened his door with a trembling hand, when quick as a flash of lightning he rushed from the cage with a wild scream of delight, and in a moment was beyond the walls of the prison! The instinct of freedom was too powerful to be resisted, though I had indulged the fond hope that he would have remained with me. But he taught me the lesson, which can never be unlearned by either country, prisoner or bird, that Nature will not be denied, and that Liberty is more to be desired than fetters of gold.

Natalya Gorbanyevskaya (1936–) is a Russian poet and dissident intellectual who took part in a demonstration in 1968 in Red Square, Moscow, against the Soviet invasion of Czechoslovakia. She was arrested, then released as she was pregnant, but re-arrested in 1969 following the appearance of a *samizdat* book by her. As dissidence was considered by many Soviet psychiatrists as a symptom of mental illness, she was transferred to a prison psychiatric hospital, where she wrote *The French Horn*.

The French horn

The french horn of the train sighs, weeps a little,
an unattainable myth.
Through the prison bars a match gleam trickles,
the whole world is eclipsed.

The horn takes wing, into the night it sweeps.
To flick through tracks
like notes. Oh how am I to reach
that rainy platform!

Forsaken, sleepless, deserted,
deserted without me —
cloud tatters like letters drift down
to your concrete,

and inscribing the puddles with full stops,
with hooks and tails,
their treble voices ring out after
the departed train.

Eva Hermann, a German Quaker, was imprisoned by the Nazis in 1943 for giving food and shelter to Jews. She was released by the Allies in 1945.

In prison — yet free

The time spent behind prison walls brings understanding which could be gained in no other way. When, suddenly, the whole of what seemed an assured existence falls about your ears in rags and tatters; when you are, physically at least, cut off from all the members of your family and circle of friends, and are completely thrown upon yourself in surroundings of hostility and indifference; when the earth beneath your feet and the very air you breathe are suddenly taken away; when all assurances are gone and all supports withdrawn and you stand unprotected and exposed, then you know that it is indeed a fearful thing 'to fall into the hands of the living God'.

When imprisonment has lasted a certain time, it ceases to be a punishment. You have come a long way from normal life and gradually find new standards. What once seemed grey on grey gradually takes on colour, even if the shades and variations are weak. Some reach this stage quickly, some more slowly. It took me a year to reach it. It is only after this has happened that you can ask for the meaning of it all, for it is only then that you can hear the answer; only then, that you are capable of gathering up the fruits that lie hidden in the experience . . .

The fighting front came nearer and nearer. We found ourselves in a small munitions factory, which was so lightly built that it would fall like a pack of cards with the first bombs, and the heavy machinery would bury us in the air-raid shelters. The factory stood at the entrance to the village, just behind the tank trap. Those of us who were political prisoners did not expect that we should be allowed to survive the end of the Third Reich. We thought annihilation faced us.

But I lived in that joy, that I had not understood [previously]. I had ceased to wait. I knew that no sentence, no reprieve, no American, could make me freer than I was.

That does not mean that external freedom, when it came at last, was a little thing. One became amazingly receptive after two years' 'dearth of the pure elements of earth'. What it means to have around me hills and meadows, fields and forests after prison grilles and walls; the scent of flowers instead of smoke and steam from damp clothing; bird chorus instead of the grind of machinery day and night — that cannot be put into words.

Vera Laska was born in Czechoslovakia and, whilst a student, became a member of the underground, helping to organize escape routes for French prisoners-of-war during the early days of World War II. She was later arrested and sent to the concentration camps. Liberated in 1945, she became a US college professor and writer.

Cherishing freedom

The eyes register but the brain resists belief. Cattle cars fit for eight animals jammed with a hundred people. No water. Food, yes, all smells melting into one nauseating wave that engulfs me. My precious orange peel is overcome by garlic. A little window, nailed shut with pine boards. Laboriously I split away part of one with my fingers. Air. I see the name of a station. Polish. Days glide into nights. Three? Four? I am with people I do not know. We are the result of emptied jails and ghettos and police stations. The woman next to me is dead. Now she takes up two spaces. I have to stretch over her toward the slit in the window.

The stench of excrement is overpowering. The woman on the floor emits a putrid smell. There are over a dozen corpses by now in the wagon. They are taken off, thrown on the platform. A bucketful of water is hurled in, cooling those at the middle. Perhaps they were able to swallow a mouthful. Most of the precious liquid drips down through the floorboards. It only intensifies the stench of human waste and vomit. Women cry, shriek, tear their hair. One is laughing hysterically. I repeat to myself: *cogito ergo sum*; as long as I think, I still exist. But thoughts are becoming hazy. Perhaps I am not even here. But I am hanging on to the large hook over the window, not high enough to hang myself. No, I have no intention to oblige the unleashed demons of bestiality and do away with myself.

Dawn, the bleakest, most wretched, shocking, mortifying dawn of my life. The apocalypse of a doomsday where forlorn souls loom against the reddish glow. The long train comes to a screeching halt, the doors are being opened. Pandemonium. The living stepping on the dead to get out. Air, breathe deeply, air, as much as you want, air . . .

It was the fear of dying, of steady mental anguish visited upon us by virulent malevolence, that time whipped into an agonizing ordeal, keelhauling our souls day after day, night after night, without letup, that was so hard. What made us endure it? Partly moral support that we gave each other. The five of us who stood so many roll calls together were a closely knit unit. Olga, who managed to keep up her spirits and with it ours; her sister Alice, who often saved our sanity with her lovely voice, singing us into dreams of an esoteric past; Verice, who even at the gates of hell preserved her purity and never succumbed to malice . . .

Ribizli from Rumania, all of twelve or thirteen years old. She had bright, lively eyes, our Pygmalion . . . She remains in our hearts as the breath of spring in our darkest winters.

How did I survive the physical and mental dehumanization? I believe through a fortuitous constellation of an originally healthy body, accidental luck, and above all a strong will, that constructive force that rules emotions and guides intuition and imagination, and channels sentiments and temperament into a disciplined personality. Those who despaired did not last long. Broken hearts could not protect abused bodies . . .

I know what life is all about for I have tasted death. The experience did not break me; it made me stronger. While the black lace of sorrow will forever be draped over my heart, paradoxically I am capable of enjoying happiness more than those who did not savour the wages of fear. I gained the gift of knowing how to live life to the fullest, body and soul . . .

I constantly enjoy the sunrise at daybreak or the frolicking of the wind in the treetops. I rejoice over the laughter of a child and the beauty of a book. I am happy that I have food to eat and a clean bed to sleep in. I pity all those who do not know how to appreciate their plenty and thus shortchange themselves of so much gratification and pleasure. Above all I cherish my freedom to listen and speak without fear.

Those without a conscience involuntarily taught me to deepen mine. The carriers of hate and evil elevated love and good into a sharper light. It is not enough not to be bad. Damn the neutrals sitting on fences not minding other people's sufferings, for they are cowardly henchmen of evildoers . . . Only by reaching out a helping hand and by actively opposing wrongdoing do we earn the right to be called human . . .

Weep not for the survivors of the purgatory called Holocaust, for theirs is the ultimate glory in triumph: they outlived the evil of their tormentors, and by their very lives overcame it. Learn from them; for nobody, but nobody, knows how to savour the sunlight and the raindrops, the free flight of the birds and the smile of the flowers as those who were once denied dignity, beauty and the simplest things in life that make it worth living.

John Lilburne (1614–47) was the leader of the Levellers, a radical republican movement of the English Civil War period. He was several times imprisoned for his opposition to the Commonwealth, which he considered did not grant full liberty of conscience to 'freeborn Englishmen'. In June 1653 he was arrested and imprisoned for writing pamphlets which met with Cromwell's disfavour. He was acquitted by the court, but such was his popularity that he was held in prison for two years thereafter. While in prison he wrote to John Fowke, Lord Mayor of London.

The mournfullest cry

My Lord,

I know you are a rational wise man, endowed with a large stock of brains, and understand very well the fundamental laws and liberties of England, for which many years ago you were a sufferer; and, I am confident, you have not the least cause in the world to be my enemy for any unhandsomeness that ever I acted against you. And yet you committed me to prison, and sent me on the way to my execution at Tyburn, which you know very well I have borne with patience and contentedness without much grumbling against you or any others that have been administrators in that injustice, tyranny and oppression that I now suffer, and, through the strength of the Almighty, my never-failing rock of salvation, undergo with comfort and rejoicing.

I beseech you further, that I am like to be murdered without mercy or compassion, by lies and falsehoods, and the letter of a most unjust and ingenious Act of Parliament and have no legal magistracy left in England, now to appeal unto for my preservation.

In which regard, I humbly beseech you to permit me to vend and sell within your jurisdiction all such moderate, sober, and rational vindications of my own unspotted innocency as are grounded upon truth and the fundamental laws of England; in the failure of which you do unavoidably compel me forthwith most bitterly to cry out of my sorrows, calamities and cruel bloody tyranny that is exercised upon me by your Lordship and your under-officers, and to make the mournfullest cry to the body of the honest and free people and soldiers of England that either my pen or my brains can invent or devise.

There is nothing in reason that the General shall desire at my hand, but he shall command. But if nothing will satisfy his indignation but the last drop of my innocent blood, I do hereby declare before God, angels, and men that he doth hereby compel me to endeavour to the utmost of all the power I have in the world to sell my life to him at as dear a rate as ever Samson sold his to the Phillippians.

From my unjust imprisonment, and yet soul-rejoicing and heart-cheering captivity in Newgate, this 1 July 1653.

Richard Lovelace (1618–57) was a country gentleman who in 1642 presented to the Long Parliament a petition on the King's behalf. A previous petition had been ordered to be burnt by the common hangman, and his action, indicative of resistance, was not popular. Lovelace was committed to prison, but bailed after seven weeks.

To Althea from prison

When Love with unconfinèd wings
    Hovers within my gates,
And my divine Althea brings
    To whisper at the grates;
When I lie tangled in her hair
    And fettered to her eye,
The birds that wanton in the air
    Know no such liberty.

When flowing cups run swiftly round
    With no allaying Thames,
Our careless heads with roses crowned,
    Our hearts with loyal flames;
When thirsty grief in wine we steep,
    When healths and draughts go free,
Fishes that tipple in the deep
    Know no such liberty . . .

Stone walls do not a prison make,
    Nor iron bars a cage;

Minds innocent and quiet take
   That for an hermitage;
If I have freedom in my love
   And in my soul am free,
Angels alone, that soar above,
   Enjoy such liberty.

Henri Perrin was one of a number of French Roman Catholic priests who volunteered during World War II to work as forced labourers in Germany so as to be able to minister to French 'exiles'. Their ministry was carried out secretly. Perrin went to a factory in Germany in 1943, but was arrested in December of the same year and accused of religious propaganda. He admitted to being a Catholic priest, and was imprisoned until April 1944, when he was expelled to Paris.

Jailbirds, but free

All the same, it was no joke being a convict. Those dreadful whitewashed walls I was always kicking my feet against, the doors that were always shut, the keys, the policemen; always shut in, bullied, guarded; we were like animals turning around and around vainly in their cages. Going, coming, entering, leaving — for some people this was all that liberty ever meant, and the actual subjection caused them much suffering. But what was even worse was the depression, the isolation, waiting — waiting for the unknown time when it would all be over. Sometimes the frightful thought found its way into one's mind — supposing they have forgotten me? Perhaps my dossier was lost — burnt in the raid? Knowing nothing, understanding nothing, waiting without being able to say anything, without being able to ask anything for weeks or even months . . .

Yet still, over all these limitations and humiliations, I felt astonishingly and profoundly free; I felt a flame, a secret little life of liberty beating away inside me, a liberty I could never lose. They could keep me locked up; they could take me to a concentration camp tomorrow, they could torture me and make me cry out with pain, but they could never touch the sanctuary where my soul watched, where I was alone master. They might deceive me, abuse me, weaken me; they might get words out of me which they could take as an admission; they could kill me. But they could never force my will, for it could never belong to them; it was between myself and God, and no one else could ever touch it.

How could they expect to reduce a Christian to slavery so easily? Did they really think that walls and chains and warders could bind Christians' activities? Poor wretches! For months now I had been seeing the very opposite thing happening.

Working, and being in cell 44, put me in touch with a large group of men. I felt here, as formerly in the camp, a wish to make them as far as possible into a fraternal community, animated by the desire not to think only for oneself, but to put oneself at the service of everyone. I wanted this even more here, where selfishness would be a far greater torture to us all, and where the need for friendship and mutual assistance was far more urgent, considering the extreme confusion, weakness, and destitution of some of the prisoners . . .

We all felt that the best element of our common life was our evening prayer. We always formed a circle in the middle of the room after roll-call. Everyone was free to do as he wished, and no one objected if someone preferred not to join us and was frank enough to keep his liberty in the matter. After a moment's recollection we made the sign of the cross in silence, and then one of the prisoners would say the *Our Father* and *Hail Mary* in his own language. In this way we prayed in German, Italian, Latin, Polish, Czech, Hungarian, Dutch and French. Usually I said a few words first, suggesting an intention, for someone leaving the concentration camp next day, for the mother of one of us killed in a raid a year ago, for the women who sent us the eggs we had just eaten, and so on. We often prayed for our homelands, for those at home, and those away. Every evening there was something new to pray for. After the prayer we said goodnight in various languages, and those who felt like it shook hands. There were days when everyone did, and they were the days when we had real community.

An American essayist, poet and social critic, **Henry Thoreau** (1817–62), was a strong individualist who wrote *Walden*, a book about his experiment in living close to nature. He believed it wrong to pay poll-tax and during his first year at Walden went to jail rather than pay it. His essay *Civil Disobedience* is a classic exposition of an individual's right to oppose government policies.

I will breathe after my own fashion

I have paid no poll-tax for six years. I was put into a jail once on this account, for one night; and, as I stood considering the walls of solid stone, two or three feet thick, the door of wood and iron, a foot thick, and the iron grating which strained the light, I could not help being struck with the foolishness of that institution which treated me as if I were mere flesh and blood and bones, to be locked up. I wondered that it should have concluded at length that this was the best use it could put me to, and had never thought to avail itself of my services in some way. I saw that, if there was a wall of stone between me and my townsmen, there was a still more difficult one to climb or break through, before they could get to be as free as I was. I did not for a moment feel confined, and the walls seemed a great waste of stone and mortar. I felt as if I alone of all my townsmen had paid my tax. They plainly did not know how to treat me, but behaved like persons who are underbred. In every threat and in every compliment there was a blunder; for they thought that my chief desire was to stand the other side of that stone wall. I could not but smile to see how industriously they locked the door on my meditations, which followed them out again without let or hindrance, and *they* were really all that was dangerous. As they could not reach me, they had resolved to punish my body; just as boys, if they cannot come at some person against whom they have a spite, will abuse his dog. I saw that the State was half-witted, that it was timid as a lone woman with her silver spoons, and that it did not know its friends from its foes, and I lost all my remaining respect for it, and pitied it.

Thus the State never intentionally confronts a man's sense, intellectual or moral, but only his body, his senses. It is not armed with superior wit or honesty, but with superior physical strength. I was not born to be forced. I will breathe after my own fashion. Let us see who is the strongest.

Reha Isvan was one of the founder members of the Turkish Peace Association which was prohibited after the military coup in Turkey in 1980. In 1983, she was sentenced to eight years imprisonment, initially in Metris military prison. With her in prison was another woman peace protestor, **Berin Uyar**. They became friends in prison, though Reha Isvan was an older and better-known figure in the peace movement. Berin Uyar was released before her friend, and subsequently wrote to her in prison. Reha Isvan's husband, Ahmet, a trade unionist, was also imprisoned.

A prison friendship

I start my letter with warm and heartfelt greetings. It has been exactly fourteen and a half months since the large iron door closed after me with a loud clang and I last saw your hands clasping the iron bars, looked at your bright eyes, and heard for the last time the voices of all our friends, saying goodbye. And since that day, I could not free myself from a feeling of guilt — as if it was me who had imprisoned you. When you were temporarily released, you reported these very same feelings. I thought you were exaggerating. But how right you were.

While you were out on bail, you wrote at least two letters a week. You said that you wished it were possible to write every moment, to share all the beauty you saw with us, and that you remembered us in the blueness of the Bosphorus, in the screams of the seagulls, with every morsel you tasted, with any flower scent . . . You knew very well that for a prisoner letters are as indispensable as breathing. I can imagine now how moved you shall be while reading this letter, how at night after everybody on the ward is asleep you will get up and read it again — a bit wistfully, smiling, happily and in anger. But I know they will not give you this letter.

If you had been here, you would have been very angry with me. 'Think a little first, dear Berin', you would have said, 'don't rush'. You are right. How difficult it is to write about you . . . as difficult as to talk of longing, love, friendship, the smell of spring that leaked sometimes through the iron bars.

At first we were in different wards. When you were first taken out to the yard, we rushed to the windows. It was very cold. Behind the bars, in a yard surrounded by high, cold cement walls, a lonely woman, with carefully combed hair, wrapped in her coat, very straight, with a smiling face . . . This was our first impression of you. After the first few rounds in the yard, you started to run. Some people laughed. Some said, 'She will drop out after a couple of rounds.' But the first day you ran 12 rounds and then started to do some exercises. You kept this routine every day, regardless of the rain, snow or heat. We who were young enough to be your daughters and granddaughters, decided to start a sports activity, gave speeches on the benefits of sports, and dropped out one by one; whereas you exercised without uttering such big words, as part of your daily life.

How is that terrible arthritis of yours? In the morning you had to perform special exercises for at least ten minutes in order to be able to move your joints. I am worried that the cold and wet cells of Metris will have made it much worse now. We understood how much you suffered when you groaned silently early in the morning, or from your facial expressions, which you tried to hide.

Do you remember that day when we were thrown into the same ward? What a terrible day it was . . . All the cells had been ransacked, many of us beaten, every single piece of our belongings gone through. We had to wait until the guards were gone before expressing our joy at being together, hugging like mother and daughter. Later the difference of 26 years between our ages disappeared and we developed a friendship full of respect, love and trust.

How we decorated our ward! We put up pictures on the walls, made covers, arranged parties with songs and dances. We changed that horrible place into a home. The chess and backgammon sets we made from breadcrumbs, are they still there? Do you still arrange backgammon tournaments? You never accepted defeat. When you lost, you said: 'Well, there's nothing to be done, if one loses in gambling, one wins in love', reminding us of Ahmet Isvan and, when you won, you challenged anyone who claimed to be a master in the game. Your joy for life infected all of us. When they saw you, all the girls were ashamed of their dowdiness and tried to get themselves into shape. Everybody loved you.

Is the food still as bad? It must be even worse. I am sure the prison administration does not allow you diet food, although they know you suffer from high blood pressure and liver problems. You were right not to make a special demand for it. The administration tries to make the prisoners beg all the time, and uses their needs against them. But you, and we, never succumbed to the prison.

You couldn't take part in the scramble when 40 people tried to wash under a single shower in one hour, but tried to wash yourself with the pan of lukewarm water (which usually became cold) which we saved for you after everybody was finished. But, do you know what we liked most about you? After these baths you set your hair as if you were going visiting the next day, on cold winter nights putting a frilled bonnet on your head. Unfortunately the black band you put on your eyes at night, so that the light which was continually on would not bother you, reminded us of the hours and days we spent at the lst Department (the torture centre).

I see from your photographs in the newspapers that you continue to wear the white dove which I made from bread crumbs. I am very proud of it. I remember how we managed to save that dove from all the searches and ransacking. Three years is not a short time. The bridge formed by this tiny dove carries your voice to us, shouting, 'we do not give up, we resist, we shall defy the enemy by refusing to bow down.'

I learned so many beautiful things from you . . . love, understanding, resistance, honour. I cannot express all that I feel. Our deeper, warmer conversations I leave to the days when we shall meet in the future, when we shall sit by the Bosphorus, under the great elm, sipping blood red tea from narrow waisted glasses, deeply breathing the air of freedom.

9. Guards

You are illegal [to KGB officer].
Alexander Solzhenitsyn

It was he who decided when Winston should
scream with pain, when he should have a
respite, when he should be fed, when he
should sleep, when the drugs should be
pumped into his arm. It was he who asked
the questions and suggested the answers. He
was the tormentor, he was the protector, he
was the inquisitor, he was the friend.
George Orwell, 1984

Born of a well-to-do Uruguayan family, **Luis Perez Aguirre**
(1941–) was ordained a Jesuit priest in 1970. He founded a
community for abandoned children, a Mothers' Committee
for the Disappeared and the Uruguayan branch of Service
for Peace and Justice. For these activities, he was awarded
the *Légion d'honneur* by the French Government. Arrested
many times before the fall of the military government in
1986, subsequently he gave an interview on his experiences.

In a limited situation

Torture was a sophisticated technique, and kind of diabolic because
they work in a very scientific way. They always follow a certain
pattern. They started with psychological pressure, with threats and
things like that. Even the imprisonment situation was really harsh.
They hang you for many hours, mainly from your hands and feet, put
together. You stay there for many times, and then because you are
upside down you lose consciousness.

After that they start a new technique. They submerge your head
under water until you suffocate and pass out. When you have
recovered they do it again. They go on and on. It is terrible. Also they
use the *picana elétrica*, an electrical tool that they use mainly on the
genitals. I have all over my body the marks of torture.

They prepare everything to eliminate you with guns. They put you
on a wall and they say they will shoot you and that is the end; a
simulated [execution]. It is really a very painful situation and you hear
the banging of the guns and then you even lose the sense of time and if
you are alive or if you are dead or whatever, and it is a terrible thing.

One time there were some being tortured, standing next to each
other. After one session one of the girls was in very bad shape and
called for help from the guards. Then she passed out and fell to the
ground. I could see her out of the bottom of my hood and I asked the
guard to get her some help, for she would die unless attended to. He
did nothing so I took off my hood — which was a very dangerous thing
to do, because usually if you do that it is the end. They were standing
there naked and with blood all over. I saw the guard by the door with
his rifle. Tears were running down his face because of the girl and
because his orders did not allow him to do anything for her, but just to
stand guard.

I think that a spiritual training is really important and I always say
that I owe to the Jesuit training my capacity for resisting. You are able
to control yourself spiritually and you are able to discern in each

moment what you have to do and you get to know your capacities and your limits and also your possibilities. You get to know very profoundly yourself, examining every day your conscience and that helped me very much in those days, yes.

I knew a man who was under torture many times and once he asked me to teach him how to pray, because he did not know how to pray. What he was doing was just counting to 1,000 back and forth. He did not know how to pray by heart, and he offered that as a prayer because nobody taught him how to pray and he needed to do it. Then I realised how important are those prayers we learn as children from our mothers, very simple prayers that we know by heart, but for those situations it is the only thing we can do, just to repeat, as Jesus on the cross repeated psalms by heart. He was doing that during the torture and I realised how important it is. In those moments when you are in a limited situation you just are able to repeat some prayers and offer that. That man was just counting because it was the only way for him to pray at that moment. I taught him the Our Father and he was very grateful.

An active worker for peace and a member of the Campaign for Nuclear Disarmament (CND), **Dorothy Birtles** took part in a peaceful protest at a US Air Force base in England in 1983. She was then 60. She was arrested and fined £10.

Lonely after the nick

I received a telephone call from Police Constable 'Smith'. 'For my sins, madam, I am the warrant officer at Cowley Police Station.' 'For *my* sins, surely,' I replied. Then he said he would be glad if I would go along 'when convenient' to pay the £10 and £10 costs.

I explained that my principles would not allow that. PC 'Smith' quite understood. So he said he was required to arrest me for non-payment and I would have to spend 24 hours in the cells at the police station, which in practice meant overnight. 'When would you like to come?' 'Surely,' I replied, 'I've got to come whenever you say?' 'Oh no, we try to suit people's convenience,' said the constable. So I said I'd like to go that night and we settled for 6.00 pm.

'Would you prefer to come under your own steam or should I call for you? Cowley is a lot nicer than Holloway,' he said (I believed him), 'nice and warm so you needn't bring many clothes, just some washing things. We'll give you a nice breakfast and you can go home at 8.00 am. We're all nice at Cowley.'

He arrived at 6 o'clock. 'Take your time, no hurry; did you know the bedroom window's open? Would you like someone to watch the house?' And off we go in the police car — oh, the disgrace - to B------Road!

I was taken to St Aldates Police Station because Cowley could not accommodate me. I felt like parting with a friend, saying goodbye to PC 'Smith', but first he oversaw my admittance at St Aldates.

The duty officer stared when we went in. 'It's a detention,' said PC 'Smith'. The duty officer continued to stare in disbelief. 'We don't take respectable ladies here.' 'She's a CND lady and we're painting the cells at Cowley.'

'Don't you want me either?' I asked, feeling like Orphan Annie.

Then I was frisked and my possessions listed. 'Have you got anything you could hurt yourself with?' I was asked. 'No, I'm not suicidal, but if I'm driven to it do use my Kidney Donor Card.'

'Please don't do anything like that, madam; both of us are here until 8.00 am tomorrow.'

He let me keep my necklace on, with the proviso that I did not try to strangle myself, but my 'Peace' badge was confiscated lest I cut an artery. My chocolate, apple, crossword book and frilly nightie were returned with the rest of my knick-knacks, but my torch was taken (what could I have done with that?). I was allowed to keep pen and paper.

At frequent intervals throughout the evening a face appeared at the spyhole: 'Are you all right, love? Warm enough? Would you like some more blankets? Something to eat? Some books?'

I spent a quiet night in Female Cell Two. The light was left on all night (for observation), so I put the mattress on the floor and slept under the bed. At 6.15 am they brought hot tea, two fried eggs, two rashers of bacon, and two slices of well-buttered toast, all beautifully cooked (eaten with a spoon so I would not injure myself).

It was nice to go home — but lonely after the nick.

Dennis Brutus (1924–) is one of South Africa's leading poets. He was arrested in 1963 and held on Robben Island for his anti-apartheid activities until 1965. In 1966 he went to the USA where he is a professor of English. He has been a leading figure in the international campaign to enforce a cultural and sporting embargo on South Africa.

Through the bars

I remember rising one night
 after midnight
and moving
through an impulse of loneliness
to try and find the stars.

And through the haze
the battens of fluorescents made
I saw pinpricks of white
I thought were stars.

Greatly daring
I thrust my arm through the bars
and easing the switch in the corridor
plunged my cell in darkness.

I scampered to the window
and saw the splashes of light
where the stars flowered.

But through my delight
thudded the anxious boots
and a warning barked
from the machine-gun post
on the catwalk.

And it is the brusque inquiry
and threat
that I remember of that night
rather than the stars.

A Catholic priest born in the pre-1939 Polish Ukraine, **Wladyslaw Bukowinski** (1904–74) was in concentration camps and internal exile during World War II, but decided to remain in the Ukraine after the war despite its incorporation into the Soviet Union. He continued to serve as a priest and was imprisoned three times, serving in all 13 years.

A slap in the face

It was during the winter of 1947–8, when I was in a large camp in the town of Bakul, Chelyabinsk district, in the Urals. We lived in large barracks in very primitive conditions. Visiting other barracks was strictly forbidden. Throughout the night the camp was patrolled by pairs of NKVD (security police) sergeants. If one of these patrols caught some unfortunate person taking a night-time stroll it would take him at once to the punishment cell, where he would have to spend at least three days.

My problem was hearing confessions. In summer this presented no difficulty, but in winter it could be done only at night, when everyone was asleep . . .

For several nights I had been preparing a fellow Pole, called Boleslaw, for his first confession. He was a very pleasant intelligent man, about 25 years old. He lived in a much better barrack than I did, since he was not an ordinary worker, but a *desyatnik*, i.e. the leader of a group of ten workers on a building site. We had agreed to use this better barrack for our religious purpose. All went according to plan. After several nights of preparation Boleslaw made a very satisfactory confession of the sins of a lifetime. After the confession we had a friendly chat which lasted quite a long while. It was well after midnight when I set off back to my own barrack, which was at the far end of the camp. Suddenly a torch flashed and a voice shouted 'Halt! Who goes there?' I had stumbled on a patrol. I knew these sergeants, and they knew me as 'the priest'.

It all happened very quickly. 'It's the priest,' said one of the sergeants. 'What are you doing wandering about the camp at night, priest?' asked the other. The first sergeant came up to me, administered a stinging blow to my right cheek and said 'Go on, get lost!' I did not turn the other cheek as the Gospel says one should, but merely returned to my barrack very angry and upset. 'If I were not worried about getting Boleslaw into trouble,' I thought to myself, 'I would report that sergeant at once to the camp commandant. Let them send me to the punishment cell — what right has he to insult me like that?'

After a few minutes I began to reflect upon the incident. That patrol ought really to have packed me off to the punishment cell at once, but instead the sergeants had confined themselves to meting out a summary penalty. This was a kind of humanitarianism on their part, 'Soviet humanitarianism' if you like, but nonetheless unmistakable. Had I not been treated with a certain degree of mercy and even affection? Was not that slap on the face perhaps intended not so much as an insult, but rather, in those circumstances, as something in the nature of a patronising pat on the back? Would it be fair to depict as persecutors men who had, after all, shown me kindness?

S.A. David (1925–) is a Sri Lankan Tamil, born in humble circumstances, who became a qualified architect. After working abroad, he returned in 1972 to organize relief and development work among the Tamils through the Gandhi Society, of which he became president. He was arrested in 1983, but escaped after two months imprisonment.

A pure ray of compassion

Nearly twenty soldiers surrounded me, ordered me into a corner. Someone gave a command and a soldier hit me on my chest. I urinated. They ordered me to take off my shirt and trouser. All of them had a hearty laugh at my nudity and there was loud obscene comments. They ordered me to walk out past the soldiers and, as I went, they struck me with hands and legs. I was taken to a solitary cell and locked up. In the morning, fellow Tamil *detenus* distributing brushes for cleaning and pouring tea cheered me up. From then on during morning and evening inspection Commander ----- would threaten to kill me. Soldiers on guard would come with leather belt and razor blades and order me to put my hands out of the iron grill door, threatening to cut off my fingers. They would order me to stand up on the concrete bench, keep my hands raised and rotate. They would scold me in obscene language and curse the Tamils.

The attack on the Tamil *detenus* became very frequent and more vicious. Almost every other day and whenever he was in the mood, Commander ----- would come drunk with a glass of arrack in his hand and open the cells, strip the *detenus* and assault and kick and curse them. I could hear cries of pain and groans throughout the nights and early mornings and see naked colleagues hanging head down from window bars. I saw naked *detenus* being chased around the courtyard and being assaulted and kicked by six to eight soldiers with PVC pipes and iron rods in their hands.

One day Commander ----- came drunk and opened my cell, ordered me to strip and hit me on my head and face. My lips split and started bleeding. He ordered three soldiers to trample my back and legs and hit me on my buttocks. They left me exhausted on the bench.

I was kept handcuffed for four days and nights continually. On cold night my hands and legs became benumbed. I felt numbness creeping towards my chest. I was in mortal panic. Uncontrollable shivers seized me. I was falling away from the concrete bench. In the midst of these bodily and mental tortures a pure ray of boundless compassion has left an indelible mark on my soul. I experienced to the very limit of its content the compassion of the great Buddha. This is the nature and action of a Singala Army Sergeant. As the *detenus* were being beaten and kicked and hanged he would look with tear-filled eyes at us and, when all was quiet, open the cells and apply balm and rub down and cover us with warm clothes.

All the sad moments I have gone through are as nothing for this rare meeting and companionship of this great soul. How noble and how great Sri Lanka could have been if its leaders could have had in their soul a hundredth of the compassion in the soul of this Sergeant.

A former Director of Health in the Egyptian Ministry of Public Affairs, **Dr Nawal El Saadawi** (1930–) was dismissed in 1973 because of her political activities. She was detained without charge for three months in 1982. She has published several works of fiction and non-fiction, many of which have been translated into several languages.

I had to impose my will

Repeated knocks; I get up and go to the door.

Long black shadows behind the glass window. And the sound of heavy breathing. A shiver runs through my body. I am all alone in the flat. My husband left before dawn, my son and daughter are out and will not be back before night.

Hesitant, apprehensive, I do not open the door. Fingers trembling, I open the glass window.

My eyes widen in amazement . . . a large number of men armed with rifles and bayonets, sharp eyes penetrating the narrow steel bars and a harsh voice saying in a commanding tone: 'Open the door!'

I shut the glass window. My body is trembling. Under my ribs, my heart is thumping violently.

The banging becomes more violent. The walls of the flat shake. Deep inside I am trembling. In my head a voice tells me to open the door, while another voice, springing from some deep-seated place inside me, from somewhere deep in my memory, in my childhood, tells me decisively: 'Don't open! Don't surrender!'

I heard the sound of the door breaking, like an explosion. They encircled me, panting. Long, lean faces wet with sweat. Open panting mouths. Curved noses like the beaks of predatory birds. A group of them closed in around me like a chain of iron. I heard their leader say: 'Take her to the car.'

The armed procession walked out of the entrance to the building. People in the street stood at a distance, staring at the procession. The men leaped into the vehicles. The officer led me to one of the vehicles. He told me to get in, to sit between himself and the driver. I refused: 'I will sit next to the window.'

The officer looked at me in surprise. Only now I saw his face. Curly black hair, black eyes, thick black moustache, full lips revealing white teeth as he said: 'That's not allowed . . . it's against instructions.' His voice was harsh, but it contained a ring of weakness and his eyes, despite their dark gleaming blackness, contained resignation and a sort of obedience to orders or submission to fate.

He tried to persuade me to sit between himself and the driver. I refused to sit between two men, especially in such heat. Two strange bodies drenched with sweat of hatred. From the outset, I had to impose my will. I did not know where they were taking me. To prison or to death. Nothing mattered except to sit in the seat I wanted and after that what would happen would happen.

The officer looked me in the eyes. I stared at him, unblinking. His eyes blinked and he looked to the ground. Then he climbed in ahead of me and sat next to the driver. I climbed in after him and sat next to the window and the door.

I felt the air move as the car started off. I took a deep breath. My willpower had won. It was only a small victory but it was important because it was the first.

But I am not normal. Something serious has happened. In the twinkling of an eye, I no longer belonged to this world outside the car, nor to those people walking in the street or riding their cars or going home. Behind me I noticed rifle butts sticking out of the car. My mind was still unable to grasp it.

A huge black door appeared before me, like the doors of the castles and fortresses of the Mamaluk period. A number of armed men, like a troop of inquisitors, came to meet us, rifles and long pointed bayonets like the spikes they used to stick into witches to look for signs of the devil. Their eyes as sharp as glass, their glances encircle me, cover me from the front, from behind, and from head to toe.

One of them banged on the door with the butt of his rifle. In the opening a bald head appeared, sharp eyes darting around quickly. He raised his hand in greeting when he saw the officer and ducked back inside.

I saw a corridor. At the end, a black shadow, head swathed in a white turban. Above the head, a light bulb, like one red open eye. He raised his hand in greeting. He struck the concrete floor with his rifle butt and clicked the metal heels of his boots together.

Then a hole opened in the wall and the ground swallowed me up.

Both **Joje Kozlevcar** and **Francis Haiderer** were keen Esperantists incarcerated in Dachau concentration camp. They were political prisoners as opponents of the Nazi regime. Kozlevcar came from Yugoslavia and was arrested in 1944; Haiderer was an Austrian who had been in Dachau since 1941. L.L. Zamenhof developed Esperanto in the late nineteenth century as a global language.

Esperanto in a concentration camp

Joje Kozlevcar

We finally reached the station of the small town of Dachau, completely exhausted. There ready for us was a detachment of Gestapo with chained dogs. They lined us up; beating with rifle butts and bites in the leg from trained dogs helped to expedite matters. That was repeated from the station to the main gate of the concentration camp. The gate opened, we entered, then it shut; to many, forever!

The first impression was that death menaced from all sides — from electric wire round the whole camp, from the guard towers behind the wire, from the crematoria, from the huts and from the Gestapo.

Immediately after arrival they separated us and placed us in the rooms of large huts; they put 300 internees in every room, although constructed for 120 persons. They completely undressed us, took away our clothes and changed them for special camp clothes on which we had to sew a red triangle (political internees) with the letter of our country (Y) on it. At the same time we received an internment number (mine was 61058) which accompanied us throughout our stay in Dachau. We had to sew the number to jacket and trousers.

A small group decided that we would pass free time by educating our people, using lectures, stories, entertainments, and other events. I myself expressed readiness to lecture concerning Esperanto as a means of making progress during our imprisonment.

All 300 internees of the room assembled and occupied the bed-planks in the room. In my lecture I did not wish simply to promote Esperanto, but to show the listeners the practical use of this international language during a voyage I made through the Baltic. I described the value of Esperanto for the person knowing no foreign language.

Through this lecture I enthused the prisoners so that they wanted more such lectures. The adjacent room asked that I present the same lecture in their room, which of course I did. But friends drew my attention to the fact that what I had undertaken was very dangerous; it could be considered sabotage. I was not afraid. Colleagues told me that in other huts there were other Esperantists. I became inquisitive. Firstly, I succeeded in contacting a good Austrian Esperantist worker, Haiderer. He had a low concentration camp number and was a pre-war official of the Workers Esperanto movement. We all met and decided to found an Esperanto circle. The programme was to link Esperantists in the camp and help them as far as possible. We fulfilled this programme. Every Sunday, when we were free, we used to come together in the camp pathways and converse in Esperanto.

The remaining internees knew us well and were ready to help and guard us. Esperantists showed solidarity among themselves. To me, for example, they did a great service, which saved me from transport to stone-breaking or other heavy manual labour. Because I did not have a profession necessary to the German war industry, I remained in the concentration camp without assigned work. That kind of person the Gestapo sent where heavy work was needed. The other detainees organised for me regular employment in the nursery for medicinal plants. There I was sheltered from the 'transport'.

Our group also arranged a commemoration day in honour of the anniversary of the death of Dr L.L. Zamenhof. Through reciting Zamenhof poems and speeches concerning Zamenhof we modestly celebrated his genius.

At the end, when no one knew whether he would survive the suffering, our little group grew, though we were capable of thinking of nothing else but saving our emaciated bodies.

Francis Haiderer

In January 1945 there was a big 'transport' from another concentration camp, evacuated because the Eastern Front was coming nearer. We prepared a poster and fixed it in one of the huts, saying 'Esperantists, let us meet at 19.00 hours at hut 81'.

At the designated hour we waited for new people but no one came. Only the known faces of a few of our members unsuspectingly looked around. Suddenly an SS man came and asked in good Zamenhof language, 'Who speaks the Esperanto language?' I approached him and said, half in German, half in Esperanto, '*Jawohl Herr Hauptmann, mi parolas Esperanto.*' He drew me forward several steps and said, 'Go through the huts, find me the poster. Be glad that *I* saw the poster. If another SS man had found it I do not know what would have happened. Be careful in future and work more secretly. Before 1933 I

was a member of the Esperanto group in Nuremburg.' He went out
and I saw him no more. This episode shows that even in a dangerous,
inhuman epoch one can be faithful to noble ideals.

Victor Nekipelov (1928–) was tried in May 1974 for
circulating *samizdat* (underground) poetry. A Soviet citizen,
he is a qualified chemist and has medical training. He was
held for two months in the Serbsky Institute, controlled by
the Ministry of Internal Affairs, for psychiatric analysis. He
was then ruled to be of sound mind and sentenced to two
years in a labour camp.

An island of the gulag

The Serbsky used a combination of barbital sodium (medinal) and
caffeine to drug the patients. First, caffeine was injected under the
skin. A little while later, medinal was slowly injected into a vein. In
certain doses, the soporific effect of medinal and the stimulating effect
of caffeine combined to cause euphoria, simultaneously suppressing
the will, so that the subject developed an irrepressible desire to talk,
answer questions, and do what others wanted. The injections were
administered by the nurse in the presence of the attending psychiatrist,
who conducted the questioning.

Many zeks (prisoners) were given tablets or injections of aminazin,
propazone, tryptophan, and other such substances. The doctors had
no right, of course, to apply compulsory treatment to those they were
examining or to anyone who had not been assigned such treatment by
law. This applies also to the use of drugs for repressive purposes.

Tabakova, my attending psychiatrist, my psychiatric destiny, had
the pretty but tired face of a waitress in a Russian tearoom. I must say
that none of the women doctors I met at the institute were intellectual
or showed signs of their professional standing and scientific dignity as
do the women one usually meets at scientific institutes. These were the
ordinary, familiar women we see in buses, shops, or the subway. They
flaunted their new clothing before one another, squeaked along the
corridor in their new platform shoes, and ran by with tea kettles at
lunchtime. They did, however, distinguish themselves from their
colleagues in clinics or institutions of higher education in one respect.
All these faces — the men's too — were marked by a deep-seated
boredom that concealed and effaced both their science and their intellect. There they would go, bulging folders under their arms, seemingly
enormously busy, or dutifully make the daily rounds, perfectly

oblivious to their wards and conversing with them like sleepwalkers.

Tabakova was always rushing somewhere. 'Well, we shall be speaking again.' Or: 'Starting tomorrow, we shall be speaking very, very often.' Every last doctor fed his charges a daily diet of such tomorrows. The doctors would make promises and then break them. Perhaps one conversation a month would take place, and that would be enough. Why complicate life? Working with the criminal-case file was simpler, and the doctors got used to it.

Gentle and polite during our talks, Tabakova had a low, throaty voice. Honey tongue, heart of gall. She was also rancorous and touchy. 'Why are you lecturing me?' she blew up once. 'Why are you asking me questions? It's I who should be asking you questions, and you should be answering them as you're supposed to.'

'I am a psychiatrist with twenty years' experience, and I know what I'm doing!' she almost shouted another time. She would lose her smile and her beauty, and sitting opposite me was no longer a great-great-great-granddaughter of Hippocrates, but an ordinary prison warden with a whip in her hand.

After studying for the Roman Catholic priesthood in South Africa, **Rommel Roberts** (1949–) changed direction and became a Quaker in 1974. He had been engaged for some time in community work in Crossroads shantytown. He was imprisoned in 1978 for one month because of this activity, and in 1980 for three months for his part in organizing a bus boycott. He still works in South Africa on peace work and conflict resolution.

A new reality

The finality of the clang of the cell door as it was slammed reinforced a terrible sense of personal emptiness and vulnerability. My sense of who I was, my identity and ambitions were suspended. I was totally stripped . . . I scrutinised my cell for traces of other human beings in an attempt to hold onto reality against the perpetual feeling of utter weakness.

The stripping of all dignity and ability to control attacked my grip on the situation. The uniform police saw me as an animal, a terrorist who was untouchable and who had to be locked up forever or alternatively liquidated entirely. A situation where the only humans with whom one comes into contact have dehumanised you so entirely can be very demoralising . . .

The interrogations lasted an eternity and, although there was never any physical violence, the possibility was always there. What they did do, however, was attack my sense of personal dignity, my faith in personal relationships and most particularly my hope for any future at all. There was always the prospect of indefinite detention, and even of life imprisonment . . .

The isolation and lack of human contact were extreme. I remember my guard saying to me that I would even grow to long for him. This in fact did happen. If one has no human contact whatsoever, one can rapidly lose one's sense of identity, become morose and gradually degenerate into suicide material. I found that in periods of isolation, when I was having no human contact, I came closest to suicide.

That was the first stage of my confinement, the encounter with the thing I most feared. Only in actually living through this thing, the unknown, was I able to pass through it and finally conquer it . . . I had to relinquish my will; to be led rather than to control. I rediscovered the sense of a spirit within one, a power giving direction and sustaining strength in life. I had known all of this in theory, but had never made the radical application of it in my own life. It opened up a whole new perception of things. I began to see things around me in a totally different light. For example, my cell became a sanctuary for me. I could retire there after an interrogation session in total peace. I had a rejuvenating perspective on things. My apprehension of my cell, imprisonment and, most particularly, my relationship with my guards changed radically. I began to see the world around me from a different vantage point. My attitude towards the security police was loving, rather than antagonistic.

In this spirit I found new ways of dealing with the situation. For example, my relationship with one of the guards who brought me food developed. He had at first made a point of not speaking to me. I began to greet him and gradually he started to respond until we were eventually talking to one another. He even began to share his food with me. I was thus more and more in a position to be the stronger one as I learned from him that he was not at all happy in his job. It became evident to me that these guards were themselves dehumanised and imprisoned as I was. The application of Christian love where I was able to love my enemies showed love breaking down its opposite, and the fear that had had a hold of me became powerless. The whole horror of the environment lost its threat. The guard that I had begun to talk to influenced other guards and what had been an intolerable situation became considerably better.

So in this seemingly hopeless situation, I was able to come to terms with fear, and to find out the source of true motivation and sustaining power. Once I had relinquished my will, and saw things with new spiritual eyes, I found that it didn't matter what happened. I could be in prison for the next twenty years and know that my life's task could be there.

Bertrand Russell, philosopher and mathematician (1872–1970), was also a celebrated campaigner for peace and human rights. In 1918 he was sentenced to six months' imprisonment for an article in the journal of the No-Conscription Fellowship, and in 1961 he received a two-month sentence for speaking against nuclear war, commuted to a week because of his health.

A person accustomed to reading

1918: I was placed in the first division, so that while in prison I was able to read and write as much as I liked, provided I did no pacifist propaganda. I found prison in many ways quite agreeable, I had no engagements, no difficult decisions to make, no fear of callers, no interruptions to my work. I read enormously; I wrote a book, *Introduction to Mathematical Philosophy*. I was rather interested in my fellow-prisoners, who seemed to me in no way morally inferior to the rest of the population, though they were on the whole slightly below the usual level of intelligence, as was shown by their having been caught. For anybody not in the first division, especially for a person accustomed to reading and writing, prison is a severe and terrible punishment. I was much cheered, on my arrival, by the warder at the gate, who had to take particulars about me. He asked my religion and I replied 'agnostic'. He asked how to spell it, and remarked with a sigh: 'Well, there are many religions, but I suppose they all worship the same God.' This remark kept me cheerful for about a week.

10. A Higher Duty

An unjust law is no law at all.

St Augustine

What men call conscience — an innate sense of right and wrong — neither reason nor man-made laws can affect. It is useless to invoke the authority of the constitution or to threaten pains and penalties. Such things matter not one jot when men's consciences are aroused.

Conscientious Objector, 1916

I have not spoken for fear of punishment and to avoid the same, but I have spoken for my most bounden duty to the crown, liberties, laws, and customs of this realm of England; but most specially to discharge my conscience in uttering the truth to God's glory, casting away all fear by the comfort which I have in Christ, who saith, 'Fear not them that kill the body, and cannot kill the soul; but fear him that can cast both body and soul into hell-fire.' He that for fear to lose this life will forsake the truth, shall lose the everlasting life; and he that for the truth's sake will spend his life, shall find everlasting life.

Archbishop Thomas Cranmer *executed 1556*

A fervent socialist, **Clifford Allen** (1889–1939) became chairman of the No-Conscription Fellowship in 1915. He was first arrested in 1916, and in May 1917 wrote to the prime minister from military prison on behalf of absolutists — those conscientious objectors who would do no work whilst in prison. He was released conditionally in December 1917 on health grounds.

The value of liberty

I have today received my third successive sentence of imprisonment with hard labour. This time my sentence is for two years.

I think it is right to make known to you that, like other men similarly situated, I have recently felt it my duty to consider carefully whether I ought not for the future to refuse all orders to work during imprisonment. I have decided that it is my duty to take this course. This will mean that I shall be subjected to severe additional punishments behind prison doors. Provided I have the courage and health to fulfil this intention, I shall have to spend the whole of my sentence in strict solitary confinement in a cell containing no article of any kind — not even a printed regulation. I shall have to rest content with the floor, the ceiling and the bare walls. I shall have nothing to read, and shall not be allowed to write or receive even the rare letters or visits permitted hitherto, and shall live for long periods on bread and water.

But forced service under conscription is morally useless. Once allowed that the state has the right to interfere in the lives of its members to the extent of demanding the taking or the sacrifice of life against their moral convictions, or the absolute disposal of their service without their consent, and you have embarked upon a system of oppression that a hundred Russian Revolutions or American high-minded interventions will never compensate.

We are then so resolutely opposed to war and militarism, and so conscious of the value of liberty, that we will not condone conscription in any shape or form.

We have persisted and shall persist in this refusal, although we are fully alive to the horror of repeated imprisonment. No man or woman who has not experienced this test of sincerity can be expected to form an estimate of the torment of its silence and loneliness. The only men who seem able to develop a true understanding of its terror are the soldiers who have faced the dangers of the trenches and who shrink from the very thought of the alternative of prison.

Our persistence is based upon something more reasoned than a mania for the torture of prison. We have surely shown unmistakably that we are actuated by motives and opinions which, however unpopular, entitled us to be no longer classed and treated as the lowest of criminals. Nor has there been any question about the genuineness of our opinions. And yet you are imposing sentence after sentence of imprisonment upon us . . .

There never were prisoners more full of hope and overjoyed with the chance of service that has fallen to them. You will never break these men; they are indomitable. A decision involving such consequences must arise from a man's profound conviction that by this means alone can he remain faithful to the spiritual guidance, the possession and expression of which he holds more precious than his own life. You have given him his chance of realising in his own life the unity of all that makes a man strong and free and sincere, you have made him feel equally the unity of all that is most eternal in the life of the world. You have made him an irresistible force in the gathering struggle to defeat everything that leads away from freedom, whether it be amongst individuals, amongst classes, or amongst nations.

'Bram' Fischer (1908–65), son of a prime minister at one of the Afrikaner Boer republics, trained as a lawyer at Oxford. A leading barrister, he was the lead defence attorney in many major political trials in South Africa, including the 'Rivonia' trial which sent Nelson Mandela to prison for life. By then, Fischer was himself a member of the underground South African Communist Party, for which he was arrested in 1964.

Granted bail, he estreated and continued to work underground until his capture in November 1965. Given a life sentence, he was released shortly before his death.

The excerpt below is from his speech from the dock in his own defence.

When laws become immoral

When a man is on trial for his political beliefs and actions, two courses are open to him. He can either confess to his transgressions and plead for mercy, or he can justify his beliefs and explain why he acted as he did. Were I to ask forgiveness today I would betray my cause. That course is not open to me.

There is another reason for my plea. I accept the general rule that for the protection of a society laws hould be obeyed. But when laws themselves become immoral and require the citizen to take part in an organised system of oppression — if only by his silence or apathy — then I believe that a higher duty arises. This compels one to refuse to recognise such laws. It can never be easy for the normal citizen of a State to break the law. If in addition he has been trained as a lawyer, as I have, his instincts are reinforced by his training. Only profound and compelling reasons can lead him to choose such a course. The laws under which I am being prosecuted were enacted by a wholly unrepresentative body, a body in which three-quarters of the people of this country have no voice whatever. These laws were enacted, not to prevent the spread of communism, but for the purpose of silencing the opposition of the large majority of our citizens to a Government intent upon depriving them, solely on account of their colour, of the most elementary human rights.

Few whites recognise them. Most accept the application of the 180-day law as a normal procedure. But the facts remain and they are the result of an attempt to use the criminal law in order to suppress political beliefs. In such circumstances the administration of criminal law ceases to have integrity. It becomes an inquisition instead. It leads to the total extinction of freedom. It adds immeasurably to the deep race hatred.

All the conduct with which I have been charged has been directed towards maintaining contact and understanding between the races of this country. If one day it may help to establish a bridge across which white leaders and the real leaders of the non-whites can meet to settle the destinies of all of us by negotiation and not by force of arms, I shall be able to bear with fortitude any sentence which this Court may impose on me.

Mohandas K. Gandhi (1869–1948), a lawyer, began his political career opposing discrimination against Indians in South Africa. He later organised the campaigns of non-violent resistance to British rule in India. He advocated *satyagraha* (truth-force) campaigns which became internationally influential in the use of non-violence as a means of exercising political pressure. Although an observant Hindu, his teachings drew upon both European thinkers and Christianity. He was imprisoned many times. In 1922 he was sentenced to six years, of which he served two, for incitement to disaffection by Indians towards the colonial government. Excerpted are parts of his address to the court in 1922.

A virtue to be disaffected

I am satisfied that many Englishmen and Indian officials honestly believe that they are administering one of the best systems devised in the world, and that India is making steady, though slow, progress. They do not know that a subtle but effective system of terrorism, together with an organized display of force on the one hand, and the deprivation of all powers of retaliation or self-defence on the other, have emasculated the people and induced in them the habit of simulation. This awful habit has added to the ignorance and the self-deception of the administrators.

Section 124, A, under which I am happily charged, is perhaps the prince among the political sections of the Indian Penal Code designed to suppress the liberty of the citizen. Affection cannot be manufactured or regulated by law. If one has no affection for a person or system, one should be free to give the fullest expression to his disaffection, so long as he does not contemplate, promote, or incite to violence.

I hold it to be a virtue to be disaffected towards a Government which in its totality has done more harm to India than any previous system. India is less manly under the British rule than she ever was before. Holding such a belief, I consider it to be a sin to have affection for the system.

In fact, I believe that I have rendered a service to India and England by showing in Non-Cooperation the way out of the unnatural state in which both are living. In my humble opinion, Non-Cooperation with evil is as much a duty as is Co-operation with good. But in the past, Non-Cooperation has been deliberately expressed in violence to the evildoer. I am endeavouring to show to my countrymen that violent Non-Cooperation only multiplies evil, and that, as evil can only be sustained by violence, withdrawal of support of evil requires complete abstention from violence.

Non-Violence implies voluntary submission to the penalty for Non-Cooperation with evil. I am here, therefore, to invite and submit cheerfully to the highest penalty that can be inflicted upon me for what in law is a deliberate crime, and what appears to me to be the highest duty of a citizen.

Martin Holladay (1955–) is a carpenter from Vermont, USA. In February 1985, he entered the grounds of a

Minuteman II nuclear missile silo near Odessa, Missouri. There he mounted a cloth banner reading 'Swords into Plowshares', and spray-painted 'No!' on the silo's concrete lid. He was arrested and charged with two federal counts: destruction of government property and destruction of national defence material. He was found guilty on both charges and sentenced to eight years in prison. He was released in September 1986 after an appeal against the length of sentence.

Moral somnolence

It is relatively quiet tonight in dormitory 8-G in Danbury Federal Prison. The inmates are resting on their bunks, for the most part, after a day at their job assignments. Now I hear the jingling of keys, which is still the sound that notifies prisoners, as it has for centuries, of the approach of a guard. It is a random 'sanitation inspection'. The guard, a young man about my age, approaches the corner of the crowded dormitory where my bed is located. He notices a slight stain on the concrete wall, a mark made by the water which drips down the wall when it rains. The guard looks at me, points to the water-stain, and orders, 'Wash the wall.'

Needless to say, most prison guards are not familiar with the techniques of consensus decision-making. The hierarchical structure of the Bureau of Prisons comfortably assumes that compulsion is legitimate. In essence, the model of the guard/prisoner relationship is that of master and slave.

The request of the guard — let's call him Mike — for me to wash the wall is not like the request of a room-mate or lover. There is, in Mike's words, no sense of, 'The bathroom's a mess. I'd clean it myself, but I'm bushed from a hard day at work. Do you think you could clean it tonight?' Mike is saying, 'Wash the wall. I don't want to hear whether you think the wall is or isn't dirty. If you don't wash the wall, I'll handcuff you and take you to disciplinary segregation.' This is what I mean by the master/slave model. If Mike opens his heart to the possibility of a loving relationship between us — if he begins to care how I feel — then he will soon be confronted with the contradiction between our embryonic relationship and the duties of his job.

So what is the non-violent response to an order from a prison guard? Gandhi believed that those arrested for civil disobedience should be 'model prisoners', unless they were ordered to perform actions which were intrinsically degrading or morally abhorrent. While I don't believe that I have any obligation to be a model prisoner, I usually decide, 'Don't sweat the small stuff.'

What is important is to avoid moral somnolence. It is precisely the false religion of blind obedience to human authority which must be resisted if we are to avoid a nuclear catastrophe. When the prison guard or the policeman or the judge issues the order, 'You must kill your neighbour,' the Christian is called to say simply, 'No.'

The example is not an idle one. The history of Nazi Germany shows how likely it is that the majority will accept the option of obeying the order to kill neighbours when the option is linked to social conformity. In fact, the bourgeois virtue of civil order is often deadly, even demonic. It sometimes seems as if we would rather join in the endorsement of a massacre than ruffle the feathers of our boss or give rise to gossip at the post office. And I would point out that in the United States today, the legal structure has ordered the citizenry to cooperate in the construction of an oven large enough to roast all humanity; and for the most part, we choose to obey this order. As each order comes down, we must look into our hearts for a loving, non-violent response, whether the order is 'Wash the wall' or 'Pay taxes to Caesar.'

Meanwhile, back in Danbury Prison, here I am, washing the wall with my sponge, wondering how often my response to a guard's order is due to clear thinking, and how often it is due to the desire to avoid solitary confinement.

I ponder the wall between the guard and me, a wall symbolized by the handcuffs on his belt. Within my heart I carry my own handcuffs as well, which I struggle to recognize: it is all too easy, for instance, to divide the people of Danbury into two camps, the keepers and the kept, and thus fail to see all the opportunities for the expression of love. In spite of the barriers of handcuffs and prison regulations, love always finds a few chinks, and therein lies our hope.

In 1834, six Dorchester farm labourers tried to form a trade union, for which they were sentenced to seven years transportation for conspiracy. Following nationwide protests, they were released in 1836. They became known as the Tolpuddle Martyrs. **George Loveless** (1797–1874) was one of them. He later became a Chartist, then settled in Canada.

Forming a trade union

On the 15th of March, we were taken to the Countyhall to await our trial. As soon as we arrived we were ushered down some steps into a miserable dungeon, opened but twice a year, with only a glimmering of light; and to make it more disagreeable, some wet and green brushwood was served for firing. The smoke of this place, together with its natural dampness, amounted to nearly suffocation, and in this most dreadful situation we passed three whole days. As to the trial, I need mention but little; the whole proceedings were characterised by a shameful disregard of justice and decency; the most unfair means were resorted to in order to frame an indictment against us; the grand jury appeared to ransack heaven and earth to get some clue against us, but in vain; our characters were investigated from our infancy to the then present moment; our masters were inquired of to know if we were not idle, or attended public-houses, or some other fault in us; and much as they were opposed to us, they had common honesty enough to declare that we were good labouring servants, and that they never heard of any complaint against us; and when nothing whatever could be raked together, the unjust and cruel judge, John Williams, ordered us to be tried for mutiny and conspiracy, under an act 37 Geo. III cap. 123, for the suppression of mutiny amongst the marines and seamen, several years ago, at the Nore. The greater part of the evidence against us, on our trial, was put into the mouths of the witnesses by the judge. I shall not soon forget his address to the jury, in summing up the evidence: among other things he told them, that if such Societies were allowed to exist, it would ruin masters, cause a stagnation in trade, destroy property, and if they should not find us guilty, he was certain they would forfeit the opinion of the grand jury. I thought to myself, there is no danger but we shall be found guilty, as we have a special jury for the purpose, selected from among those who are most unfriendly towards us — the grand jury, landowners, the petty-jury, land-renters. Under such a charge, from such a quarter, self-interest alone would induce them to say 'Guilty'. The judge then inquired if we had anything to say? I instantly forwarded the following short defence in writing, to him: 'My lord, if we have violated any law, it was not done intentionally; we have injured no man's reputation, character, person, or property; we were uniting together to preserve ourselves, our wives, and our children, from utter degradation and starvation. We challenge any man, or number of men, to prove that we have acted, or intend to act, different from the above statement.' The judge asked if I wished it to be read in court. I answered 'Yes'. It was then mumbled over to a part of the jury, in such an inaudible manner, that although I knew what was there, I could not comprehend it.

Having established his first ministry in Montgomery, Alabama, as a Baptist pastor, **Martin Luther King** (1929–68) assumed the leadership of the US civil rights movement following a bus boycott in the mid-1950s. He followed the non-violent principles of Mahatma Gandhi, and received the Nobel Peace Prize in 1964. From Birmingham Jail in 1963 he wrote to his fellow clergy who disagreed with his leadership of public demonstrations. He was assassinated in 1968.

Thinking long thoughts

One may well ask, 'How can you advocate breaking some laws and obeying others?' The answer lies in the fact that there are two types of laws: just and unjust. I would be the first to advocate obeying just laws. One has not only a legal but a moral responsibility to obey just laws. Conversely, one has a moral responsibility to disobey unjust laws.

In no sense do I advocate evading or defying the law, as would the rabid segregationist. That would lead to anarchy. One who breaks an unjust law must do so openly, lovingly, and with a willingness to accept the penalty. I submit that an individual who breaks a law that conscience tells him is unjust, and who willingly accepts the penalty of imprisonment in order to arouse the conscience of the community over its injustice, is in reality expressing the highest respect for the law.

We who engage in non-violent direct action are not the creators of tension. We merely bring to the surface the hidden tension that is already alive. We bring it out in the open, where it can be seen and dealt with. Like a boil that can never be cured so long as it is covered up but must be opened with all its ugliness to the natural medicines of air and light, injustice must be exposed, with all the tension its exposure creates, to the light of human conscience and the air of national opinion before it can be cured.

In your statement you assert that our actions, even though peaceful, must be condemned because they precipitate violence. But is this a logical assertion? Isn't this like condemning a robbed man because his possession of money precipitated the evil act of robbery? It is wrong to urge an individual to cease his efforts to gain his basic constitutional rights because the quest may precipitate violence.

Perhaps I must turn my faith to an inner spiritual church, the church within the church, the true *ekklesia* and the hope of the world. But again I am thankful to God that some noble souls from the ranks of organized religion have broken loose from the paralysing chains of conformity and joined us as active partners in the struggle for freedom. They have left their secure congregations and walked the streets of Albany, Georgia, with us. They have gone down the highways of the South on tortuous rides for freedom. Yes, they have gone to jail with us. Some have been dismissed from their churches, have lost the support of their bishops and fellow ministers. But they have acted in the faith that right defeated is stronger than evil triumphant. Their witness has been the spiritual salt that has preserved the true meaning of the gospel in these troubled times. They have carved a tunnel of hope through the dark mountain of disappointment.

Over the past few years I have consistently preached that non-violence demands that the means we use must be as pure as the ends we seek. I have tried to make clear that it is wrong to use immoral means to attain moral ends.

One day the South will recognize its real heroes, with the noble sense of purpose that enables them to face the jeering and hostile mobs, and with the agonizing loneliness that characterizes the life of the pioneers. They will be old, oppressed, battered Negro women, symbolized in a seventy-two year old woman in Montgomery, Alabama, who rose up with a sense of dignity and with her people decided not to ride segregated buses, and who responded with ungrammatical profundity to one who inquired about her weariness: 'My feets is tired, but my soul is at rest.' They will be the young high school and college students, the young ministers of the gospel and a host of their elders, courageously and non-violently sitting in at lunch counters and willingly going to jail for conscience' sake. One day the South will know that when these disinherited children of God sat down at lunch counters, they were in reality standing up for what is best in the American dream and for the most sacred values in our Judaeo-Christian heritage, thereby bringing our nation back to those great wells of democracy which were dug deep by the founding fathers in their formulation of the Constitution and the Declaration of Independence.

Never before have I written so long a letter. I'm afraid it is much too long to take your precious time. I can assure you that it would have been much shorter if I had been writing from a comfortable desk, but what else can one do when he is alone in a narrow jail cell, other than write long letters, think long thoughts and pray long prayers?

William Laud (1573–1645) was born in Reading, England,

and educated at Oxford. He was ordained in 1601, and became Archbishop of Canterbury in 1633, being a strong supporter of King Charles I and opponent of puritanism. As such, he was brought down by parliament in the general upheaval of the puritans' struggle against the king. He was accused of treason and imprisoned in the Tower of London. At his trial, the judges refused to find him guilty of treason under existing laws. Parliament then passed an ordinance under which he was beheaded on Tower Hill on 10 January 1645.

He made this speech from the scaffold, 'giving the paper into the hands of his chaplain. Then laying his head upon the block, he said aloud "Lord receive my soul", which was the signal given to the executioner, who very dextrously did his office.'

I am coming as fast as I can

This is an uncomfortable time to preach; . . . and how I have looked to Jesus the author and finisher of my faith, he best knows. I am now come to the end of my race, and here I find the cross, a death of shame. But the shame must be despised, or no coming to the right hand of God. For my self, I am a most grievous sinner many ways, by thought, word and deed: I cannot doubt but God hath mercy in store for me (a poor penitent) as well as for other sinners. I have upon this sad occasion ransacked every corner of my heart; and yet I have not found (among the many) any one sin which deserves death by any known law of this kingdom. And yet I charge nothing upon my judges; for if they proceed upon proof I, or any other innocent, may be justly condemned. And though the weight of my sentence be heavy upon me, I am quiet within, as ever I was in my life. And though I am not only the first Archbishop, but the first man that ever died by an ordinance in Parliament, yet some of my predecessors have gone this way, though not by this means.

The last particular (for I am not willing to be too long) is myself. I was born and baptized in the bosom of the Church of England, established by law. This is no time to dissemble with God, least of all in matters of religion: and therefore I desire it may be remembered, I have always lived in the Protestant religion established in England, and in that I come now to die.

Now I am accused of high treason in Parliament, a crime which my soul ever abhorred. It was said 'Prisoners' protestations at the Bar must not be taken'. Therefore I must come to my protestation, not at the Bar, but at this hour and instant of my death; in which I hope all men will be such charitable Christians as not to think I would die and dissemble, being instantly to give God an account for the truth of it. I do therefore here in the presence of God and his holy angels take it upon my death, that I never endeavoured the subversion of law or religion. There is no corruption in the world so bad as that which is of the best thing within itself; for the better the thing is in nature, the worse it is corrupted. And [Parliament] being the highest court, when it is misinformed or misgoverned, the subject is left without all remedy.

But I have done: I forgive all the world, all and every of those bitter enemies which have persecuted me; and humbly desire to be forgiven of God first, and then of every man, whether I have offended him or not, if he do but conceive that I have. And so I heartily desire you to join in prayer with me.

O eternal God and merciful Father, look down upon me in the riches and fulness of all thy mercies. And since thou art pleased to try me to the utmost, I humbly beseech thee, give me now in this great instant, full patience, proportionable comfort, and a heart ready to die for thine honour, the King's happiness, and the church's preservation. And my zeal to this is all the sin which is yet known to me in this particular of treason for which I now come to suffer. But otherwise my sins are many and great: Lord pardon them all, and those especially (whatever they are) which have drawn down this present judgment upon me. And when thou hast given me strength to bear it, do with me as seems best in thine own eyes: And carry me through death, that I may look upon it in what visage soever it shall appear to me. Lord, I am coming as fast as I can.

Andy Mager (1962–) was indicted in 1985 for refusing to register for the draft in the USA. He had already served 35 days for participating in protests against cruise missiles. He made his own defence and final speech to the court before being sentenced to six months detention.

Resistance is a long tradition

I believe that individual people must take risks in our own lives in order to change the world around us. Appeals to the government to change are simply not enough. Refusing to register is in many ways a very personal decision. I don't claim that it is what everyone should do. But the government passed a law requiring that I fill out a card, in case they want to send me to war. It gives my consent and participation in preparation for war. Not only do I believe that I could not in good conscience fill out that card, but that under the Nuremberg Accords I have a responsibility not to do so. I believe the government's ability to wage wars around the world and violate the treaties it has signed depends upon the cooperation of the people they expect to do the fighting for them.

I believe my resistance to this war is part of a long tradition of social change — which includes the Boston Tea Party, the underground railroad helping slaves to escape, the unionization of the labour movement, the civil rights lunch counter sit-ins, the abolition of child labour laws and the withdrawal of United States troops from Vietnam. All of these efforts helped gain a greater degree of freedom and democracy in this country. Many of the people involved were called traitors, communists and lawbreakers. They were jailed, beaten and sometimes killed. In retrospect, how do we look at them? These lawbreakers included: Thomas Paine, Harriet Tubman, Susan B. Anthony, Martin Luther King and many others who are recognized as people who helped make this country a better place for all.

In court I am told that I am in the wrong place, that this isn't the place for moral and political issues to be addressed. We are at a time in history where if we don't prevent war it may destroy our world. I don't claim that my individual act of refusing to register will by itself end war. But it is a step. It's the response of a concerned person reacting to a world which in many ways seems to be tottering at the edge. I ask you to join me in exploring how we will end war.

Born in Macedonia, then part of Bulgaria, in 1915, **Venko Markovski** developed Macedonian as a literary language and was recognized as Bulgaria's leading poet. After World War II, Macedonia became part of Yugoslavia and Markovski became a deputy in the Yugoslav parliament. In 1956, by then an opponent of President Tito's policy, Markovski circulated an anti-Tito poem for which he was imprisoned; technically, however, he 'disappeared' for at that time it was the practice to imprison well-known figures under a fictitious name to mask their real identities.

Held on Goli Otok, an island in the Adriatic, Markovski was released in 1961 and allowed to go to Bulgaria.

Right in front of you

I am listed here as Veniamin Milanov Tosev [to prove] that in

Yugoslavia there are no poets in prison. The public makes no association with the name Veniamin Milanov Tosev.

Among the guards were individuals who were taking correspondence courses in an attempt to earn a degree. One of these guards, knowing I was a writer, came up to me one day and said: 'I was told you are a writer. You have knowledge of literature. I have a request . . .'

'Please, what do you want to know about literature?'

'Tell me about Macedonian literature.'

'Whom are you interested in?'

'Venko Markovski.'

'Is it possible you don't recognize Venko Markovski?'

'I don't know him.'

There was an unpleasant pause. I felt sorry for this man who was ordered to guard someone without knowing whom he was guarding. I spoke to him as follows:

'The best way for you to learn about Venko Markovski is to read his poetry written in Croatian. In this way you will understand Markovski the poet, the Partisan, the public figure, and you will pass your exam easily. But if you rely on me to tell you about Venko Markovski, you will find yourself — after you fail your exam — in the very place where Markovski now finds himself.'

'What do you mean by that?' the guard asked. 'Where is he in fact?'

'Right in front of you, here on Goli Otok.'

'Can it be that you are really he?'

'Yes, I am here under another name.'

The guard walked away silent and confused.

The warden obviously thought that since he had physical possession of his prisoners he disposed of their minds and souls as well. But he was mistaken; the body is one thing and the soul is another. There is no way to bribe the human conscience once it has committed itself to the struggle for the rights of its people.

In 1977 the Christian Institute of Southern Africa was declared unlawful by the South African government. Its director was the Rev. Dr **Beyers Naude** (born 1915) an Afrikaner and a minister of the Dutch Reformed Church. The institute was inter-racial. He refused to give evidence to a commission set up by the government to enquire into the institute, and was sentenced to 30 days imprisonment or a fine. A local minister paid the fine, and he was released after one day. At his trial he read into the court record a sermon he gave when considering whether to become director of the institute even if his church refused him permission and he had to relinquish his ministry.

The anchor of inner faith

Your Worship: we bring you this morning the word of God from *Acts 5:29*, which reads as follows: 'We must obey God rather than men' and to understand what these words mean for the Church and society, but also for you and me, we must first have a clear understanding of all that happened.

Peter speaks forcefully and to the point: 'If God asks anything all other things must give way.' This does not mean that a person should not obey human power and authority. On the contrary, 'Let every person submit himself to those powers which have been put over him,' says Paul. When, however, the will and way of man comes into conflict with the will and the way of God, then man must know: Now I must obey God rather than man.

But how does the person know that it is God who speaks? Through our conscience? And how do we know that our conscience is always right? How did Peter know this? How could he prove it? The fact is he could not, he stands defenceless before his judges and before the people. All that he has as anchor is that inner assurance of faith which God has given him through his Spirit, and which he gives to all who after much agonizing are willing to stand in complete dependence before God, completely willing to be convinced by God concerning the obedience he expects from us.

I know some will say — is it not presumptuous to make an analogy between this history and the situation in which we find ourselves today? Only the Holy Spirit can convince each of you to what extent *Acts 5* is relevant to our situation. In so far as I am concerned I sought for light for my decision in other parts of the Scriptures; I also tried to find reasons why I could cut my ties with the Christian Institute, to continue comfortably and happily in my work in the congregation. But time and time again, at times with great agonizing, fear and resistance in my heart, the Lord brought me back to this part of the Scripture, as if he wanted to say: Whatever this text may mean to others this is my answer to you: obey God rather than man.

And now I bring you the light as God gave it to me during the past few days through many events, sometimes with resistance and resentment on my side. The various decisions of the Synod mean in spirit and in practice that the God-given right and freedom of the minister and layman to witness prophetically to the truth of God's word is now so restricted that the minister of the Gospel is no longer in principle given the freedom to express his deepest Christian convictions and to express them at such a place and time as God reveals to him through his Word and Spirit. This is why the choice before me is a choice between religious conviction and submission to ecclesiastical authority. For me there is only one way, to be obedient to God; thus for me God's Word and God's Way. Therefore I must go.

The philosopher **Socrates** (469–399 BC) was charged under the democracy of Athens with heresy and corrupting the minds of the young, and sentenced to death by drinking hemlock. He could have escaped with the help of his friends, but he decided to give loyal obedience to constitutional authority. Plato recorded his speech to the court.

Death does not matter

I am subject to a divine or supernatural experience. It began in my early childhood — a sort of voice which comes to me; and when it comes it always dissuades me from what I am proposing to do, and never urges me on. It is this that debars me from entering public life, and a very good thing too, in my opinion; because you may be quite sure, gentlemen, that if I had tried long ago to engage in politics, I should long ago have lost my life, without doing any good either to you or to myself. Please do not be offended if I tell you the truth. No man on earth who conscientiously opposes either you or any other organized democracy, and flatly prevents a great many wrongs and illegalities from taking place in the state to which he belongs, can possibly escape with his life. The true champion of justice, if he intends to survive even for a short time, must necessarily confine himself to private life and leave politics alone.

I will offer you substantial proofs of what I have said; not theories, but what you can appreciate better, facts. Listen while I describe my actual experiences, so that you may know that I would never submit wrongly to any authority through fear of death, but would refuse even at the cost of my life. It will be a commonplace story, such as you often hear in the courts; but it is true.

The only office which I have ever held in our city, gentlemen, was when I was elected to the Council. You decided that the ten commanders who had failed to rescue the men who were lost in the naval engagement should be tried *en bloc*; which was illegal, as you all recognized later. On this occasion I was the only member of the executive who insisted that you should not act unconstitutionally, and voted against the proposal; and although your leaders were all ready to denounce and arrest me, and you were all urging them on at the top of your voices, I thought that it was my duty to face it out on the side of law and justice rather than support you, through fear of prison or death, in your wrong decision.

11. Hope

You can live three weeks without food
You can live three days without water
You cannot live three minutes without hope.

Rabbi Hugo Gryn

From tomorrow on, I shall be sad —
From tomorrow on!
Today I will be gay.

What is the use of sadness — tell me that? —
Because these evil winds begin to blow?
Why should I grieve for tomorrow — today?
Tomorrow may be so good, so sunny,
Tomorrow the sun may shine for us again;
We shall no longer need to be sad.

From tomorrow on, I shall be sad —
From tomorrow on!
Not today; no! today I will be glad.
And every day, no matter how bitter it be,
I will say:
From tomorrow on, I shall be sad,
Not today!

Jewish child
Terezin concentration camp, Czechoslovakia, 1944

Russian novelist **Fyodor Dostoevsky** (1821–81) was arrested in April 1849 for belonging to a circle of young men which discussed radical ideas. He spent eight months in solitary confinement and was then condemned to death. On 22 December he faced the firing squad, only to be reprieved at the last minute and given four years' imprisonment. He wrote on the same day to his brother Mikhail.

A mock execution

It is decided! I have been sentenced to four years at hard labour in a fortress (I believe in the Orenburg Fortress), to be followed by service in the ranks. Today, this 22nd of December, they carted us off to Semyonovsky Square. There, they read us all our death sentence, allowed us to kiss the cross, broke a sword over each of our heads, and attired us for execution (white shirts). The three of us were placed at the post for the execution to be carried out.

They were calling three names at a time. I was in the second group and so I had no more than one minute left to live. I thought of you, brother, of all your family; at the last moment you, you alone were in my mind, and it was only then that I realized how much I love you, my dear brother!

Then they sounded retreat. Those who were tied to the post were led back, and they announced that His Imperial Majesty was granting us life. After that they read us our actual sentences.

Brother, I have not lost courage and I do not feel dispirited. Life is life everywhere, life is within ourselves and not in externals. There will be people around me, and to be a *man* among men, to remain so forever and not to lose hope and give up, however hard things may be — that is what life is, that is its purpose. I have come to realize this. This idea has now become part of my flesh and blood. Yes, this is the truth! The head that created, that lived by the superior life of art, that recognized and became used to the highest spiritual values, that head has already been lopped off my shoulders. What is left is the memories and the images that I had already created but had not yet given form to. They will lacerate and torment me now, it is true! But I have, inside me, the same heart, the same flesh and blood that can still love and suffer and pity and remember — and this, after all, is life.

The books (I still have the Bible) and some manuscripts — rough sketches of a play and a novel (and a completed story, 'A Child's Fairy Tale') — have been taken away from me and I suppose will be turned over to you.

When I turn back to look at the past, I think how much time has been wasted, how much of it has been lost in misdirected efforts, mistakes, and idleness, in living in the wrong way; and, however I treasured life, how much I sinned against my heart and spirit — my heart bleeds now as I think of it. Life is a gift, life is happiness, each minute could be an eternity of bliss.

Now, at this turning point in my life, I am being reborn in another form. Brother! I swear to you that I will not lose hope and will keep my spirit and my heart pure.

Viktor Frankl was born in Vienna. In 1942 he, his wife, his parents, his sister and his brother were sent to Nazi concentration camps. Only he and his sister survived. A doctor, he was employed as such for part of his time in the camps. He later became an eminent professor of psychiatry, teaching in the USA and Vienna.

Questioned by life

Man *can* preserve a vestige of spiritual freedom, of independence of mind, even in such terrible conditions of psychic and physical stress. We who lived in concentration camps can remember the men who walked through the huts comforting others, giving away their last piece of bread. They may have been few in number, but they offer sufficient proof that everything can be taken from a man but one thing: the last of the human freedoms — to choose — one's attitude in any given set of circumstances, to choose one's own way.

The prisoner who had lost faith in the future — his future —was doomed. With his loss of belief in the future, he also lost his spiritual hold; he let himself decline and became subject to mental and physical decay . . .

A few days previously a semi-starved prisoner had broken into the potato store to steal a few pounds of potatoes. The theft had been discovered and some prisoners had recognized the 'burglar'. When the camp authorities heard about it they ordered that the guilty man be given up to them or the whole camp would starve for a day. Naturally the 2,500 men preferred to fast.

On the evening of this day of fasting we lay in our earthen huts — in a very low mood. Very little was said and every word sounded irritable. Then, to make matters even worse, the light went out. Tempers reached their lowest ebb. But our senior block warden was a wise man. He improvised a little talk about all that was on our minds at that moment. He talked about the many comrades who had died in the last few days, either of sickness or of suicide. But he also mentioned what may have been the real reason for their deaths: giving up hope. He maintained that there should be some way of preventing possible future victims from reaching this extreme state. And it was to me that the warden pointed to give this advice.

I spoke about the future. I said that to the impartial the future must seem hopeless. I agreed that each of us could guess for himself how small were his chances of survival. I told them that although there was still no typhus epidemic in the camp, I estimated my own chances at about one in twenty. But I also told them that, in spite of this, I had no intention of losing hope and giving up. For no man knew what the future would bring, much less the next hour. Even if we could not expect any sensational military events in the next few days, who knew better than we, with our experience of camps, how great chances sometimes opened up, quite suddenly, at least for the individual. For instance, we might be attached unexpectedly to a special group with exceptionally good working conditions — for this was the kind of thing which constituted the 'luck' of the prisoner . . .

Not only our experiences, but all we have done, whatever great thoughts we may have had, and all we have suffered, all this is not lost, though it is past; we have brought it into being. Having been is also a kind of being, and perhaps the surest kind.

Then I spoke of the many opportunities of giving life a meaning. I told my comrades (who lay motionless, although occasionally a sigh could be heard) that human life, under any circumstances, never ceases to have a meaning, and that this infinite meaning of life includes suffering and dying, privation and death. I asked the poor creatures who listened to me attentively in the darkness of the hut to face up to the seriousness of our position. They must not lose hope but should keep their courage in the certainty that the hopelessness of our struggle did not detract from its dignity and its meaning. I said that someone looks down on each of us in difficult hours — a friend, a wife, somebody alive or dead, or a God — and he would not expect us to disappoint him. He would hope to find us suffering proudly — not miserably — knowing how to die.

The purpose of my words was to find a full meaning in our life, then and there, in that hut and in that practically hopeless situation. I saw that my efforts had been successful. When the electric bulb flared up again, I saw the miserable figures of my friends limping toward me to thank me with tears in their eyes.

Henrique Guerra (1937–) was born in Angola and attended secondary schools there and in Lisbon where he also studied at the School of Fine Arts. During the latter period he was arrested for political activity in support of the Popular Movement for the Liberation of Angola (MPLA). He has shown paintings in art exhibitions in Luanda and has written short stories and an economic study of Angola.

Prison song

that companion
went out with tears in his throat
and I saw
that he was not weeping from sadness
he was weeping with unshakeable confidence
that from tears should rise laughter
as hands make bread
and I stayed
pinned in my solitude

that comrade
on going out of the prison cell
carried
and left
the crying of unshakeable confidence
that feet would journey on hard ground
that the hands raised
to make bread
would be raised
so that there should be wheat instead of prison bars

   . . . from cactuses do flowers rise
songs will sprout on this wall

Juana (1957–) is a Chilean woman who, when a student, was imprisoned in 1981 by a military court for political activities. After four years she was tried by a civil court and given three months' imprisonment, so that she was released and sent into exile. She now lives in France. She corresponded with an English 'befriender'.

I have life

I was overjoyed to receive your letters . . .

The moment your letters arrived someone came and said to me 'they requisitioned four letters for you from outside, in the guardroom'. Here everybody who visits us is checked, and the correspondence too. After, the letters are passed to the senior wardress and afterwards to the prisoner. Just imagine, I was longing for the moment for them to hand them to me. And today about 12.30 a.m. they call me. I was shaking all over. My uncertainty continued, since lunch was signalled so I had to wait longer. At last we got out to the yard and in the company of my closest friends we began reading. In the complete world that we share, correspondence too has become everybody's. We were all thrilled. Suddenly I even feel that we know each other. The frontiers that separate us are broken by these letters of yours.

You know in this jail at the present time it is winter and the days and nights in this prison make you shiver with cold. The clothing isn't adequate. The cold gets into your bones. This place is very near to the Andean *cordillera*. Every morning when I get up I look through the barred window, I greet the light and the dawn and I look at the new day with hope for a future of brotherhood. I can see that immense, majestic *cordillera*, all white purity, like that I wait for here, calm and silent. The sadness of the bare trees that I can see, the earth without its greenery seem to me like the death of a bird that is calm as it waits to fly again in the breezes and the sky. I should so much like to talk to you about my life, my dreams, about darkness and dawn.

The fact is that my mouth has not learned to stay silent, my words aren't sealed. Sometimes I write for a long, long time, I don't know how so many words spring from me . . .

Still, if there is something I haven't lost, it is the joy with which I live this life. I'm the one with most laughs and smiles. It is hard for me to be inactive. As well as being fine for talking, I really stir things up all day and with my friends we laugh a lot. So the days move on without our realising it. The hours of this long cold night are shortened . . .

The warmth and tenderness of love reaches me from people like you. I have life, and day by day I walk in belief in it. I go beyond the wall and the grille. It is impossible to hide me and shut me in, I fly free, like that dove that comes home every day. I shall tread in the tracks that others left; my eyes will shine with a light that has not grown dim. All men in the world shall build a brotherhood for the future, with faces without sorrow, no children in prison, a world where this present one of death and torture will be only a memory of a bad moment in time.

I won't pass on to another sheet since I should begin to struggle at it, and this way it is more authentic.

Hope you'll write soon and long.

A leading Moroccan poet, **Abdellatif Laabi** (1934–   ) founded in the late 1960s two literary magazines which had a significant influence throughout North Africa. By 1972 King Hassan's regime was highly unpopular, and in that year Abdellatif Laabi was arrested along with others of the intelligentsia. During imprisonment he continued to write, and his work was smuggled out and published. He was amnestied in 1980. In 1983 he received the 'persecuted poet' prize of the Poetry International Festival.

A long way to cherry time

It's still a long way to cherry time
and to hands filled with immediate
        presents
the open sky greeting the fresh morning
        of freedoms
the joy of talking
and the happy sadness

It's still a long way to cherry time
and to cities filled with wondrous silence
to greeting the fragile dawn of our loves
the pang of meetings
the mad dreams turned into daily duties

It's still a long way to cherry time
but already I can feel it
it palpitates and rises
germinating in the warmth
of my passion for things to come
. . .
Everything's fine
I tell you
don't laugh
    don't have any doubts
Hope
    is a serious matter

when it's rational
of course it's not an army
or a magic wand
but it's a sure guide
an excellent diviner
Believe me
one must hope

Bishops **Latimer** (1485–1555) and **Ridley** (1500–55) were eminent Protestants who opposed the Catholic policies of Queen Mary, and were condemned as heretics by a committee of Convocation at Oxford. They were burnt at the stake together in front of Balliol College in 1555.

Human candles

Then the smith took a chain of iron, and brought the same about both Dr Ridley's and master Latimer's middles; and as he was knocking in a staple, Dr Ridley took the chain in his hand, and shaked the same, for it did gird his belly, and looking aside to the smith, said: 'Good fellow, knock it in hard, for the flesh will have his course.'

Then they brought a fagot, kindled with fire, and laid the same down at Dr Ridley's feet. To whom master Latimer spake in this manner: 'Be of good comfort, Master Ridley, and play the man. We shall this day light such a candle, by God's grace, in England, as I trust shall never be put out.'

A Romanian, **Olga Lengyel** was deported to Auschwitz/Birkenau in 1944, along with her parents, husband and two sons. Only she survived.

Human dignity

To achieve such a degradation they employed a stupid, brutalizing and disconcertingly useless discipline, incredible humiliations, inhuman privations, the constant menace of death and, finally, a sickening promiscuity. The entire policy was calculated to reduce us to the lowest moral level. And they could boast of results: men who had been lifetime friends ended up by hating each other with real repugnance; brothers fought each other for a crust of bread; men of formerly unimpeachable integrity stole whatever they could. The prisoners of Auschwitz–Birkenau who carried piles of stone, only to drag them to their original places the next day, could see but one thing: the revolting sterility of their effort. The weaker individuals sank more and more into an animal existence where they dared not dream of eating their fill, but only of taking the worst edge off their gnawing hunger. All they asked was to be a little less cold, to be beaten a little less often, to have a bit of straw to cushion the rough boards and occasionally to have a whole glass of water for themselves even though it came from the polluted water supply of the camp. One required an extraordinary moral force to teeter on the brink of the Nazi infamy and not plunge into the pit.

The priests and nuns in the camp proved that they had real strength of character. One rarely met that except in deportees who were animated by faith in an ideal. Apart from the clerics, only the active members of the underground, or the militant communists, had that spirit. Yet I saw many internees cling to their human dignity to the very end. The Nazis succeeded in degrading them physically, but they could not debase them morally. Because of these few, I have not entirely lost my faith in mankind. If, even in the jungle of Birkenau, all were not necessarily inhuman to their fellowmen, then there is hope indeed.

A native of Poland, **Rosa Luxemburg** (1870–1919) was a leading Social Democrat and opposed to World War I. She spent most of the war years in jail, and on release became a co-founder of the German Communist Party. She was murdered by right-wing ex-soldiers. In 1916, she wrote from Wronke prison to her friend, Sonja Leibknecht.

The lovely song of life

This whining tone, this 'alas' and 'alack' about the 'disappointments' which you have experienced — disappointments which you blame on others, instead of just looking into the mirror to see the whole of humanity's wretchedness in its most striking likeness! And when you say 'we' that now means your boggy, froggish friends, whereas earlier, when you and I were together, it meant *my* company. Just you wait, I will treat 'you' in the plural.

In your melancholy view, I have been complaining that you people are not marching up to the cannon's mouth. 'Not marching' is a good one! You people do not march; you do not even walk; you creep. It is not simply a difference of degree, but rather of kind. On the whole, *you* people are a different zoological species than I, and your grousing, peevish, cowardly and half-hearted nature has never been as alien, as hateful to me, as it is now. You think that audacity would surely please you, but because of it one can be thrown into the cooler and one is then 'of little use!' . . .

For you people, the simple words of honest and upright men have not been spoken: 'Here I stand, I can't do otherwise; God help me!' Luckily, world history, up until this point, has not been made by people like yourselves. Otherwise, we wouldn't have had a Reformation, and we probably would still be living in the *ancien régime*.

As for me, although I have never been soft, lately I have grown hard as polished steel, and I will no longer make the smallest concession either in political or personal intercourse.

I swear to you: I would rather do time for years on end than struggle 'along with your heroes, or generally speaking, have anything to do with them!'

Do you have enough now for a New Year's greeting? Then see that you remain a *Mensch!* Being a *Mensch* is the main thing! And that means to be firm, lucid and cheerful. Yes, cheerful despite everything and anything — since whining is the business of the weak. Being a *Mensch* means happily throwing one's life 'on fate's great scale' if necessary, but, at the same time, enjoying every bright day and every beautiful cloud. Oh, I can't write you a prescription for being a *Mensch*. I only know how one *is* a *Mensch*, and you used to know it too when we went walking for a few hours in the Südende fields with the sunset's red light falling on the wheat.

The world is so beautiful even with all its horrors, and it would be even more beautiful if there were no weaklings or cowards. Come, you still get a kiss, because you are a sincere little dear. Happy New Year!

Arrested in March 1977, **Anatoli Sharansky** (1948–) was sentenced to 13 years imprisonment as a refusenik, i.e., one who agitated to be allowed to emigrate to Israel. He was released in 1986 and now lives in Israel.

The psalms and survival

After Papa's death I decided, in his memory, to read and study all hundred and fifty Psalms of David (in Hebrew). This is what I do from morning till evening. I stop only to eat, take walks, do eye exercises, and glance at the newspapers. Gradually, my feeling of great loss and sorrow changes to one of bright hopes. I am denied the right to visit Papa's grave but when, in the future, I hear these wonderful verses, these lines that encompass the lives of all the Jews in Israel, and not only there, I shall remember Papa. It will be as if I had erected a memorial stone to him in my heart, and he will be with me all the days of my life.

The Book of Psalms which my wife sent to me just one month before my arrest was my evidence of spiritual connexion with my people, with my country, with my wife. It was increasing my strength. I felt it was much easier for me to survive. I think that everybody can become a hero in this sense of the word because the other thing you must do is be firm in your principles and be sure in yourself; rely on yourself, not be afraid to follow your principles in any circumstances.

It was a unique experience which permitted me to test myself. I had some ideas and some principles in which I thought I believed, but whether I was really firm in these principles, whether they were really my principles or simply something which I found to be attractive at some moment, had to be tested.

Alexander Solzhenitsyn (1918–) is an internationally known writer and dissident who was imprisoned in Soviet concentration camps for many years before being exiled. Awarded the Nobel Prize for Literature, his writings include memorable exposés of concentration camp life. He now lives in the USA.

A prison walk

The walk was bad on the first three floors of the Lubyanka. The prisoners were let out into a damp, low-lying little courtyard — the bottom of a narrow well between the prison buildings. But the prisoners on the fourth and fifth floors, on the other hand, were taken to an eagle's perch — on the roof of the fifth floor. It had a concrete floor; there were concrete walls three times the height of a man; we were accompanied by an unarmed jailer; on the watch tower was a sentinel with an automatic weapon. But the air was real and the sky was real! 'Hands behind your back! Line up in pairs! No talking! No stopping!' Such were the commands, but they forgot to forbid us to throw back our heads. And, of course, we did just that. Here one could see not a reflected, not a secondhand Sun, but the real one! The real, eternally living Sun itself! Or its golden diffusion through the spring clouds.

Spring promises everyone happiness — and tenfold to the prisoner. Oh, April sky! It didn't matter that I was in prison. Evidently, they were not going to shoot me. And in the end I would become wiser here. I would come to understand many things here, Heaven! I would correct my mistakes yet. O Heaven, not for them but for you. Heaven! I had come to understand those mistakes here, and I would correct them!

The walk in the fresh air lasted only twenty minutes, but how much there was about it to concern oneself with; how much one had to accomplish while it lasted.

There, alone beneath that bright heaven, you had to imagine your bright future life, sinless and without error.

12. Loyalty

If I am only for myself, what am I?
Hillel

Maybe I better tell you that if it were more
than jail, if it were my life, I would give it
for what I think democracy is and I don't let
cops or judges tell me what I think
democracy is.

Dashiell Hammett *On his refusal to give
names to the US House Un-American Activities
Committee in 1951*

Senator **Benigno Aquino** was an opposition leader in the Philippines under the Marcos government. He was imprisoned in 1972 and in 1977 sentenced to death by a military tribunal for alleged subversion. The sentence was commuted and he was released in 1979, went to the USA for surgery, and then was warned that his life would be at risk if he returned. In 1983 he did so, and was assassinated as he left the plane at Manila airport. His wife subsequently became President of the Philippines. In 1973 he wrote the following letter to the military tribunal.

To die with honour

Sirs, I know you to be honourable men. But the one unalterable fact is that you are the subordinates of the President. You may decide to preserve my life, but he can choose to send me to death. Some people suggest that I beg for mercy. But this I cannot in conscience do. I would rather die on my feet with honour, than live on bended knees in shame.

My friends and relatives have been harassed. Some have been detained. The witnesses I intend to call are all afraid. I want to save all from further agony.

I have therefore decided not to participate in these proceedings: first, because this ritual is an unconscionable mockery; and second, because every part of my being — my heart and mind and soul — yes, every part of my being is against any form of dictatorship. I agree we must have public order and national discipline if the country is to move forward. But peace and order without freedom is nothing more than slavery. Discipline without justice is merely another name for oppression. I believe we can have lasting peace and prosperity only if we build a social order based on freedom and justice. My non-participation is therefore an act of protest against the structures of injustice that brought us here. It is also an act of faith in the ultimate victory of right over wrong, of good over evil. In all humility, I say it is a rare privilege to share with the Motherland her bondage, her anguish, her every pain and suffering.

A new Zealand sheep farmer, **Archibald Baxter** (1882–1970) was a political opponent of conscription. In 1917 he was arrested for refusing to serve, and put on a troopship for

France, where punishments applicable to soldiers in the field could be meted out. Although technically a soldier, he continued his opposition, and was eventually transferred to a mental hospital (unnecessarily, in his view). Before that, he was sentenced to '28 days Field Punishment No. 1'.

No. 1 Field Punishment

The sergeant took me over to the poles, which were willow stumps, six to eight inches in diameter and twice the height of a man, and placed me against one of them. It was inclined forward out of perpendicular. Almost always afterwards he picked the same one for me. I stood with my back to it and he tied me to it by the ankles, knees and wrists. He was an expert at the job, and he knew how to pull and strain at the ropes till they cut.

The weather became very cold and rough. With the change in the weather the other prisoners were no longer out on No. 1, but we two conscientious objectors were, morning and afternoon, as usual. I thought nothing could make the punishment worse than it was, but I soon found that cold, stormy weather greatly increased the suffering. I began to find it almost impossible to sleep at nights from restlessness and pain. I was alternately burning hot and shivering with cold, and the constant pain in my joints woke me whenever I did doze off from exhaustion. The kindness of the other men in the tent to me I can never forget. They insisted on making my bed for me, and often, I know, would put their own blankets and overcoats under me to make it a little easier for me.

It is hard to say if I would have lasted out the whole of my sentence — I was going down physically every day — if something had not occurred a few days before it was up. A day came — one of those days in early March that outdo the middle of winter in cold and storm. There was a blizzard blowing, with the temperature below zero and the snowflakes freezing as they fell. I was not expecting to go out, for I did not imagine that they would tie us up in such weather. We were tied to the poles as usual.

The storm blew in our faces and in a very short time we were white with snow from head to foot, the flakes freezing so rapidly that they clung in spite of the gale. The cold was intense. A deadly numbness crept up till it reached my heart and I felt that every breath I drew would be my last. Everything grew black around me, although I was still quite conscious. Suddenly loud voices sounded behind us and an angry red-faced sergeant appeared beside the poles.

'What's all this bloody business?' he shouted. 'At first I thought they were posts; but when I went closer to look I saw the hats. I never saw such a damned thing done in all my life.'

Here the compound sergeant, who had come hurriedly out to meet him, made some remark which I could not hear.

'I don't care who they are or what they've done,' the stranger shouted. 'It's what you're doing to them I'm concerned about. I didn't think men could do such a thing. I'll make it known everywhere. Take them off at once.'

That ended it for us. We were not put on again.

I remember always the gentleness and humanity of the ordinary soldiers who were close to me in those times. Once, when I had been maltreated by an officer while I lay on the ground, being too weak to do otherwise, they carried me very gently, and quietly cursed the authorities who were punishing me. Later they were penalized for being too lenient with me. When three of them pulled me out of a shellhole, and said 'Stick with us,' I felt that I could not let them risk their own lives for me under a false impression, so I told them I was an objector. They said they knew all about me and understood quite well what I was standing for. The ordinary soldiers were not antagonistic. When I starved at the last, they too were near starving, but would certainly have given me some of their meagre rations if I had told them of my situation. If the soldiers had not looked after me I would undoubtedly have died. My feeling towards them resembles a prayer that something good might always follow them, and that the light should shine upon them. Nor, for that matter, do I have any feeling of hostility towards the officers whose duty it was to do me harm. They, unlike the soldiers, had become part of the military machine, but submerged themselves in it; and it was the military machine I was opposing, not them as persons.

John Brocklesby (1889–1962) was a Methodist lay preacher from Yorkshire who refused to accept that he was 'deemed to have enlisted' for war service under the Military Service Act, 1916. He was accordingly arrested on 11 May 1916, and jailed in Richmond Castle, where some of his graffiti can still be seen on the wall of one of the prison cells. After 18 days he was sent to France and court-martialled. He was released in 1919.

To the last ditch

I still think of my first night 'in the army' as the most uncomfortable night in my life. There were about thirty men in a guard room designed for fifteen. There were five broad shelves hinged to the wall each providing sleeping room for three men. The men who couldn't get on a shelf were parked on the floor, almost filling the floor space. The stench of humanity and drunks was nothing to the crowning stench of a filthy latrine in the corner, of which the drain was choked and urine was seeping across the guard-room floor. The floor space was almost filled, but there was a space around the stream of urine. I, as the last comer, had to pick a dry patch and edge off as far as possible. I did not feel happy, nor that I was suffering in a noble cause. I knew that these inconveniences were paltry compared with the sufferings brought to millions by the cursed war. Two blankets had been doled out, one for mattress and one for cover, but I had no pillow. I had brought my Teachers' Bible, which for many years had given light and strength. This served for a pillow, and I considered myself better served than Jacob.

[Within a few days Brocklesby and others were drafted to Boulogne, France.]

At Henriville Camp the OC told us that as we were now on active service the penalty for refusing to obey orders was death; he would give us 24 hours to think it over. We were set at liberty and walked around the town. We seemed to throw off all our problems for that day, but as we walked up the hill towards the camp I said, 'Well chaps, we're up against it now.' 'How far are you prepared to go?' I asked. 'To the last ditch!' they all said one by one. It was the most thrilling experience of my life.

In due course we were court-martialled. The CO had told us there would be no martyrs' crowns because no one would know what had happened to us. It was no time for clever backchat, so I made no answer; though it did occur to me as being a curious idea that the army controlled the issue of martyrs' crowns.

[They were sentenced to death, commuted to ten years imprisonment.]

There was a field postcard in use in the army in 1916 designed to lighten the work of censoring letters. There were several stereotyped statements and the soldier had to cross out those which did not apply. Two of these which I well remember might have been specially designed for my needs:

'(a) I am being sent to base.
 (b) I have not heard from you for a long time.'

I crossed off the last three letters of 'base' and everything in the second but the second and third letters of 'you' and the word 'long'. I made my cancellings look as haphazard as possible but thought it looked blatantly clear. Yet it evaded the overworked censor and told the folk at home:

'I am being sent to b . . . ou . . . long.'

[By this means sympathetic MPs in England were able to locate Brocklesby and the rest of the party. They had been sent to an active service area, where they could be shot without the knowledge of Parliament. Brocklesby was later sent to a prison in England.]

It was during one of my terms in the basement that I received a gift of great beauty; the thickest walls cannot exclude God's blessings. Sounds floating in at the window indicated that there was a garden-party or fête in progress quite nearby. I could picture the whole scene, the sunlit lawn, the neat borders, the happy children all unconscious of the horrors in France, unconscious even of the incarcerated law-breakers a few yards distant. It might have been just one of those happy social money-raising schemes for church or charity which are flowers of peacetime. But then, oh then, a brass band struck up and played, 'Where my caravan has rested.' What a lovely bucolic piece! I have one other similar memory, when a local orchestra came and played the Eroica for us. Oh, gift of God! I knew the Eroica well as an arrangement for four hands on the piano; I had often played it at college but this was the first time I had heard it with its superb orchestral colour. How I blessed those musicians for their Christlike kindness in coming to play to those in prison.

[Brocklesby was placed on the Home Office Scheme, but deliberately absconded in protest at being given war work to do. He was re-arrested at his home.]

On Saturday morning the most gentlemanly Police Officer I have ever met, PC Kaye, called for me. He suggested that I should walk to the railway station while he followed some distance behind, so that it would not appear I was under arrest. He was full of such considerate ideas to save me from any unpleasant feelings. So he brought me to Armley Gaol. We stood before the desk of the reception clerk and he asked me what my sentence was. I said, 'Ten years!' Poor Kaye winced as if struck across the face. I thanked him but never saw him again.

The COs designated as Methodists were visited regularly by a Methodist minister called Wardell, for whom I shall ever feel deep gratitude. His first visit was memorable. His first words were:

'Well, young man, what are you here for?'

'I am here because my conscience will not allow me to take part in the war.'

I shall never forget his reply. It gave me something to wrestle with for months.

'It is very difficult to understand,' he said very gravely, 'how conscience drives men in exactly opposite directions. Both my boys joined the army as a matter of conscience, and one has paid with his life.'

Poor bereaved Mr Wardell! Before he left he had to tell me that his remaining son had followed his brother. Yet never (I must emphasise this) did he by word, look or gesture, express any condemnation of my attitude. In his pastoral visits and especially in the Methodist service he conducted he was all that a minister should be. His sermons were as carefully presented to our group of seven or eight as if we had been a congregation of 500. I had a Methodist Tune Book with me in my cell and I was appointed organist for the services. Although I had only a harmonium, it was a service of love and joy.

George Mangakis, born in 1923, was a professor in penal law at Athens University when the colonels' regime enforced his dismissal in 1969. Later that year he was imprisoned and tortured as an opponent of the regime. He was sentenced to 18 years, but released and exiled in 1973. He returned to Greece after the fall of the regime and became Minister of Justice.

A fundamental unity

I think of my companions. The political prisoners I have come across in my various prisons. The ones who resisted and are now pacing across their cells, taking those three little jerky steps forward, then backward. They are all made of the same stuff, even though they may be very different persons in other respects. They all possess a very rare sensitivity of conscience. A truly unbelievable sensitivity. It becomes manifest in tiny details, as well as on big occasions. When they speak, they exercise the utmost delicacy with regard to the other person's feelings. They are always at your side with a glass of water, before you have time to ask for it. I want to give an example of this extraordinary sensitivity. Some days ago, one of us was about to be released. He was in the prison hospital. He could have left directly from there, but he delayed his departure for a week, so as to come and say good-bye to us. Seven days of voluntary prison just to say good-bye to his friends. That is what I mean. These people, then, have truly taken upon themselves the entire predicament of our times. They are consciously carrying the burden of our people's trampled honour. And in so doing they feel close to all those who are persecuted on earth. Through a fundamental unity they grasp the meaning of all that is happening in the world today. It is the unity of man's yearning to be free of oppression, no matter in what form. Whoever resists oppression is a brother to them, no matter who or where he is, scattered in the innumerable prisons of my own and other countries.

We often talk about the dignity of man. It is not an abstraction; it is a thing which I have actually experienced. It exists in our very depths, like a sensitive steel spring. It has absolutely nothing to do with personal dignity. Its roots lie much deeper. Throughout the nightmare of the interrogation sessions, I lost my personal dignity; it was replaced by pure suffering. But human dignity was within me, without my knowing it. There came a moment when they touched it; the questioning had already been going on for some time. They cannot tell when this moment comes, and so they cannot plan their course accordingly. It functioned suddenly, like a hidden spring that made my scattered spiritual parts jerk upright, all of a piece. It wasn't really me who rose to my feet then, it was Everyman. The moment I began to feel this, I began to overcome the questioning ordeal. The effort was no longer only for myself. It was for all of us. Together we stood our ground.

Guillermo Marin (1950–) was a student who helped to run Christian projects in the slums of Bogotá, Colombia, acting as a spokesperson for them to the authorities. In 1986 he was arrested, tortured, shot and left for dead during 48 hours' detention by the security police. He fled the country in 1987, and is now a chemical engineer living in England.

A lucky escape

As I left a meeting to walk to my bus-stop I was stopped by a man holding a pistol to my head. With two or three others I was blindfolded and bundled into a truck. Inside the truck my shirt and shoes were removed and I was laid on my face on the floor of the truck. The men put their feet on my back and beat me with the butts of their guns. I was driven for what seemed like 40 minutes, eventually arriving at a place where I was led to another truck. While being moved from one vehicle to another, still blindfolded, I could hear the wind in the trees and the sound of a river. In the new truck I felt very alone. I still held the bus-fare coins in my hand — my only link with reality. They were taken from me when the soldiers heard the chink of the coins.

The second vehicle was set up as a torture-chamber. I was tortured there for 48 hours without a break except for questioning.

The body of the truck was separated from the driver's cab by a wooden partition door. Two men were in there all the time, presumably to ensure a quick getaway if they were surprised by any enquirers. The walls and roof must have been soundproofed. Small pulleys were suspended from the roof for use as implements of torture on the breasts and testicles of their victims. There were four sets of batteries with wires attached and metal rings in the floor for the attachment of limbs by handcuffs. There were also benches for the torturers to sit on. A radio was blaring loudly to cover any noise.

Fortunately for me, the batteries did not work. But I suffered what I felt was the worst torture — the *submarino*. My head was held under water until my lungs felt like bursting, then taken out. While I gasped for breath I was constantly taunted with threats of re-immersion.

Psychological torture was also used to try to get from me the names of the other people who had been at the meeting. The torturers said my wife, children and aged father would all be left without support if they killed me, which they would surely do if I did not speak up. I was told that none of their victims ever escaped with their lives; giving the wanted information was the only chance they had.

Later my chains and handcuffs were replaced by rope, a sure sign that the end was near. The torturers do that to save their metal equipment, and to avoid identification, as only government forces use such equipment. I was tied hands and feet, hooded and put into a sack. I was moved to a third vehicle, and driven for a further 40 minutes as the soldiers listened to a football match on the radio.

Then I heard bullets being put into a gun, I was forced into a kneeling position, and two shots were fired into my head. I heard a soldier say 'That's it.' I was conscious, I could feel blood running down my head.

I did not hear the truck drive away, probably because I was stunned. Then I heard the noise of what I thought were cars, but realized later were planes. I managed eventually to get the hood off my head, though my hands and feet were still tied. Some time later I was found by some people; but they turned out to be the police. I knew that if I told them what had really happened they would have to hand me back to the army. So I quickly invented a story about being beaten up and shot because of a bad debt. The police believed me and took me to a hospital. There I was known to the medical students, some of whom also worked for the poor. I was kept under an assumed name until my discharge.

Paul (c. 1–64 AD) was a Jew and a Roman citizen who became a Christian about 33 AD. He undertook missionary journeys to spread knowledge of Christianity in the Graeco-Roman world of his day, and was several times imprisoned and his life endangered. He was eventually sentenced to death and beheaded. From his Roman prison he wrote to the congregation at Philippi.

Giving confidence

When I pray for you all, my prayers are always joyful, because of the part you have taken in the work of the Gospel from the first day until now. It is indeed only right that I should feel like this about you all, because you hold me in such affection, and because, when I lie in prison or appear in the dock to vouch for the truth of the Gospel, you all share in the privilege that is mine.

Friends, I want you to understand that the work of the Gospel has been helped on, rather than hindered, by this business of mine. My imprisonment in Christ's cause has become common knowledge to all at headquarters here, and indeed among the public at large; and it has given confidence to most of our fellow Christians to speak the word of God fearlessly and with extraordinary courage.

I have learned to find resources in myself whatever my circumstances. I know what it is to be brought low, and I know what it is to have plenty. I have been very thoroughly initiated into the human lot with all its ups and downs — fullness and hunger, plenty and want. I have strength for anything through Him who gives me power.

Irina Ratushinskaya (1954–) was born in the Ukraine, Soviet Union, obtained a degree in physics and became a teacher. In 1981 she received ten days' imprisonment for demonstrating in Pushkin Square, Moscow. In September 1982, she was again arrested, and sentenced to seven years hard labour for anti-Soviet agitation. She was said to have written poetry critical of the Soviet Union. She was in solitary confinement and suffered forcible feeding in the 'Small Zone', a special unit for women political prisoners which has an exceptionally harsh regime.

She was released in 1986, and went into exile. She now lives in England.

I will live and survive

I will live and survive and be asked:
How they slammed my head against a trestle,
How I had to freeze at nights,
How my hair started to turn grey . . .
But I'll smile. And will crack some joke
And brush away the encroaching shadow.
And I will render homage to the dry September
That became my second birth.
And I'll be asked: 'Doesn't it hurt you to remember?'
Not being deceived by my outward flippancy.
But the former names will detonate my memory —
Magnificent as old cannon.
And I will tell of the best people in all the earth,
The most tender, but also the most invincible,
How they said farewell, how they went to be tortured,
How they waited for letters from their loved ones.
And I'll be asked: what helped us to live
When there were neither letters nor any news — only walls,
And the cold of the cell, and the blather of official lies,
And the sickening promises made in exchange for betrayal.
And I will tell of the first beauty
I saw in captivity.
A frost-covered window! No spyholes, nor walls,
Nor cell-bars, nor the long-endured pain —
Only a blue radiance on a tiny pane of glass,
A cast pattern — none more beautiful could be dreamt!
The more clearly you looked, the more powerfully blossomed
Those brigand forests, campfires and birds!
And how many times there was bitter cold weather
And how many windows sparkled after that one —
But never was it repeated,
That upheaval of rainbow ice!
And anyway, what good would it be to me now,
And what would be the pretext for that festival?
Such a gift can only be received once,
And perhaps is only needed once.

As an absolutist conscientious objector, **Howard Schoenfeld**, an American, refused the draft in 1941, and was imprisoned. Here he writes of one of his fellow pacifist prisoners, **Benedict**, a superb baseballer.

The prison pitcher

One day a guard entered the cell block, walked down the corridor and opened the door to Benedict's cell. Benedict, like most of the pacifists, was a fine athlete. Outside, his physical prowess was a legend in amateur athletic circles and, in particular, he excelled as a soft ball pitcher. Big muscled, strong and agile, his speed ball was so swift only one man in the prison could catch him. The prison team, built around his pitching, was tied for first place in its league, and his ability to hold the opposition scoreless had placed it there.

The Warden, a sports lover, was delighted with the unusual situation, and it did not surprise us to hear the guard offer Benedict his freedom if he would pitch the championship play-off games, which were scheduled for that day. Benedict said he would do it on condition that all the men in solitary, including inmates not in the pacifist group, were released. The guard said he would speak to the Warden about it, and we heard him trudge down the corridor.

We waited in silence till he came back. The Warden could not agree to Benedict's terms, but he offered a compromise. He would release all the conscientious objectors for the game, and Benedict permanently. Benedict refused.

Fully an hour passed before the Captain of the guards entered and released us. The prison team had lost the first game of the series, and the Warden, unable to endure further losses, had agreed to Benedict's terms.

Grinning hugely, we left our cells, and laughing at each other's pasty complexions, bearded faces, and unkempt hair, hurried out into the prison yard. A wave of applause went through the inmate stands as Benedict rushed down the field and began warming up.

Benedict summoned his strength after long weeks of demoralized living and, in a superhuman and prodigious performance, pitched batter after batter out, enabling the prison team to rally and score, and win the series.

The next day at noon the Warden released us. The midday whistle had blown and the men were already in the mess hall, eating. We straggled across the empty yard, basking in the sun, enjoying our freedom. A spontaneous wave of applause broke out among the men as the first of our group entered the hall. Surging across the hall the wave became a crescendo. Six hundred pairs of hands joined in and the crescendo became pandemonium. Guards ran up and down the aisles; they were ignored. The pandemonium increased when Benedict entered the hall, maintaining itself at an incredible pitch. But when the so-called criminals who had been in solitary came in, the convicts literally went wild, beating their metal cups on the tables, and stamping their feet.

We stood in the centre of the hall, astounded at the demonstration. It became clear to me that, although they were applauding Benedict, and all of us who had been in solitary, they were doing something more. A mass catharsis of human misery was taking place before our eyes. Some of the men were weeping, others were laughing like madmen. It was like nothing I had ever seen before, and nothing I ever expect to see again.

Born in Russia in 1923, **Jacobo Timerman** went to Argentina as a child with his family. He became a political journalist and founded a liberal newspaper, *La Opinión*. In 1977 he was abducted, tortured and held prisoner by the Argentinian army. No charges were brought against him. He was released and expelled in 1979 and moved to Israel.

Merely an eye

Tonight, a guard, not following the rules, leaves the peephole ajar. I wait a while to see what will happen but it remains open. Standing on tiptoe, I peer out. There's a narrow corridor, and across from my cell I can see at least two other doors. Indeed, I have a full view of two doors. What a sensation of freedom! An entire universe added to my Time, that elongated time which hovers over me oppressively in the cell. Time, that dangerous enemy of man, when its existence, duration, and eternity are virtually palpable.

The light in the corridor is strong. Momentarily blinded, I step back, then hungrily return. I try to fill myself with the visible space. So long have I been deprived of a sense of distance and proportion that I feel suddenly unleashed. In order to look out, I must lean my face against the icy steel door. As the minutes pass, the cold becomes unbearable. My entire forehead is pressed against the steel and the cold makes my head ache. But it's been a long time — how long? — without a celebration of space. I press my ear against the door, yet hear no sound. I resume looking.

He is doing the same. I suddenly realize that the peephole in the door facing mine is also open and that there's an eye behind it. I'm startled: they've laid a trap for me. Looking through the peephole is forbidden and they've seen me doing it. I step back and wait. I wait for some Time, more Time, and again more Time. And then return to the peephole.

He is doing the same.

And now I must talk about you, about the long night we spent together, during which you were my brother, my father, my son, my friend.

You blinked. I clearly recall you blinking. And that flutter of movement proved conclusively that I was not the last human survivor on earth amid this universe of torturing custodians. At times, inside my cell, I'd move an arm or a leg merely to view a movement that was non-violent, that differed from the ones employed when I was dragged or pushed by the guards. And you blinked. It was beautiful.

You were — you are? — a person of high human qualities, endowed certainly with a profound knowledge of life, for you invented all sorts of games that night, creating Movement in our confined world. You'd suddenly move away, then return. At first I was frightened. But then I realized you were recreating the great human adventure of lost-and-found — and I played the game with you. Sometimes we'd return to the peephole at the same time, and our sense of triumph was so powerful we felt immortal. We were immortal.

You were — you are? — extremely intelligent. Only one possible outgoing act would have occurred to me: looking out, looking, ceaselessly looking. But you unexpectedly stuck your chin in front of the peephole. Then your mouth, or part of your forehead. I was very desperate. And frightened, I remained glued to the peephole, but only in order to peer out of it. I tried, I assure you, even if briefly, to put my cheek to the opening, whereupon the inside of my cell sprang into view and my spirits immediately dropped. The gap between life and solitude was so evident; knowing that you were nearby, I couldn't bear gazing back toward my cell. You forgave me for this, retaining your vitality and mobility. I realized that you were consoling me, and I started to cry. In silence, of course. You needn't worry. I knew that I couldn't risk uttering a sound. You saw me crying, though, didn't you? You did see that. It did me good, crying in front of you. You know how dismal it is to be in a cell and to say to yourself, It's time to cry a bit, whereupon you cry hoarsely, wretchedly, heedlessly. With you I was able to cry serenely, peacefully, as if allowed to cry. As if everything might be poured into that sobbing, converting it into a prayer rather than tears. You can't imagine how I detested that fitful sobbing of mine inside the cell. That night, you taught me how we could be comrades-in-tears.

13. Memories

The prison world is penetrated by the letter. After so many efforts to forget, to refrain from loving and thinking, the entire edifice collapses.

Jacobo Timerman

Prison is sometimes
Always I love you

Unknown Uruguayan prisoner

During World War I, some conscientious objectors were held in cells at Richmond Castle after arrest. On the walls of those cells there still remain the words they wrote while awaiting court-martial. Their punishment, if posted to France for active service, could be death. Lord Derby, later to be Secretary of State for War, said condemned men 'would be shot and quite right too'.

J.T. Barker of Barnoldswick brought to memory the words of a hymn and scratched them on the wall. Their use reflects the importance of hymns and chapel-going in the formative years of some of the conscientious objectors of that day.

The hymn was written by a German, Phillipp Spitta, and appears in *Lyra Domestica*, translated R. Massie, London, 1860.

A well-remembered hymn

I know no life divided,
O Lord of life, from thee
In thee is life provided
For all mankind and me
I fear not death, O Jesus,
My life lives on with thee
Thy power shall soon free us
From death eternally

I fear no tribulation
Since, whatso'er it be
It makes no separation
Between my Lord and me
Since then, my Lord and Teacher
Hast claimed me for thine own
E'en now with thee I'm richer
Than monarch on his throne

Thus while over earth I wander
My heart is light and blest
My treasure is up yonder
My heart is there at rest
O Blessed thought I'm trying
To live to please the Lord

In faith and hope rejoicing
Through his most precious word

Architect and journalist **Czeslaw Bielecki** set up an underground publishing house in Poland. After martial law was
introduced in 1981, he went into hiding but was arrested in
1982. He was force-fed during a hunger strike in October
1985 which he waged in protest at not being allowed to see
his two sons, Kuba and Max, with whom he kept up a
regular correspondence until his release in 1986. The sons
were later allowed visits. They were nine and six at the time
of this letter.

When I want to run away with my thoughts, it only takes a moment
for me to hear the delicate whirr of the steel cable. I feel its vibrations
and the grinding of the wheels on the supports of the ski lift as up I go. I
look round for a minute hearing you shouting each other down to
draw my attention. 'Look Dad!' Suddenly Max loses his balance, falls
over grimacing with the exertion of it, and feels he's about to lose hold
of the lift. But no, not at all, he somehow manages to get up, his clown
legs go through drunken movements, his skis start to slide apart, and
now they almost cross. Somehow, miraculously, Max has found his
balance and forgotten about fear. The little rascal grins and shouts
out: 'Did you see?!'

Kuba goes up in a crouching position. I hear his shouting and
answer with an 'I can see!', watching him from the corner of my eye,
for if I were to continue this pleasure but for a second, it would be too
late for me to let go. Somebody's saying something to me.

I concentrate on the same spot on the wall and can still hear the
whirring of the cable and the whispering of the snow under my skis.

There is yet another way for us to be together.

If at any moment you feel like being with me, just face the sun and
close your eyes. (I also do this every now and then when I'm on a
walk.) You will then see red, pulsating clouds: that is our common
blood flowing under the vaulting of our eyelids. Now all you need do is
open your eyes to see that we are united by the same earth, sky and
sun. They are so big they cannot be kept apart by iron bars. Even the
shadow of a passing bird could be the same mark I saw a while ago on
the beaten ground of the Mokotow exercise yard.

I haven't had a letter from you for two weeks. This is the jubilee, the
tenth letter I'm about to send (not counting the time I wrote to both of
you separately).

Recently two letters, which I sent a month ago, were returned by the censors.

Perhaps you also put more than you should into your letters! The last letter I received from you was the one with the photograph of Irys. I also had one from Grandma and Grandpa.

I feel fine. I can't complain about my stomach. It's not its fault they won't put me on a diet! I try to make do by eating as little as possible. I've lost four kilos. I can go down another five — why carry such weight! — before there's any need to get worried. I still read a lot and go through my gymnastics diligently: five x 100 exercises daily i.e. 100 press-ups, 100 knee-bends, 100 circuits lying on my back etc. Please write to me during your holidays and tell me where you are and what you're up to.

Max, how are you getting on with your house-cum-bed-cum-slide? I send you all my love.

Your Dad

PS. I found the enclosed feather on a walk.

A village craftsman (a tinker) of Elstow, near Bedford, England, **John Bunyan** (1628–88) became a Baptist pastor in his early twenties after undergoing a religious conversion. In 1660 he was jailed for public (unlicensed) preaching, and confined until 1672 in Bedford prison. Whilst there he wrote his autobiography, *Grace Abounding to the Chief of Sinners*. During a second term of imprisonment, he wrote the first part of his most famous work, *Pilgrim's Progress*. He later became a well-known non-conformist preacher. His eldest daughter, Mary, was born blind.

Had home to prison again

Being again delivered up to the Gaolers hands, I was had home to Prison again, and there have lain now compleat twelve years, waiting to see what God would suffer these men to do with me. In which condition I have continued with much content through Grace, but have met with many turnings and goings upon my heart both from the Lord, Satan, and my own corruptions; by all which I have also received much conviction, instruction, and understanding, of which I shall only give you, in a hint or two, a word that may stir up the Godly to bless God, and to pray for me; and also to take encouragement, should the case be their own, Not to fear what men can do unto them.

I never had in all my life so great an inlet into the Word of God as now; the Scriptures that I saw nothing in before, are made in this place and state to shine upon me; Jesus Christ also was never more real and apparent than now; here I have seen him and felt him indeed.

I never knew what it was for God to stand by me at all turns and at every offer of Satan to afflict me, as I have found him since I came in hither; for look how fears presented themselves, so have supports and encouragements; yea when I have started, even as it were at nothing else but my shadow, yet God as being very tender of me, hath not suffered me to be molested but would with one Scripture and another strengthen me against all.

Before I came to Prison, I saw what was a-coming, and had especially two considerations warm upon my heart; the first was, How to be able to endure, should my imprisonment be long and tedious; the second was, How to be able to encounter death, should that be here my portion. By Scripture I was made to see that if ever I would suffer rightly I must first pass a sentence of death upon everything that can properly be called a thing of this life, even to reckon my Self, my Wife, My Children, my health, my enjoyments, and all, as dead to me, and my self as dead to them. And I reasoned with myself; if I provide only for a prison, then the whip comes unawares; and so does the pillory; again if I provide only for these, then I am not fit for banishment; further, if I conclude that banishment is the worst, then if death come, I am surprised; so that I see the best way to go through sufferings, is to trust in God through Christ, as touching the world to come.

But notwithstanding these helps, I found myself a man, and compassed with infirmities; the parting with my Wife and poor Children hath oft been to me in this place as the pulling the flesh from my bones; and that not only because I am somewhat too fond of these great mercies, but also because I should have often brought to my mind the many hardships, miseries and wants that my poor family was like to meet with, should I be taken from them, especially my poor blind Child, who lay nearer my heart than all I had besides; O the thoughts of the hardship I thought my blind one might go under, would break my heart to pieces.

Poor Child! thought I, what sorrow art thou like to have for thy portion in this world? Thou must be beaten, must beg, suffer hunger, cold, nakedness, and a thousand calamities, though I cannot now endure the wind should blow upon thee: but yet recalling my self, thought I, I must venture you all with God, though it goeth to the quick to leave you: O I saw in this condition I was as a man who was pulling down his house upon the head of his Wife and Children; yet thought I, I must do it, I must do it. I had also this consideration, that if I should now venture all for God, I engaged God to take care of my concernments; but if I forsook him and his ways, for fear of any trouble that should come to me or mine, then I should not only falsify my profession, but should count also that my concernments were not so sure if left at God's feet, while I stood to and for his name, as they would be if they were under my own tuition, though with the denial of the way of God. This was a smarting consideration and was as spurs unto my flesh. I thought also of the glory that he had prepared for those that, in faith, and love, and patience, stood to his ways before them. These things, I say, have helped me, when the thoughts of the misery that both my self and mine might, for the sake of my profession, be exposed to, hath lain pinching on my mind.

Born in 1915, **John Hamlin** was, together with his wife (Frances), a Presbyterian missionary in China from 1947 to 1951. They were both expelled from the country after being held in solitary confinement for six weeks and questioned on charges of enmity to the new Chinese Republic. They later went to teach in Thailand. Here John Hamlin reflects on his period in detention.

The baseball game

I had begun my baseball game which I later perfected. By sitting on the bed and throwing a small stone against the wall, I could tell by where the stone fell how much of a run or hit the man made. If it fell on a brick within the given area, it was a one base hit. If on a longitudinal crack, it was a two base hit; a latitudinal crack meant a three base hit; and if it landed where the two joined, it was a home run. Outside the area was out, and certain bricks marked with an 'S', with water squeezed out of my wash cloth from saved morning-wash water, meant a strike. I drew a baseball diamond on my bed horse and used bits of matchsticks for one team, and bits of broom straw for the other, keeping score with more straws.

On Sunday I had no ball games, but did more walking, going through the Psalms as far as I could remember them. The spiritual benefits distilled from pain were great. Complete loss of self-determination taught me dependence on God and submission to His will. The 130th Psalm was my constant companion. The many verses where we are told to wait on the Lord came to mind as I tried this waiting. I gained a deeper understanding of Christian truths before taken for granted. I tried to surrender my treasured freedoms, and my loved ones, and my very life into His care. I tried to be a prisoner of the Lord instead of the Chinese 'People'.

Nazim Hikmet (1902–63) was born in Turkey, but left when the country was occupied by the Allies in 1920. He eventually returned to Turkey, where he was imprisoned as a suspected communist on three occasions, the last beginning in 1938. He was released in 1951. He gained a high reputation as a poet.

Your duty to spite the enemy

Just because you did not give up your hopes
for the world, for your country, and for humanity,
they either send you to the gallows
or put you in jail
for ten years, for fifteen years
or, who cares, for even longer.
Never say,
'I wish I were swinging
at the end of a rope like a flag.'
You must keep on living.
Perhaps living is not a pleasure any more
but it is your duty
to spite the enemy,
to live one more day.
In your jail one part of yourself may be all alone
like a stone at the bottom of the well,
but the other part of you
should mingle so with the crowds of the world
that in your jail you will tremble
with every rustling leaf forty days away from you.
It is sweet but dangerous
to wait for letters,
and to sing sad songs,
to keep awake till morning
with your eyes fixed on the ceiling.
Look at your face whenever you shave,
forget your age,
protect yourself from lice
and from the spring evenings.
And then you should never forget

how to eat your bread to the last crumb
and how to laugh heartily.
And who knows,
maybe your woman doesn't love you any more
(don't say it is a small matter;
to the man in jail
it is like a young limb broken off the tree).
It is bad to dream about the rose and the garden;
and good to dream of the mountains and the seas.
I would advise you
to read and write without any rest,
to take up weaving
and to cast mirrors.
So it is not impossible to spend
ten, fifteen years in a cell
or even more;
it can be done —
provided under your left breast
that precious gem
the jeweled heart stays bright.

Joseph Müller (1894–1944) was a German Catholic priest who was arrested in May 1944 on a charge of being politically unreliable, and executed the following September in Brandenburg prison. On the day of his death he wrote a farewell letter to all who knew him.

Farewell, my home

Now my last earthly greeting comes to you from my cell. What shall I say in the circumstances? Oh, my heart is so full of joy now that I am on the way home to the Father. I have known all these days that my sacrifice would be accepted. It is now eleven-thirty. In one hour I shall be at home; I shall have left you so far as this earth goes, but nothing can separate us from the love of Christ.

I send a farewell to your world with a countenance glowing with gratitude. Farewell, you little hut, my cell, poor and faithful, you my silent friend — you were my last church and my last pulpit. Farewell, all that lies behind me — you churches in which I served as a priest, you streets and lanes with your kind and your stony people. Farewell, my home, my last place of work, and say to everyone that the priest who lived in you lies in his last chains and is now about to die on his last journey as all men die whom Christ's life and death have benefited. I have just read the Twenty-second Psalm and said my last earthly prayer for all who stand at my hard bier.

In January 1977 **Alicia Partnoy** (1955–) was arrested by the security forces in Argentina for distributing literature during a strike. She was kept blindfolded and handcuffed for three months, and held a further two and a half years without charge. She was then exiled to the USA, where she now lives. She is married with one child, a daughter named Ruth.

A puzzle

For a while now I've been trying to recall how Ruth's face looks. I can remember her big eyes, her almost non-existent little nose, the shape of her mouth. I recall the texture of her hair, the warmth of her skin. When I try to put it all together, something goes wrong. I just can't remember my daughter's face. It has been two months since I've seen her. I want to believe that she's safe. I've tried not to remember too much, to avoid crying, but right now, I want to imagine her face, to put together the pieces of this puzzle.

Perhaps if I tried to bring to mind some scenes when we were together. For example, that day while coming back from my parents: I was pushing her stroller along the street, when suddenly she looked up at the roof of a house. An immense dog was impatiently stalking back and forth. Ruth pointed to the dog with her little finger. 'Meow,' she said, since she was only used to watching cats climb up high. Thrilled, I kissed her; that kiss was a prize I awarded myself for such a display of wisdom by my child. I stopped the stroller to kiss her . . . but how did her face look? I can only remember her small triumphant smile.

One morning I was travelling to a suburban neighbourhood with my baby and two bags. The night before some friends of mine had been kidnapped. Since they knew where I lived, I thought of moving out for a few days just to be safe. But I can't remember my daughter's face on that bus. I know that she was wearing the pink jacket, that I had the bag with stripes, the same one my mom used to take to the beach. I have perfect recall of every item in the bag — but I try so hard and I still can't remember my daughter's face. I could describe her toys, her clothes. If only I had her picture. But again, maybe it's better this way. If I could look at a picture of her face, I would surely cry . . . and if I cry, I crumble.

Rudolph Reder was born in Poland in 1881. On the outbreak of World War II, he was a chemist in the Ukrainian city of Lvov. As a Jew, he was arrested by the German occupying forces in 1942 and sent to Belzec, a concentration camp south of Lvov. After a few months, he was sent under escort to Lvov to pick up a load of sheet metal. All but one of his guards left to see the town after the lorry was loaded. The remaining guard fell asleep, and Reder escaped. A Polish friend hid him at great risk until the city was liberated by the Russians in 1944.

In this excerpt, he describes the gassing-machine at Belzec, one of the early extermination methods, and a return visit he made to the site of the camp in 1946.

The death machine

The engine was big, 1½ by 1 metre. It made a roaring noise, and from time to time it made a louder noise. It was running so quickly that one could not see the spokes as the wheels went round. It ran for exactly 20 minutes and then they stopped it. The Ukrainian guards immediately opened the doors of the death chambers. They opened outwards on to ramps. Then they threw out the bodies, so that they quickly formed a heap of corpses. Every day they used 80–100 litres of petrol.

Two guards attended the engine, and when it broke down they called me, as a supposed craftsman. I examined it and I saw glass tubes which were connected to pipes leading to the chambers. I considered that the engine either created high pressure and caused a vacuum, or the petrol produced monoxide in order to kill the inmates. The cries for help and screams of agony of the suffocating people closed in the chambers lasted 10 to 15 minutes. They were terrifyingly loud at first, and then they died down, and the moans became quieter. In the end everything became silent.

The piercing cries were in different languages because foreign transports arrived besides the Polish Jews. There were Czech, French, Dutch, Greeks and even Norwegian. I do not remember German Jews.

The foreign Jews arrived in exactly the same wagons as the Polish Jews, but dressed well and properly equipped with luggage and food, confident that work was awaiting them. But the attitude of the German murderers towards them was exactly the same as to the Polish Jews, and the method of murder was exactly the same. They perished in the same ruthless way and in the same hopeless grief.

When, after 20 minutes of suffocation, the guards slid away the airtight doors the corpses were in an upright position. Their faces were as if they were asleep, unchanged. The mouths were open a little, the hands clenched, often clutching at the lungs. Those next to the doors would fall through the open doors like dummies.

On his return to Belzec, 1946

When the Red Army chased the German 'bandits' from Lvov, I was able to go out to God's world, to look around without pain and fear, and to breathe clean air. For the first time since my slavery began, I could allow myself to think and feel. I wanted to see again the place where they suffocated those who yearned to live.

When I returned, I talked with the people who lived nearby. They told me that in 1943 there were fewer transports because the extermination of Jews was transferred to the Auschwitz gas chambers. Then in 1944 the Germans dug up the grave-pits, poured petrol on to the corpses and burnt them. Dark, thick smoke spread for many kilometres around. The stench was carried by the wind for long distances. For many weeks they were grinding the bones day and night. The wind was blowing like fine dust through fields and forests.

When the 'production' of artificial fertiliser from the piles of human bones was finished they filled in the open graves carefully, levelling the surface. In this way both the horrible acts of the Germans and the graves of the Jews of Belzec were transformed into a luscious greensward.

I said goodbye to my informants and walked away, on my own. The branch railway-line had not disappeared, but I followed its familiar road. It led me through living, scented pines to a huge glade, where there was peace.

14. Prison conditions

These are not chains, they are ornaments.
St Cyprian

For this I can say, I never since played the coward, but joyfully entered prisons as palaces, telling mine enemies to hold me there as long as they could: and in the prisonhouse I sung praises to my God, and esteemed the bolts and locks put upon me as jewels, and in the Name of the eternal God I always got the victory, for they could keep me there no longer than the determined time of my God.

   If any one has received any good or benefit through this vessel, called William Dewsbury, give God the glory; I'll have none, I'll have none, I'll have none. I have nothing to do but die.

William Dewsbury *An early Quaker who spent many years in prison, writing a week before his death in 1688*

Bangladesh (formerly East Pakistan) gained its independence in March 1971. Many of those who had supported the Pakistani government were persecuted. Particularly targeted were intellectuals, large numbers of whom were imprisoned under dubious legal powers. One such **anonymous detainee** smuggled this letter out of a Bangladeshi jail in 1973.

Our animal farm

It is exciting and thrilling to write to you from inside this dungeon, this jail with about three thousand animals romping about where the standard accommodation is one thousand and fifty only. So you can feel the price of space, living space, here in our animal farm. We are all bi-ped animals, treated and fed like them, and here we are about a hundred in one room, sufficient for hardly thirty, a goodly number of principals, professors of colleges and varsity, advocates, local leaders. Not a bad joke indeed, quite sadistic in approach, all herded in and clamped inside as collaborators with the 'occ. army'. It is over a *lakh* (over 1,000) in jails and camps by now, besides thousands killed, maimed, robbed, looted and burnt. Extortion is the national pastime and profession, famine at the door, armed brigands raiding the countryside freely, economy totally shattered, transport dislocated. It is all beyond one's imagination, a total transformation, or should I call it a new experience, a new realisation?

You are lucky, having been out of the country, all of you fortunate beings, better stay out and get fixed.

Shocking and surprising — the foreign press did not care to know, to probe this staggering human tragedy. How is that they do not realise it is a police state? Imagine me here, and why? What fault, what crime? Simply because I was honest, upright, conscientious and outspoken? Simply because I could not, did not, fall in line with them?

A senior government official in Addis Ababa, Ethiopia, **Mesfin Bekelle** (a pseudonym) was a churchgoer who was arrested following the assumption of power by a left-wing government in 1977. He now lives in exile.

Terror fills the prison

For the 900 prisoners in the prison there are toilet spaces for eight people at a time and two showers. The occupants of each cell take turns and one is not allowed to visit the toilets or showers other than in the cell's turn. At the height of the Red Terror there were up to 85 people packed into cells four metres by four metres. It was impossible to sit or stand without doing so on top of one another. The doors are opened for meals and to visit the toilet once in the morning, once in the late afternoon. Sometimes prisoners — five to ten at a time — are allowed to sit outside in the sun.

At night the prison guards, after putting fetters on some of the prisoners' feet and arms, will push them in and lock the doors. There is one small barred window in each room, close to the roof. The temperature rises and people take off their clothing and sit or sleep in their underwear. Fleas and bedbugs start coming out of their hiding places in the rough stone walls. Perspiration starts to condense on the ceiling and cold drops start falling back on the prisoners. The ceilings have turned black. Often up to sixty per cent of the prisoners are sick from torture and can barely move; they have to be helped to the toilet. The smell in the cells from untreated wounds is unbearable.

The guards will open the doors between 4:30 and 5am. Everyone has to get up, stack away their bedding, wash, visit the toilet and eat breakfast before the interrogators arrive. Starting from about 8:30am one person from each room will stand at the door to listen to the names called by the prison officials. Provided that it is not for torture, everyone is anxious to be called; it is an opportunity to walk to the office in the fresh air. There are calls for interrogation in the afternoon as well; the interrogators often work Saturday afternoons and Sundays, as well as coming to work early in the morning and leaving late in the evening. They do it for the overtime pay.

As the end of the day approaches everybody starts worrying because, when somebody is due to be taken away, it is around this time that the security officer in charge of the prison comes. Around 5:30pm he orders everyone back to their rooms, to finish dinner and to close the doors by 6:30pm. This is an indication that some prisoners are to be taken away for execution. Terror spreads and everyone says to himself, 'Could it be my turn today?' At 6:30pm the security policeman pulls a piece of paper out of his pocket and reads out the names and the corresponding room numbers. As prisoners hear their names they start walking out, shouting slogans, depending on which nationality within the Ethiopian empire they belong to. Others just cry aloud. Many, out of fear, cannot control their bodily systems and so wet their pants as they walk out. Terror fills the prison. Soon it will be quiet; people will be gone forever. They are taken to some corner in the outskirts of Addis Ababa to be shot and buried *en masse*.

Before the guards come to lock the doors, a few prisoners from each room who are seriously sick are taken out to sleep in the open space between the two buildings. Some who have stinking wounds have lime-juice poured over them to reduce the smell. Amongst these two or more will be found dead in the morning, when they will be taken away by prison guards.

It is a new day but almost the same things that happened yesterday will be repeated. When the families of those taken away last evening and those who died last night come to deliver food, they will be told that their friends are not around any more. They will immediately realize that their relatives have been executed and will start crying. This is the manner in which they learn of the death of their loved ones.

Solicitor's clerk **James Brightmore** was an English conscientious objector who had served eight months in prison in 1917 when he was returned to his (nominal) army depot. He was then 23 years old. He was punished by the depot commander, and wrote to his nearest relative, his aunt. Despite the fears expressed in his letter, he was not executed but transferred to a special work camp for objectors.

The pit

This is the best stuff [cigarette paper] I can find to write what may be my last letter. Everything has been taken off me, and I should not have this pencil but for chance. I was sentenced to 28 days' detention in solitary confinement. The confinement was in a pit. When it was 8 ft. deep water was struck, but they continued until it was 10 ft. The bottom is full of water, and I have to stand on two strips of wood all day long just above the water line. Sitting is impossible; the sun beats down, and through the long day there are only the walls of clay to look at; a dead mouse is floating in the water as I write and half-a-dozen bottles. This is torture worse than those of ancient days; already I am half mad.

I am to be sent to France, and yesterday was passed fit. I was taken before the doctor to be examined, but refused examination, knowing that whether judged fit or not I should be passed, because it is ordered that I am to be sent out. I hunger-struck for two days in the hole here, but found I was getting too weak to resist, and my brain, too, seemed to be giving under the strain.

I wish I could only see your letters. I could be re-assured or know your wishes. As it is, I feel sentenced to death, knowing that within a few days I shall be in France and shot. The fact that men are being sent to France at all is proof positive to me that the military authorities have captured the machine and are able to do as they like with us.

It is nothing but cold-blooded murder to send men into the trenches to be shot like dogs for disobedience. I am not afraid to die, but this suspense, this ignorance, linked up with the torture of this pit, have plunged me into misery, despair, madness, almost insanity. The hardest thing is leaving you three dear ones behind, and the suffering and anxiety I am bringing upon you. All these weary months of imprisonment we have lived on hopefully; now the cup is being dashed from our hands, and in 'Liberty's' name.

A dissident from an early age, **Vladimir Bukovsky** was born in the Urals, USSR, in 1942. He was imprisoned several times and also placed in a psycho-prison where the authorities tried to prove that, as a dissident, he must be mentally ill. Instead, he denounced psychiatric abuse. He was exchanged for a Chilean communist in 1976, and now lives in the West.

In the punishment cell

The most unpleasant thing of all was the sensation of having lost your personality. It was as if your soul, with all its intricacies, convolutions, hidden nooks and crannies, had been pressed by a giant flat-iron, so that it was now smooth and flat as a starched shirt-front.

This is particularly noticeable when you are alone in the punishment cell, in the box. There you get no paper, no pencil and no books. They don't take you out for exercise or to the bathhouse, you get fed only every other day, the only window is blocked, and the one electric light-bulb is set in a niche right at the top of the wall, where it meets the ceiling, so that its feeble light barely illuminates the ceiling. A ledge jutting out from the wall is your table, another your chair — ten minutes is as long as you can sit on it. At night they issue you a bare wooden duckboard for a bed, and blankets or warm clothes are forbidden. In the corner there is usually a latrine bucket, or else simply a hole in the floor that stinks to high heaven all day. In short, it's a concrete box. Smoking is forbidden. The place is indescribably filthy. Gobs of bloody saliva adorn the walls from the TB sufferers who have been incarcerated here before you. And right here is where you start to go under, to slip down to the very bottom, into the ooze and the slime. The words they have for it in jail express it exactly — you 'go down' to the box, and you 'come up' again.

You spend your first two or three days down there groping round the entire cell — maybe somebody has managed to smuggle some tobacco in and has left a bit behind, or has tucked a fag-end away somewhere. You poke into every little hollow and crack. Day and night still mean something to you. You spend most of the day walking up and down, and at night you try to sleep. But the cold and hunger and boredom wear you down. You can doze off for only ten to fifteen minutes at a time before leaping up again and running for three-quarters of an hour to get yourself warm. Then you doze off for fifteen minutes again, huddled either on your duckboard (at night) or on the concrete floor (by day), with one knee drawn up under you and your back to the wall, until it's time to jump up again and start running.

Gradually you lose all sense of reality. Your body stiffens, your movements become mechanical, and the more time passes the more you turn into some sort of inanimate object. Three times a day they bring you a drink of hot water, and that water affords you indescribable pleasure, melting your insides, as it were, and bringing you temporarily to life. For about twenty minutes or so, an exquisite ache permeates your entire being. Twice a day, before you use the latrine, they give you a scrap of old newspaper and you read it greedily, devouring every word, several times over. In your mind's eye you run over every book you have ever read, everyone you have ever met, every song you have ever heard. You begin doing additions and multiplications in your head. You remember snatches of tunes and conversations. Time comes to a halt. You fall into a stupor, starting up and running about the cell for a while, then lapsing into a daze again, but it doesn't help the time to pass. Gradually the patches on the walls start to weave themselves into faces, as if the entire cell were adorned with the portraits of prisoners who have been here before you — it is a picture gallery of all your predecessors.

An English lawyer came to Moscow and contacted the director of the Institute with a request for a meeting with me.

'Bukovsky?' he repeated, with a frown. 'I don't remember. I'll have to look and see if we've got a patient of that name.' And he started riffling through some papers on his desk. 'Oh yes, here he is. He was found to be suffering from schizophrenia, but the treatment has helped a lot and we shall soon be discharging him.'

In this way the eight-month scientific argument over my psychiatric condition was brought to an abrupt end. No certificates, no explanations, no apologies. I beg your pardon, who detained you? You simply imagined it all.

And for another three months after my release my mother continued to receive belated replies from the various departments of the Public Prosecutor's Office: 'No grounds have been found for your complaint. The investigation is being carried out according to normal judicial practice. Your son has been detained in accordance with the law.' Truly we were born to make Kafka live.

After being first arrested in 1917 in a demonstration for women's suffrage, **Dorothy Day** (1897–1980) became a leader in the struggle for social justice in the USA. She founded the *Catholic Worker* and its Houses of Hospitality for the destitute in the 1930s. She was repeatedly imprisoned. In 1955 she was imprisoned for refusing to take shelter during an air-raid drill in New York. She considered it a mockery to suggest that there could be a shelter against nuclear attacks.

Graciousness is an old-fashioned word

From the time one is arrested until the time one leaves a prison every event seems calculated to intimidate and to render uncomfortable and ugly the life of a prisoner.

I can only hint at the daily, hourly repetitive obscenity that pervades a prison. Shouts, jeers, defiance of guards and each other, expressed in these ways, reverberated through the cells and corridors at night while, rosary in hand, I tried to pray.

Noise — perhaps that is the greatest torture in jail. It stuns the ear, the mind. Everything was exaggeratedly loud. Television blared from the 'rec' room on each floor in the most distorted way. One heard not words or music but clamour. The clanging of gates (seventy gates on a floor), the pulling of the master lever which locked all the cells of each corridor, the noise of the three elevators, the banging of pots and pans and dishes from the dining room — the shouting of human voices — all these made the most unimaginable din.

Most cells for the five hundred or so prisoners, or girls held in 'detention', are cemented and tiled halfway up the front, and then barred to the ceiling; about ten bars across the front of the cell, perhaps five bars to the gate, which is so heavy one can hardly move it. It is the crowning indignity for the officer to shout, 'Close your gates!' and to have to lock oneself in. The open bars at the top enable one to call the guard, to call out to other prisoners, to carry on some friendly intercourse. The 'cooler' is meant to be a place of more severe punishment than the cell, of course, so it is completely closed in.

When I lay in jail thinking of war and peace, and the problem of human freedom, of jails, drug addiction, prostitution, and the apathy of great masses of people who believe that nothing can be done — when I thought of these things, I was all the more confirmed in my faith in the little way of St. Therese. We do the minute things that come to hand, we pray our prayers, and beg also for an increase of faith — and God will do the rest.

I was getting pushed here and there, told what I could or could not do, hemmed in by rules and regulations and red tape and bureaucracy. It made me see my faults, but it also made me see how much more we accomplish by cultivating a spirit of trust.

The whole experience of jail was food for my soul. I realized again how much ordinary kindness can do. Graciousness is an old-fashioned word but it has a beautiful religious tradition.

In 1944 Albania came under communist rule and the government began to repress all religious bodies in the country. The Roman Catholic Church bore the brunt of this policy. In 1945 **Giacomo Gardin**, a member of the Society of Jesus, was arrested and sentenced to six years imprisonment and two years hard labour. In 1951 he was sent to an internment camp, released in 1955 and expelled to Italy.

A sweet word

May 1948

Again we are chosen and transported to work in the swamps of Beden, also in southern Albania, in order to work on the irrigation there. We are experiencing horrible days. The speed of the work is taking its toll of our already depleted strength. Beside the hundreds of other prisoners, there are fifty-eight priests suffering and working alongside them. We are part of a special squad composed solely of clergy. The thud of the soldiers' gun butts descending and the bark of their commands form a common symphony between sunrise and sunset. Five fellow priests soon succumbed. Others followed. During the course of the day's work, our squad of clergy attains the first place and receives our prize: a red flag.

March 1950

It is the end of the winter and we are returned to work. Our destination is no longer the swamps, but the construction site of the railroad in central Albania. The work has changed, as has the face of the countryside, but the treatment is the same — brutal and inhuman. As in the beginning, so now, oppressed by fatigue and malnutrition. I am assaulted by the feeling of being a priest who does not exercise his vocation, feeling completely lost. Doubts circulate through my mind, as to why I was ordained a priest, only to find myself confronted by my present situation. An attack of anxiety in a moment. I realize that I can do much through my mere presence and my name in capacity as a priest and Jesuit, here, in this place of torment and martyrdom. This experience teaches me more every day. A word of relief, of consolation, in passing by someone, whose strength sapped, has fallen down not only physically, but spiritually as well, hating everything and everyone; a sweet word and the touch of a gentle hand which gives me the opportunity to strengthen the belief in God and the Faith, for a suffering Muslim; the tenderness in a small piece of bread, taken from my daily portion and given to a fellow prisoner whose bread has been denied — all these excite my soul in the monotonous passage of days and months, and brightening the image of a new ministry. I feel uplifted, if not sanctified. So I am not a lost one, after all.

A distinguished Croatian writer, **Vlado Gotovac**, born in 1920, was imprisoned in Yugoslavia in 1972 for anti-government activities. He spent four years in jail. In 1981 he was sentenced to a further two-year term of imprisonment in Stara Gradiska prison.

'I am God to you'

Stara Gradiska, quite a new experience for me. I entered a real kingdom of dankness which made its incursions everywhere: on all sides there was rust and mildew and a suffocating miasma. Then there were the evening horrors and the nightly attacks of rheumatism — and ever-present filth, stench and putrefaction; everything an endless chain of things being churned into garbage, things rotting away before one could even get a glimpse of them . . .

In my cell were 32 of us — murderers, housebreakers, swindlers, a man sentenced for terrorism, and myself, nearly all serving long sentences. For the most part they were brutish, cruel, crafty men, prepared to do anything to improve their lot. The prison staff are aware of this and exploit it: they make skilful use of promises, privileges, and work places, demanding in return 'co-operation' —

first and foremost denunciation and provocation of political prisoners. Thus Djuro Kopic, serving a sentence for murder, had a knife made, with the intention of killing me one night; and he was convinced that he would not be punished. His scheme miscarried; but he was rewarded for his initiative with a job in the prison surgery.

Political prisoners in Stara Gradiska are billeted not only with murderers, pickpockets, housebreakers and sexual deviants, but also with men sentenced to care and medical treatment — disturbed alcoholics, insane people, mental deficients, and men almost completely ravaged by syphilis. This terrifying crew is handled in a completely arbitrary and thoughtless manner. At any moment anything is possible. Chief Milosevic said: 'I am God to you. No one can come to your rescue.'

No books from outside are allowed in Stara Gradiska, no published material; and nothing may be written except letters.

Almost every day some prisoner would swallow a spoon or a piece of wire, or stick a knife into his stomach, taking care not to injure the intestines — not something everyone can manage! Sometimes someone would cut off a lump of his flesh. All this to get out of Stara Gradiska, at least for a while; to escape from hunger, beatings, the cold and damp, the solitary confinement; just for a breathing spell in hospital.

Sometimes in the afternoon, the duty education officer and Chiefs would organise boxing matches between insane prisoners. The winner received a prize of cigarettes. The wretched fighters would hammer away at each other awkwardly and crazily, but with merciless tenacity. These humiliating exhibitions raised storms of laughter and cynical cheers. On these occasions I was particularly saddened by the fate of Slavko Rajs, a childish youth who was in prison because of his unpredictable fits. I managed to befriend him by giving him paper and paints, as he enjoyed painting. When I was released, a whole collection of his water colours and drawings was taken from me. I managed to get away with one moving memento of him and Stara Gradiska, a drawing on which he had written a dedication to me: 'This place is accursed of God; a lasting keepsake from your good and faithful comrade and friend, Slavko Rajs.'

Born in England, **Cedric Mayson** is a Methodist minister who went to South Africa in 1953 and became a South African citizen. He spent 15 months in jail awaiting trial for high treason, including several months in solitary confinement. Granted bail during his trial in 1983, he fled the country.

Contextual theology

I spent eleven months as an ordinary awaiting-trial prisoner in the historical monument of Johannesburg's Fort. About one hundred other whites, who the authorities would not release on bail, were there for every crime including murder, robbery with violence, theft, vagrancy, fraud, bilking, and drug running. The cells were wire cages seven feet high and when I lay on my back with outstretched arms I touched all four walls at the same time. Each cell had a rusty galvanized shit pot, a bed mat, and some filthy blankets. In the yard were three toilets none of which had seats, with walls three foot high but no doors, and several rows of basins all in the open air: the most public lavatory I had ever seen. In the corner of the yard stood a door before which we queued for 'graze up'. In the exercise period some tried to play games if a ball was available, and others to walk up and down, but there were so many people that the dodging and bumping made it difficult. Many just sat and talked, or just sat. Sometimes there were fights, or public sexual performances, or bullying, or arguments, or grief, or comments on those who were high on smuggled drugs. To one side stood the open door to the Visitors Room where twenty people were crammed together and had to shout through the bars to be heard in a bedlam of sound.

In this environment I was asked to take morning prayers. Clearly it would have been utterly useless to rehash a normal church service or a typical church prayer in either language or subject matter. It had to arise directly out of our own experience there and then, the experience of prisoners with other prisoners in a prison yard — and it is incredible how much of the Bible was written by or about people in prisons. From that time onwards I seldom had a free moment in the yard because so many wanted to talk something through.

The point is simply this: our theology must arise out of the context of our lives.

Born in 1932 in Hanoi, Vietnam, **Nguyen Chi Thien** was first arrested in 1958 for attempting to publish some of his poems, and sentenced to two years hard labour. In 1961 he was committed to a 're-education' camp, and has since spent over 23 years in camp or prison. In 1985 he was awarded the Rotterdam Poetry Prize.

No poetry, no

My poetry's not mere poetry, no,
but it's the sound of sobbing from a life,
the din of doors in a dark jail,
the wheeze of two poor wasted lungs,
the thud of earth tossed down to bury dreams,
the clank of hoes that dig up memories,
the clash of teeth all chattering from cold,
the cry of hunger from a stomach wrenching wild,
the throb-throb of a heart that grieves, forlorn,
the helpless voice before so many wrecks.
All sounds of life half lived,
of death half died — no poetry, no.

The founder in 1609 of a Catholic society for women, the
Institute of the Blessed Virgin Mary, **Mary Ward** (1585–1645)
was imprisoned for nine weeks in Anger Convent, Munich,
in 1631. She and her devotees eschewed the cloistered life
and the nun's habit. In 1630, an order for suppression came
from Rome. With some of her followers, she fled to
Yorkshire, England, her birthplace, where a convent of her
society was finally set up in 1686. Her prison letters were
written in lemon-juice, which becomes visible when
heated. For writing paper she used the wrapping paper of
parcels sent in to her by other sisters.

My palace, not prison

From my palace, not prison, for truly so I find it.

Paper I have none, nor must not have, but what you send things
folded in, and that will be enough. I have little or no liquid left. We
can only once a day read what you write, wanting fire. Your last
papers I cannot warm till night.

I am in cloister, I trow, and closed up we are in one little pretty stair
on the first floor, joining upon the Grot where they bury, and the
deceased saints lie. Our habitation is the place of the despaired of the
sick — we did as it seems displace one that is every moment a-dying,
and she hath been sick these three years and hath spit up all her lungs
— where sometimes we fry and sometimes we freeze, and there do all
that we have to do, two little windows close walled up, our door
chained and double locked and never opened but at the only entrance

and departure of our two keepers. The night we came were placed beds near to our door, where night and day four nuns keep guardia. Mass and sacraments are not feasts for us to frequent. For all this the chamber we inhabit hath all in it could be wished. Indeed I say true and marvel at it, but our Lord gives no more than Lady-like, and what is most easy to be borne. Be sure no complaints be made, nor notice taken of these things.

I must write in such haste as God knows what I shall say. Let us use this manner warily or else we lose all.

In Frankfurt in the early 1960s, twenty of the staff of Auschwitz concentration camp were tried and found guilty of crimes under German law. **Otto Wolken** of Vienna was a physician and ex-inmate who gave evidence.

A doctor in a concentration camp

[In the prisoner dispensary] There were bandages made of crêpe paper, a little cotton wool, a batch of ichthyol ointment, a batch of chalk, a few aspirin tablets; and after the arrival of the first transport from Hungary we had Ultraseptil, a sulfa drug the Hungarian doctors brought with them. Yes, and once we got potassium permanganate. We tried to make a therapeutic ointment out of it. Every wound was treated with ichthyol ointment. We had to put something on it. Eczema was treated with chalk to make it less visible. I attached an aspirin tablet to a string in the dispensary and said: 'In case of slight temperature, lick it once; in case of higher fever, twice . . .'

One hurried to get to the latrine. That was a concrete trough across which lay boards with round holes. There was room for 200 or 300 at one sitting. Latrine details watched to see that no one stayed too long and used sticks to chase the prisoners away. But some couldn't move so quickly, and others weren't through, and because of the strain a portion of the rectum would still protrude. When the latrine detail hit them they would run away and then once more get in line. There was no paper. Those who had jackets with linings would tear off a little piece at a time to clean themselves. Or they would steal a piece from somebody during the night to have some in reserve. The waste water of the washrooms was piped into the latrines to wash away the excrement. But again and again there were major stoppages, especially in places where the water pressure wasn't strong enough. When that happened a terrible stench spread throughout. Then pump details — 'shit details' — would come to pump out the mess.

A group of ninety children were loaded on trucks to be taken to the gas chambers. There was one boy, a little older than the rest, who called out to them when they resisted: 'You saw how your parents and grandparents were gassed. We'll see them again up there.' And then he turned to the SS men and shouted: 'But don't think you'll get away with it. You'll perish the way you let us perish.' He was a brave boy. In this moment he said what he had to say.

15. Selflessness

None of us decided in advance that we
wanted to go to jail. We simply did certain
things which we had to do and which it
seemed proper to do; nothing more, nor less.
If it is foolish to insist on living in harmony
with one's conscience, so be it.

Vaclav Havel

If my imprisonment has no end,
I shall receive all from God as a mark of
   love.
If my oppressors take all my wealth,
My heart and my mind will not be enslaved.
And if they afflict me on this earth,
My soul will rejoice in the world to come.
If they kill me, I shall sing with love
As I make my way to the house of God.
I am glad to suffer the pain he sends,
Since the reason for all comes from God.

Todras Ben Judah Abulafia *Jewish*
thirteenth-century poet

In 1973, when employed in a senior position by the Swiss multinational company, Hoffman-La Roche, **Stanley Adams** (1927–), a British citizen, gave information about over-pricing of drugs to the EEC Commission for Competition. He did this as a whistle-blower against abuse of power by a large international monopoly. In December 1974, he was arrested by the Swiss police, and charged under a 1935 law directed against economic espionage by Hitler's Germany. His wife committed suicide in January 1975 whilst he was held incommunicado. He was released on bail after three months, and found guilty by the Swiss courts, although the European Court later decided that the Commission should compensate him.

The whistle-blower

In February they started my interrogation. I wasn't questioned inside the prison but escorted by a police officer and Alsation dog to the Basle police headquarters about half a mile away. My interrogating officer was a man called Werner Wick, Commissioner Wick. The first time we met he told me that I would be brought from prison every morning, interrogated for a couple of hours, returned to the prison for lunch, and then, depending on his work load, I might or might not be questioned in the afternoon. Commissioner Wick took six weeks or more to cover the ground that had been covered in Lugano in ten hours. Every day I would be asked questions, which I answered, and the next day Commissioner Wick would come back with new questions, digging deeper into my answers. It was quite evident to me that he was being fed the new questions from somewhere. A lot of the discussion was highly technical and the knowledge was not such as was usually held by a police superintendent. I can only assume that he took my answers to someone when I had finished and was then instructed on the new questions to ask the next day in response to my answers. Sometimes it was so obvious that I laughed. It had to be my ex-colleagues at Roche who were helping him. No one else had the information. It was a farce, really. Here I was being charged by the State, prosecuted by the State, and questioned by the State, and yet it seemed that the whole affair was being stage-managed by Roche. If I hadn't been caught in the middle of it, I might have found it funny.

When the police had finally asked all the questions they had to ask, in as many different forms as possible, and as many times as possible, and with as many variations as possible, and could find no possible way of detaining me any further, they declared they had finished interrogating me. It was my view that the whole charade was merely a means of keeping me in prison as long as possible since they knew that even if I was found guilty when the case came to court I would still only be given a suspended sentence, and if I was to serve as an example to anyone else tempted to reveal the secrets of Swiss business, then it was important that I spent some time in prison.

I shall sue for damages. How, I do not know, but I will do it. And I shall do it not only for me, but for all those other potential whistle-blowers who now look at me and think, as they are meant to think, 'It's not worth it', and keep silent.

Because we need them. The world needs them if it is to survive. The fiercer the pressures to keep silent, the more urgent the need is for people to speak out.

Friends ask me now, 'Would you have done it, if you had known everything that was going to happen?' That is an impossible question to answer. But, if you leave aside the death of my wife, then I would say without hesitation Yes, and mean it. Because if I answer No, and other people answer No, then what hope will there be for my children? and my children's children?

If you have a tale to tell, then I say, tell it.

After a few minutes my eyes became accustomed to the darkness and I was able to look around me. I was in a small cell, square, with a very high ceiling. Basle was an old prison, about two hundred years old or more, and the walls were very thick. The only source of natural light was a window set high above our heads, about eleven feet up. I call it a window, because it was made of thinner material than the wall, but it had long since ceased to function as one. It was crusted in the dirt of centuries and no light passed through. A grimy neon tube which burned night and day provided the alternative. On the floor, once my mattress had been added, were four mattresses, side by side. They fitted the space from wall to wall precisely, each mattress touching the other. Between the foot of the mattresses and the door was a handbasin, a WC — open, not curtained off — and a small table, about two foot square, with four stools. And that was it.

After a day or so I decided I could trust my cell mates so I asked for their help. I explained that the European Commission had no idea that I had been arrested and I had no means of informing them as I had no contact with the outside world and would not have for some time to come. As they were all in on minor offences it seemed likely that they would be released within the next few days, and I wanted whoever got out first to take a message for me. They all agreed to help.

One of them must have been released and made contact with the Common Market as they had promised.

At first Schlieder [A European Commission official] thought it was some kind of a joke, that someone was trying to frighten him, but he checked it out through the usual diplomatic channels and discovered it was true and from then on the European Commission started putting pressure on the Swiss government to have me released.

All I knew then . . . was that I was no longer alone. The outside world knew where I was. And I had hope. When you're in prison on your own you have no one to share your happiness with, no wife, no children, no girl friend, no friends, nobody. You can't even shout through the wall and share it with another prisoner because the walls are so thick they wouldn't hear you, and if they did, they wouldn't know what you were talking about. So you hug your elation to yourself, talk to the walls, and cry as I did with happiness and relief.

The **maidservant to Madame Guyon**, the famous French mystic, was imprisoned at the same time as her mistress, both of them coming under suspicion of heresy. She was held in solitary confinement and incommunicado, but managed to smuggle a letter out to her brother in 1697. No record has been found of her name.

A letter of comfort

I do not know that I shall ever have the consolation of seeing you again. I should be glad to see you, and still more on your account than on my own. That is to say, I should be glad, if it were God's will; for I have no desires and no consolations separate from Him.

I am sensible, my dear brother, of the good disposition of your heart; and well I know that you love me. I never can forget your great care and concern in relation to my welfare, when we were about to part from each other; and how much troubled you were in seeing me forsake the advantages the world held out.

There is but little danger of my getting away from the prison of Vincennes, where I have been confined twice. I have been in prison this last time nearly three years. Whether I shall ever be released again in this life I know not. Perhaps I shall have no other consolation in this life than what I find in suffering.

I am not allowed any materials for writing; nor is it an easy thing for written communications to pass in and out of my cell. Unexpectedly, however, I obtained some sheets of paper; and, using soot instead of ink, and a bit of stick instead of a pen, I have been enabled to write this. But I do it in the utmost hazard and jeopardy. It is my hope that you will receive what I write, and that, with the Divine blessing, it may one day be a means of comforting you in my imprisonment; for it seems to me that you have a hundred times more trouble and concern about it than I have. Not a day passes in which I do not thank God that He has imprisoned me here.

I feel for those who have afflicted and persecuted us. I indulge the hope, that God will, in time, open the eyes of those among them who are upright, but have acted wrongly from false views. It is my desire, especially, that they may be led to understand and appreciate the character of Madame Guyon. We are now separated from each other; I am in this prison alone, she in another place; but we are still united in spirit. The walls of a prison may confine the body, but they cannot hinder the union of souls.

Shmuel Ha'spari (1955–) is an Israeli playwright who was called up for military service in 1985. He had previously fought in the Yom Kippur War and in Lebanon, but as a devoutly religious man, he decided he could not serve in Lebanon again.

I am not a dodger

Had I wanted, I could have neatly gotten out of this business. I could have asked for deferment of service or gone abroad. But I didn't want that. I have been brought up to be a good Jew and a good Zionist, and not to evade responsibility. I told people: 'I am a playwright and a theatre director, not a plumber. The theatre is my way of life. I cannot let myself make any concession, because afterwards I would not be able to write a single word.' I knew that if I dodged this responsibility I would afterwards become a whore – I would start writing things in which I don't believe. I regarded this refusal as a personal test. I knew that I must not fail this small test. I thought: what will happen if . . . I would have to go to prison for writing a play or for voicing a political opinion? Would I then bow down, too?

I went to Base Camp. I told the brigade commander that I am staying home, and he was astonished. For more than two hours he tried to convince me. 'Why do you need this?' he asked me. 'Soon, withdrawal will start, and the whole business of Lebanon will end. Anyway, you will be stationed in Marj Ayun, which is close to the Israeli border, and you will have no contact with the civilian population.' I said to him: 'This is hard for me, but if I have to go to prison, I will do it and hold my head high.' I am not a dodger.

The regimental commander left me alone for three hours, to deliberate with myself. Meanwhile, my comrades outside had already stowed the gear and prepared the jeeps. I knew I had to choose between my comrades, the salt of the earth, and the prison scum. I also knew that if I climb on the jeep, this would be interpreted as if I am afraid of prison — and I shrank from this conclusion. My comrades came and tried to convince me, and this was very hard. Only a combat soldier can understand this: the fellowship, the strong bond between you and your comrades, the desire to stay with them.

I stayed alone with my thoughts. It was hard. It is not easy to refuse, not at all easy. Refusal is a terrible word, especially when you are a combat soldier, most especially when you are also religious. For a religious man in Israel, it is more difficult to refuse, because you are accustomed to accept authority. For you, the operative principle is *'Dina D'malchuta Dina'* ('The King's Law is binding' — a Talmud quotation). The (religious) public, your home, your family — everything is conditioning you. It is strange to see a refuser wearing a skullcap.

I was brought before the brigade commander, to be tried by him. He again attempted to convince me. I felt that he understood my motives, but had no choice. My comrades had already departed for Lebanon, and I asked him to get it over with quickly. It took only about half a minute. There was a terrible tension in the room. I didn't look at him; he didn't look at me. While talking to me, he kept his eyes on the paper before him. I was sentenced to 35 days in Military Prison.

A French Protestant doctor of medicine, **Adelaide Hautval** (born in 1906) was transported to Auschwitz in 1943, because she insisted on wearing a yellow star, as French Jews were forced to do, while in prison for an infringement of border regulations. She did so as a protest against Gestapo treatment of the Jews. In Auschwitz she became a prisoner-doctor, but refused, at risk of her life, SS orders to take part in experiments on other prisoners. She was smuggled to another part of the camp by a German political prisoner, and survived to become a Health Inspector of Schools near Paris.

Moral choices

Each one of us carries in himself the seeds of all possible actions and from this point of view a concentration camp is a terrible touchstone. If sometimes there may be an abyss between two courses of action, at other times it is only a question of degree. For instance, was there any essential difference between the prisoner-nurses who drove patients savagely towards the gas-chamber trucks — because they themselves had been threatened with death if they refused this task — and our own little group of doctors who stood by overwhelmed but completely passive while this horror was going on?

No one can possibly know in advance how he would react in circumstances like these. One is alone with one's conscience in deciding what to do. And sometimes it was impossible to know if one had even made the right choice. In April 1945 I was at Ravensbruck. We were waiting for the Russians. The SS were evacuating the camp, but there were many patients too ill to move. Many of us thought it likely that the camp would be burned to the ground when the SS left. Our own group of doctors was absolutely firm that it would be quite wrong for us to abandon our patients whatever the circumstances. Others opposed us, saying that those who were too ill to move had no chance of surviving anyhow and that our duty lay with the patients who were well enough to be evacuated. Who was right? Who can say?

I recall these memories, which I don't enjoy thinking about, because, although many prisoners managed to resist degradation, others showed their human frailty. One must guard against the wish to play at being a magician and pretend that one could always remain a master of one's circumstances. I don't think anyone in the world has the right to judge or decide what he himself would do in the quite extraordinary conditions that had to be faced in places like Auschwitz . . .

I'm sure that all the terrible things done in the world begin with small acts of cowardice. At Auschwitz, for instance, we prisoner-doctors had to face this terrible question of the selections: that is, we were asked by the SS to decide which patients were too ill or weak to be able to work properly. And if we selected these patients we knew perfectly well that they would be dispatched immediately to the gas chambers. Many of us refused to take part in this process. I myself refused to write the words 'unfit for work' on any medical papers. And what happened was that another prisoner-doctor did it on my behalf in order that I shouldn't have my own head chopped off. If the prisoner-doctors refused to write the words then an SS doctor made the selection and we found they were taking away many of the patients who were in reasonably good health. So what happened? Some of the prisoner-doctors felt themselves obliged to make the selection after all, so as to be sure that only those who were really likely to die anyhow would be chosen. Then again there was the question of medicines. They were in desperately short supply, so in the camp hospitals we tried to reserve them for those who were likely to survive and not to give them to those who seemed to be dying. And this was already the first step down the ladder, because unjust feelings began to creep in. One would, for example, try to save someone whom one felt close to rather than someone whom one didn't know very well. All this horror was so much our daily bread that we became deadened to it. As a doctor one might spend the whole day trying to save someone whom one knew, while leaving others to die without doing a thing. We asked ourselves what was our responsibility. I said: 'Look at us here. We're responsible for what is happening, too. The fact that we're doing nothing doesn't free us from guilt.' And I shall always feel that all of us, whoever we were, took part in these crimes and that if some of us from time to time were able to refuse, it's nothing to be proud of.

What impressed me in all this Nazi experience was how vulnerable human nature is. You only have to be indoctrinated about something for months, for years, to end by believing it. And once you believe certain people to be inferior it becomes perfectly natural to subject such people to experiments and no reasoning can touch you . . .

But along with the horror and the degradation there was an enormous amount of heroism, of daily acts of courage and devotion. What I did was nothing. And besides, if I had the luck to be able to refuse, it was certainly not due to myself, but simply because I had in me an instinct which told me that there were more important things in life than saving one's own skin. There were many, many examples of heroism, of *positive* heroism. For instance, everyone who was going to be sent to the gas chambers at Auschwitz was put in a special block — Block 25. When they came back from work the prisoners were made to run, and all those who couldn't run properly were put in Block 25 ready for the gas chambers. Fifteen thousand a day. And several times others who had escaped selection took the condemned people food. I remember one young colleague of ours who was caught and pushed into the block. Several days afterwards we saw her sitting in the gas-chamber truck with the rest and as the truck went by she gave us a farewell wave — poignant but completely serene.

One should try and remember the good things. Courage and helpfulness knew no boundaries of race, social class or nationality, and my life was saved several times by German prisoners who were not Jews. There was the head of the block who brought me special food at Birkenau when I was ill; and the communist in charge of the allocation of work who somehow managed to smuggle me back to Birkenau from

Auschwitz. I think we ought to love life too much to remember only the hatred and bitterness of the past.

While living in Brussels in 1943, **Madame Jeanty-Raven** and her husband were arrested by the Gestapo for sheltering a British airman. They were a part of the resistance escape-line Comète. She was told by her lawyer (a German) of an obscure provision whereby a husband could be saved from the death penalty if the wife was mentally ill. She therefore feigned madness and was transferred from prison to a lunatic asylum, being liberated in March 1945. Her husband was executed about the same time.

Feigning madness

The doctor made a gesture waving his hands above his head. What and how escaped my attention, and my hands, like lead, were hanging by my side. 'Come, do what I did,' said the doctor. I knew that he would not repeat the gesture, and I knew I had not seen it. The doctor insisted that I should do what he had done. Then, to gain time, I asked him, 'Dr Schubert, who has told you?' 'Told me what?' he said. 'Told you that I was a very good dancer!' 'Ach! Madame Jeanty, nobody has told me anything. Go on and do what I did.' But then, like the stubborn 12-year-old child that I had decided to become, I too insisted and said, 'But I am a very good dancer, doctor, watch!' and instead of doing what he had done, I turned round and round him, smiling, curtseying until . . . he surrendered!

So, I was certified insane and sent to a lunatic asylum in Germany.

The Director of the asylum, Dr Geller, was an old gentleman who looked kind and human. I dreaded the idea that I might remain interned for any length of time. I was very depressed and felt that all my imagination had gone and that I could no longer be a lunatic . . . by choice. My only chance was to talk to Dr Geller, so I sent him a note and he agreed to see me.

I plunged in and told him that I was not mad, but pretending. His duty as a German was to report me. He did the contrary and helped me . . .

Because I was very under-fed, one day on waking up, I could not see, everything was dark and I thought I was blind. I got up to tell the sister, but fell on the floor. Sister came, put me back into bed and told the doctor on duty. He came to see me and said, 'Hunger, stay in bed.' That was all he could say.

A few hours later, Dr Geller came and told me how sorry he was that I had made no complaint about this, that he could improve my food because he was receiving money from my brother-in-law in Brussels which would enable him to give me a black-market first-class regime. I was so weak that I did not even think of asking questions. With better food and better morale I gained hope. On one of my [post-war] visits to Bonn, I asked Dr Geller [about it] and he replied in his calm manner, 'If I told you that it was my own money, you would have refused.'

You don't remain in a prison cell for months without giving time to thinking. I learned not to judge an event when it is happening, for one is too involved not to distort it. When I knew that my husband would not come back and tried to understand why it had to be so, I did. If I had resumed my blissful life with him, I could not have visited prisons or camps [after the war]. I can identify myself with a prisoner, I know what to say to him and, even more, what I must not say to him. I know despair, the key to so many crimes.

And this is how it should be. We need to know and feel that our experiences are those of other people. How can you help pain if you do not know it? Why do we often think that suffering is acceptable for others and not for ourselves? How can we measure our neighbour's grief? We cannot.

When working as a nurse in a hospital in Namibia in 1977, a Namibian citizen, **Magdalena** (a pseudonym), was arrested by the military on suspicion of giving medical supplies to the South West Africa People's Organization (SWAPO). After a month, a visiting magistrate found her not guilty. She was then about 27 years old, and had two children, but thinks it unlikely she can bear more on the evidence of her miscarriages.

I am ready for death

The police blindfolded me again and took me to the room where they torture people. They took all my clothes off me so that I was just left with my underwear on. Then they tied me up by my arms. My feet were three or four feet from the ground. They put ice in my mouth and on top of it some kind of plug. I think it was one of those things they use in mental hospitals. I felt somebody putting a string round both my thumbs and tying it very tight. I was still blindfolded but I could feel somebody tying my ears and my big toes — both of them.

After that I felt something being put in my vagina. Suddenly the whole of the left side of my body started to ache. It was very, very painful. I don't know what they did to me. Then they started on the other side. After this they did both sides at the same time. I think that it was an electric shock, but I don't really know. It hurt so badly that I lost consciousness.

Later I woke up and saw that I was lying on the floor with absolutely no clothes on me. Somebody was pouring iced water all over my body. One policeman kicked me and said that I must walk to my cell. I could not stand up. I just had to crawl. They put my dress on me and from there they took me to my cell.

Within a few minutes I saw that I was bleeding. I cannot remember what time it was. I looked down and saw the blood was streaming out of me on to the floor of the cell. Some time later one of the policemen asked me: 'Were you pregnant?' I said to him: 'I told you before that I was pregnant.'

The police came to fetch me again for more torture. I was tied upside down with my feet in rubber stirrups. I was pretty mixed up and confused, I don't really know what they asked me or what I said. They started with their questions. I remember I was just talking all sorts of nonsense. I can't remember anything I said.

After meeting the magistrate I was released from prison. They asked me to report everything to them which I heard about SWAPO or the freedom fighters. I told them I would not work for them under any conditions. They told me that they would put me back in prison if I did not help them. They said once again that they would put me away for life. I told them: 'You can put me in jail. I am ready for anything, death or more trouble.' Then I was dismissed.

In 295 AD in Tebessa, Algeria, then a part of the Roman Empire, **Maximilian**, a young man of 22 years, was brought before Proconsul Dion to be recruited into the Roman Army. He was accompanied by his father. The imperial representative and other officers of the court were also present. Maximilian was brought to the measuring post to see if he reached the standard height of the service.

A worthless thing

Maximilian: I cannot fight, I cannot do evil, I am a Christian.

Dion: Measure him. (The officers called out that his height was 5ft. 10in.)

Dion: Give him the badge [the soldiers' badge — a leaden collar].

Max: I will not suffer it, I cannot fight.

Dion: If thou wilt not serve, thou must die.

Max: I will not serve. You may cut off my head if you will. I cannot engage in earthly warfare. I am God's soldier.

Dion: Who persuaded thee to this?

Max: My own mind, and He who called me to His service.

The Proconsul turned to the father, and said, 'Advise thy son.' The father replied: 'He knows his own mind; of what use would my counsel be?'

Dion (to Maximilian): Receive the badge.

Max: I will not receive your badge: I have the badge of Christ my God.

Dion: I will send thee straight to thy Christ.

Max: Do it now; I am ready.

Dion: Mark him, and fix on the collar.

Max: I shall break it, for I count it a worthless thing. I am a Christian, and it is not lawful for me to wear on my neck a leaden seal of this kind, after having received the seal of salvation of my Lord Jesus Christ, the Son of the living God.

Dion: Consider thy youth. It is honourable in a young man to be a soldier.

Max: I can engage in no warfare but for my Lord.

Dion: But there are Christians in the Imperial armies who fight.

Max: *They* know what is allowable for *them*: I am a Christian, I cannot do evil.

Dion: Why, what evil do those commit who fight?

Max: Thou knowest what things they do.

Dion: Do not scorn the service, lest thou perish miserably.

Max: I shall not perish; for though thou shouldst put me to death, my soul will live with Christ my Lord.

Dion: Erase his name.

It was erased, and the Proconsul proceeded: 'Because with an impious mind thou hast refused the service, receive this sentence as an example for others'; and he read from his tablet, 'Let Maximilian, because of his impious refusal to enter the military service, be put to death with the sword.'

Max: 'Thanks be to God.'

When he came to the place of execution his head was severed from his body.

Adam Michnik (1946–) is a Polish writer and a one-time leading member of Solidarity. Imprisoned many times for short periods before the imposition of martial law in December 1981, he suffered a three and a half year gaol spell under martial law (1983–86).

In 1982 the French PEN Club awarded him their *Prix de la Liberté*. In 1983 he wrote the following letter to the Minister of the Interior after an offer of release conditional upon him leaving Poland.

He is now the editor of the leading Polish daily paper, *Gazeta Wyborega*.

Bound by truth

The point is, General, that for me, the value of our struggle lies not in its chances of victory but rather in the value of the cause. Let my little gesture of denial be a small contribution to the sense of honour and dignity in this country that is being made more miserable every day. For you, traders in other people's freedom, let it be a slap in the face.

For me, General, prison is not such painful punishment. On that December night it was not I who was condemned but freedom; it is not I who am being held prisoner today but Poland.

For me, General, real punishment would be if on your orders I had to spy, wave a truncheon, shoot workers, interrogate prisoners, and issue disgraceful sentences. I am happy to find myself on the right side, among the victims and not among the victimizers. But of course you cannot comprehend this: otherwise you would not be making such foolish and wicked proposals.

In the life of every honourable man there comes a difficult moment, General, when the simple statement *this is black and that is white* requires paying a high price. It may cost one one's life on the slopes of the Citadel, behind the wire fence of Sachsenhausen, behind the bars of Mokotów prison. At such a time, General, a decent man's concern is not the price he will have to pay but the certainty that white *is* white and black *is* black. One needs a conscience to determine this. Paraphrasing the saying of one of the great writers of our continent, I would like to suggest that the first thing you need to know, General, is what it is to have a human conscience. It may come as news to you that there are two things in this world, *evil* and *good*. You may not know that to lie and insult is not good, that to betray is bad, to imprison and murder is even worse. Never mind that such things may be expedient — they are forbidden. Yes, General, *forbidden*. Who forbids them?

General, you may be the mighty minister of internal affairs, you may have the backing of a power that extends from the Elbe to Vladivostok and of the entire police force of this country, you may have millions of informers and millions of zlotys with which to buy guns, water cannons, bugging devices, servile collaborators, informers, and journalists, but something invisible, a passerby in the darkness, will appear before you and say: *this you must not do.*

That is conscience.

I am certain that this letter will seem to you yet another proof of my stupidity. You are accustomed to servile begging, to police reports and informers' denunciations. And yet here you have a man who is entirely in your hands, who is being harassed by your prosecutors, who will be sentenced by your judges, and who dares to preach to you about conscience.

What impertinence!

However, you can no longer astonish me. I know that I will have to pay dearly for this letter, that your subordinates will now attempt to enlighten me about the full range of possibilities of the prison system in a country that is in the process of building communism. But I also know that I am bound by truth.

James Rowland was an American student during the Vietnam war. He considered the war unjust, and in 1966 refused induction into the armed forces. He was given an indeterminate sentence of up to four years under the Youth Corrections Act. He wrote to a friend from prison in California about his refusal.

Paying a radical's price

I think the worst kind of fear is the fear that you yourself will fail to act according to your conscience. That fear is now gone. I am one of the freest men in this country.

Prison is a break in my life, I'm burning my bridges behind me. Those left on the other shore are going to have to build their own bridges over to me if they want me. I'm no longer making the effort. The people in my past who hate me, who don't understand me, who patronize me, who tolerate me, and become puzzled by me, are gone. Friends, some good, some not so good, are probably lost. Does it matter? Well, beneath my iconoclastic exterior, I do care; but sometimes it is more important to make a stand, though your friends turn against you.

I don't feel like a martyr, and I haven't a martyr's desire to be pilloried so he will be admired. That is scant compensation. Besides, most people who question me don't have any feelings but a wonder that crazymen such as myself are allowed to run loose. Well, you just do what you have to do.

It looks like I will be here a while, as paroles for draft refusers are scarce now. To have a radical's conscience, one has to pay a radical's price, and it's worth it.

A South African, **Richard Steele** was sentenced in February 1981 to 12 months in prison for refusing to serve in the South African army. In an interview with a member of the International Fellowship of Reconciliation he reflects on his experiences.

The power of fearlessness

Whatever I was doing in my life I wanted to reflect my Christianity. In considering the issue of military service, which is obligatory in South Africa for men, I had to consider it in the light of Christian faith. Just in seeing who Jesus Christ is, someone absolutely gentle and caring and life-giving, you come to ask a simple question: would he, if he received military call-up papers, go and do military service? My conclusion was that he wouldn't. . .

From the trial I went directly to a military detention barracks in Pretoria. It was soon found out that I was a Christian. People would ask why I wasn't wearing the uniform or doing drills, so I would explain my refusal to participate in war because of my belief that life is holy. The Christian rationale would come out quite quickly. Many would come back to talk more intimately — they perhaps would want more of a personal relationship with God. It got to a stage when it became obvious we ought to get together as a group and so we met a couple of evenings a week. The prison situation is so foreign and hostile that you are forced to re-think very basic questions. So it wasn't difficult to have a bible study — in fact an ideal place.

I remember one evening, at the end, when we were about to have a time of prayer and were talking about what to pray about. One of the group suggested, 'Let's pray for the boys on the border fighting the terrorists.' I said, 'Fine. Let's do it. But let's pray as well for the SWAPO [South West Africa People's Organization] army.' That absolutely shocked him. It was the first time he'd ever thought of praying for — in his opinion — the enemy. We talked about it quite a lot, and he came to see that if you pray for one person, you should pray for another.

For myself the great crossing-point came before prison, when I had to consider the possibility of death, that I might die in prison. I could imagine that under some circumstances a person might get beaten to death. Was I prepared to die for what I believed? I realised finally that I was, and this freed me of a tremendous anxiety.

In prison itself, in refusing to obey orders, while no longer worrying about death, there was fear at first about solitary confinement or being put on 'spare diet' — bread and water — as I was at one point. One of the things I learned was not to get preoccupied with physical consequences and rather to concentrate on the actual value of what I was doing. The *power* of fearlessness is astonishing. They could threaten me with anything at all and not get me, because I wasn't afraid. This was immensely liberating to me. I could be the person I was without fearing them. They had no power over me.

In solitary confinement I spent my time on yoga, long periods of prayer, bible study, recalling and reliving events in my life. It helped simply to accept the reality of a small cell and its isolation and then expand my consciousness as far as it would go. You come to realise very clearly that God isn't locked in or out of corrugated iron walls, that Jesus suffered in similar ways and overcame the power of evil confronting him.

There is always an element of goodness in each person and the possibility of change. In detention barracks I was able to build really human relations with other prisoners and with the prison staff, though it took time. I saw profound changes in attitude toward me and toward the issue of conscientious objection.

16. Suffering

Thou hast put us to the proof
And refined us like silver

Psalm 66

It is easy to talk about Poland.
It is harder to work for her,
Harder still to die for her,
But hardest of all to suffer for her.

Graffiti *On the wall of an underground cell in
the former Gestapo headquarters in Warsaw*

As a student leader in the struggle against Cuban dictator Batista, **Jorge Valls Arango** (1933–) was imprisoned, then, on release, went into exile. He returned to Cuba after Castro came to power, called for a democratic constitution, and in 1964 was sentenced to 20 years imprisonment. His poetry was smuggled out and published. In 1984, following his release, he received the Rotterdam International Poetry Prize.

Happiness

From hell you cannot get out, but from prison you may die and get out. All sorts of physical, psychical and moral violence are exerted upon us. We have never six weeks of peace, we have never one day of safety, of tranquillity. They are always teasing, provoking, doing something to disturb and to destroy. The most important thing is not the physical violence. That has been horrible many times. It is the risk you are always running of becoming mad or becoming idiot — which has been the case with many of my companions. Some of them have gone mad and committed suicide. Some of them have even become idiot. After a time, a man doesn't know how to talk, and we live every minute defending our soul, our structure, our human identity.

In prison I have lived the three most important and happy moments of my life. Happiness doesn't depend on the place where you are, but what you are living. The first time was during Batista's period: I was captured and I was supposed to be killed. But someone knew me and put me in a cell for 48 hours. In that time I have lived such a wonderful thing that, as I was inside the cell and I was expecting my death (because I couldn't expect anything else), I said 'Oh God, this is wonderful. I am so happy that this is the best moment to leave the world.'

Then, many years after, one day a priest was in jail — we were both in the same galley — and we held mass on a prisoner's bed, the father sitting cross-legged in front of me, the consecration on the bed with a prisoner's jug and a piece of old bread, some drops of wine that we had taken into the prison the 'way of the rats' [smuggled] and I had for the first time Communion with the bread and the wine consecrated.

A third time I was inside the punishment cell, but I have been so terribly happy because of some affection, I may say recently discovered, some personal feeling, that I had the same thought as the first time: I am so happy, so happy now. It is the best time for dying. Yet that time I knew I was not going to die, that happiness was just a way of proving to me that life is neither pain nor happiness but just a taste to continue to keep on.

Born in Peking in 1915, **Nien Cheng** studied at the London School of Economics from 1935 to 1938. She married a Chinese diplomat and lived in Australia from 1941 to 1948. They returned to China following the revolution of 1949, and her husband became general manager of a large (Western-based) firm. When he died in 1957, Nien Cheng took up employment with his old firm in Shanghai. In 1966, during the upheaval of the cultural revolution, she was arrested on suspicion of being a British spy. As she consistently refused to confess to this trumped-up charge, she was held in solitary confinement for six and a half years. In 1973 she was released, possibly because of a lessening of international tension, and went to live in the USA. During her incarceration her daughter, Meiping, was beaten to death by Red Guards.

Ordeal by handcuffs

My heart was still beating very fast. In spite of the unpleasant smell in the room, I breathed in and out deeply and slowly to try to calm down and slow my heart beat. When I felt better I sat down on the wooden board and tried to look round in the dark. I was relieved not to see anything that suggested blood, excrement or vomited food left by previous prisoners. I was so tired that I put my head on my drawn-up knees and closed my eyes to rest. The only compensation for being locked in a cement box, I thought, was that without the window to admit the cold air and wind, the place was decidedly warmer than my cell.

The handcuffs felt different from the others I had worn before. I examined them with my fingers. Indeed, they were different, much heavier and thicker, with a square edge, not rounded like the others. My hands became very hot and uncomfortable. When I found it difficult to curl my fingers into a fist, I knew they were swollen. My hands became my sole preoccupation and worry. If my hands were crippled, how would I be able to carry on with my daily life when the Cultural Revolution was over? . . .

I pressed my fingers in turn. At least they were not numb. But I could tell they were badly swollen. I wondered how long I would remain manacled like this. At that moment I did not need to think of the threat to my life, only the threat to my hands. What could I do to lessen the possible damage to them? It seemed to me the swelling was caused by the tight handcuffs fitted firmly round my wrists which prevented proper circulation. When the militant female guard put her hands round the handcuffs to tighten them, she knew exactly what she was doing.

The female guard was followed by others. All of them lectured me on the advantage of . . . confessing. Now that they knew I was suffering discomfort and worrying about my hands, they did not dash away but lingered hopefully outside the door waiting for my answer.

I was having difficulty walking. For some reason I could not explain, the handcuffs were affecting my feet. Like my hands, they felt hot and painful. My shoes became so tight and unbearable that I had to kick them off. Fortunately they were soft cloth shoes so that I was able to press down the back and wear them as slippers. Now I just staggered about, for my feet could not bear even the reduced weight of my emaciated body. The stains of blood and pus on the quilt where I placed my hands became larger and more numerous as the handcuffs cut through more skin on my wrists and more deeply into the wounds. Either the weather suddenly got a lot warmer or I was feverish: I no longer felt the cold but shivered from pain whenever I had to move my hands or stagger across the room.

Several more days passed. The handcuffs were now beginning to affect my mind, probably through their effect on my nervous system. I got muddled periodically and forgot where I was. I no longer remembered how many days ago I was first manacled. Life was just an unending road of acute pain and suffering on which I must trudge along as best I could.

During moments of lucidity, I tried to discipline my mind by doing simple arithmetic . . . But after only a little while my ability to concentrate would evaporate and I would get confused again. The guards still came to the locked door. But what they said was just a jumble of words that made no sense to me.

After several more days, I became so weak that I no longer had the strength to stagger to the small window to get rice or water. I tried to refuse when they were offered to me, but whether words came out of my mouth or not I did not know. Most of the time I was so far away that I did not know what was happening around me. After drifting in and out of consciousness like that for some time, I passed out altogether.

When I opened my eyes again, I found myself lying on the dusty floor. I pulled myself together and looked up to find the militant female guard and the young man who had put the handcuffs on me standing over me. The cell door was wide open. Dangling in the hands of the female guard was the pair of heavy brass handcuffs they had removed from my wrists. The handcuffs were covered with congealed blood and pus. Probably the guard considered them repulsive, as she was holding them gingerly by the chain by just two fingers.

I remained on the floor, too exhausted to move. Although the handcuffs were removed, my whole body was aching and hot. Slowly I brought my left arm forward and looked at my hand. Quickly I closed my eyes again. My hand was too horrible to contemplate. After a moment, I sat up and looked at both hands. They were swollen to enormous size. The swelling extended to my elbows. Around my wrists where the handcuffs had cut into my flesh, blood and pus continued to ooze out of the wounds. My nails were purple in colour and felt as if they were going to fall off. I touched the back of each hand, only to find the skin and flesh numb. I tried to curl up my fingers but could not because they were the size of carrots. I prayed to God to help me recover the use of my hands.

It took me many months of intense effort at exercise to be able to raise my arms above my head; it was a full year before I could stretch them straight above me.

Ruth First (1925–82), a South African anti-apartheid activist and writer, was detained in 1963 under a provision entitling the police to hold anyone in solitary confinement for periods of 90 days. After 90 days she was released but rearrested as she left the police building. She then agreed to make a statement, intending only to impart information the police already knew. After one session, she refused to continue, realizing the danger that she might be led into betraying her colleagues. She attempted suicide and was released after 117 days.

She then went into exile. Married to Joe Slovo, head of the South African Communist Party, she remained active in the liberation struggle until assassinated by South African security agents in Mozambique. Her life story was portrayed in the film, *A World Apart*.

The excerpt below describes the circumstances of her attempted suicide.

Scent of victory

I had been given the book as an inducement to finish the statement, but I had no intention of doing that, and sooner or later they would take the book back as reprisal action; that at least. I had to make it last as long as possible, though, for I accepted that I now had no option but to adjust to indefinite detention, detention for eternity. I had never been afflicted by a fatalism quite so deep.

The days were grey and melancholy. I barely noticed the exercise periods. I had reeled back from a precipice of collapse but I felt worse than ever. I was persecuted by the dishonour of having made a statement, even the start of a statement. Give nothing, I had always believed; the more you give the more they think you know, and the more demanding they become. I had never planned to give anything, but how could I be the judge? It would be impossible to explain such an act, to live it down. Joe had always told me that my weakness was my extreme susceptibility to acceptance and fear of rejection and criticism: were these the qualities that had propelled me to make a statement? Or was it again my arrogance, my conceit that pooled experiences and rules of conduct (under interrogation) were for other people, and that I was different and could try my own way? My air of confidence had always been useful in keeping others from knowing how easily assailed and self-consciously vulnerable I was; it had worked many a time, but it could do nothing for me now. I had presided over my collapse with a combination of knowingness and utter miscalculation. My conceit and self-centredness had at last undone me. I had thought to pit myself against the Security Branch in their own lair. What had I hoped to learn? I had been stupid. Weak. A failure. By day and by night I went over this self-exposure. I was a spider caught in my own web, spinning finer and finer threads in my head to make disentanglement impossible. I felt unimaginably tired and dispirited. I could not cope any longer. I could not weigh up factors properly. No one could get near me to help me and the help I needed could not be supplied by anyone else. I spent all Sunday making a dilatory attempt at a crossword puzzle, but filling in the clues was surface activity: a decision was forming in my mind. The Security Branch was beyond doubt planning an act of character assassination against me: I would not give them information out of loyalty to my friends, but they would break me finally with some carefully introduced indication that my friends had abandoned me because I had betrayed them, or so the Security Branch would arrange for the version to be told. This abandonment I would not be able to face; and even until it happened I did not have the strength to survive. There was only one way out, before I drove myself mad, and as the truest indication to anyone who was interested that I had not let the Security Branch have it all their own way. I was anguished when I thought of the children, but what good would I be to them in mental pieces? On the flyleaf of the crossword puzzle book, with the pencil that was the property of the South African Government, I wrote a note that apologized for my cowardice, loved the children once more, tried to say words that would have a special meaning for Joe, and indicated that I had not given in, that those still free should not panic and should proceed in the knowledge that I had kept their secrets. After the last inspection of the night I reached for the phial of pills (which the wardress had left in the cell quite inadvertently) and swallowed the lot.

I had never thought about dying so I do not know how I expected to feel coming back into consciousness. I had no feeling at being witness to my own resurrection, only a bewildering confusion of time and place and circumstance. I thought I had moved away, but I was in the same cell. I seemed to find an easy, matter-of-fact acceptance that I had not succeeded. My mind was closed to the enormity of what I had tried to do.

At last I permitted myself my first scent of victory. I determined to shake off the all-devouring sense of guilt at my lapse. I had been reeling towards a precipice and I had stopped myself at the edge. It had *not* been too late to beat them back. I had undermined my own resistance, yet I had not after all succumbed. In the depth of my agony I *had* won.

Etty Hillesum (1914–43) was born a Jew in the Netherlands, took a law degree at Amsterdam University, and went on to study psychology. In 1942 the Nazis gathered all Dutch Jews into Westerbork transit camp, preparatory to removal to concentration camps, and there Etty kept a diary. In 1943 she and her family were deported to Auschwitz, where she died. This excerpt from her diary was written in September 1942.

The thinking heart

Man suffers most through his fears of suffering. The body keeps leading the spirit, when it should be the other way round. Hunger, and cold and danger are, after all, imaginary phantoms, not the reality. Reality is something one shoulders together with all the suffering that goes with it, and with all the difficulties. And as one shoulders them so one's resilience grows stronger. But the idea of suffering (which is not the reality, for real suffering is always fruitful and can turn life into a precious thing) must be destroyed. And if you destroy the ideas behind which life lies imprisoned as behind bars, then you liberate your true life, its real mainsprings, and then you will also have the strength to bear real suffering, your own and the world's.

I have not been entirely honest with myself. I shall have to learn this lesson, too, and it will be the most difficult of all — 'Oh God, to hear the suffering you have imposed on me and not just the suffering I have chosen for myself.'

The tree stood motionless out there in the grey, still morning. And I prayed, 'God, grant me the great and mighty calm that pervades all nature. If it is Your wish to let me suffer, then let it be one great, all-consuming suffering, not the thousand petty anxieties that can break a human being. Give me peace and confidence. Let every day be something more than the thousand everyday cares. All those worries about food, about clothing, about the cold, about our health — are they not so many denials of You, my God? And don't You come down on us hard in punishment? With insomnia and with lives that have ceased to be worth living?

I wish my life to turn into one great prayer. One great peace. To carry my peace about with me once again. 'Give me peace, Lord, wherever I may be. Perhaps I no longer feel Your peace because I am doing wrong. Perhaps, but I don't know.' I brood far too much about my health these days and that is no good. 'Let there be the same great calm in me that pervaded Your grey morning today. Let my day be more than just looking after the body.'

It is now close on 7 o'clock. I shall go and wash from head to toe in cold water, and then I shall lie down quietly in my bed, dead still, I shall no longer write in this exercise book, I shall simply lie down and try to be a prayer. I have felt it so often, all misery for a few days and thinking I wouldn't get over it for weeks, and then suddenly the clouds were lifted from me. But now I don't live as I should, for I try to force things. I must let things take their course and that's what I am trying to do with all my might.

'Not my will, but Thy will be done.'

Of course, it is our complete destruction they want! But let us bear it with grace.

There is no hidden poet in me, just a little piece of God that might grow into poetry.

And a camp needs a poet, one who experiences life there, even there, as a bard and is able to sing about it.

At night, as I lay in the camp on my plank bed, surrounded by women and girls gently snoring, dreaming aloud, quietly sobbing and tossing and turning, women and girls who often told me during the day, 'We don't want to think, we don't want to feel, otherwise we are sure to go out of our minds,' I was sometimes filled with an infinite tenderness, and lay awake for hours letting all the many, too many impressions of a much-too-long day wash over me, and I prayed, 'Let me be the thinking heart of these barracks.' And that is what I want to be again. The thinking heart of a whole concentration camp. I feel my strength returning to me; I have stopped making plans and worrying about risks. Happen what may, it is bound to be for the good.

Victor Jara was a popular musician and singer who was arrested during the coup which brought General Pinochet to power in Chile in 1973. With thousands of others, he was herded into a stadium in Santiago. To prevent him from writing, both his arms were smashed while he awaited execution. Shortly before he died, Jara recited this poem to fellow detainees, who memorized it.

Silence and screams are the end of my song

There are five thousand of us here
in this small part of the city.
We are five thousand
I wonder how many we are in all
in the cities and in the whole country?
Here alone
are ten thousand hands which plant seeds
and make factories run.
How much humanity
exposed to hunger, cold, panic, pain,
moral pressure, terror and insanity?
Six of us were lost
as if into starry space.
One dead, another beaten as I could never have believed
a human being could be beaten.
The other four wanted to end their terror —
one jumping into nothingness,
another beating his head against a wall,
but all with the fixed stare of death.
What horror the face of fascism creates!

How hard it is to sing
when I must sing of horror.
Horror which I am living,
horror which I am dying.
To see myself among so much

and so many moments of infinity
in which silence and screams
are the end of my song.

What I see, I have never seen
What I have felt and what I feel
will give birth to the moment.

Albie Sachs (1935–), a South African lawyer and academic, has been active in anti-apartheid activities since his student days. In 1963, he was detained under the 90-day provision and held for 167 days. After his release, he went into exile. A senior member of the African National Congress (ANC), he survived an assassination attempt by South African security agents in Mozambique in 1988. The excerpt below refers to his period of detention in 1963.

Today I am lucky

I have been very lucky in my life so far. Serious suffering never came my way for long. I regarded it as a state of mind into which some people allowed themselves to fall. Work, reading, the right company and the right attitude were all that were needed to help a person through a spell of suffering. Now I realise that suffering can be very real. At present a series of intrinsically trifling activities may control my unhappiness or, rather, enable me to live with it, but they cannot remove unhappiness from my life. Similarly, happiness is not just a state of mind: it has its base in the circumstances of life, and has to be constantly worked for. I am overcome by a feeling of amazement, almost horror, at the monks of old who voluntarily subjected themselves to a lifetime of silence and isolation. In future I shall no longer think of them as quaint or crazy personages. I shudder at their self-imposed martyrdom and wonder at the depth of religious passion which drove them to such extremes of psychological mutilation. There is no glory in their conduct: such abasement might extirpate self-pity and vanity, but it also drives out love. Self-denial is admirable when coupled with giving and love, but when it is coupled merely with personal suffering it is absurd. The pain I feel now is not ennobling, it is destructive; it is a special pain, it has no identifiable source. It does not stem from grief at a loss, or frustration at an impediment. It is unlocalised in my body. Where does it hurt? Not in my head, or my chest, or my legs, but all over, in the whole of me. The more I thresh and struggle the worse it gets. Basically I think it is an animal pain, a bodily thing due to my unnatural state of inactivity. My mind and emotions rebel at having nothing with which to engage themselves. The greatest deprivation and source of suffering is the lack of human association . . .

It is two o'clock now, I hear the chimes. My last train of thought was quite absorbing, I did not count time as it passed. That is the nearest I can come to happiness — not to be aware of time. What was it that so occupied me? I cannot remember now. Oh what can I do to shore up my enfeebled memory? I feel angry and defeated at being unable to recapture the line of thought in which I was so happily absorbed only a few minutes ago.

Elie Wiesel (1929–) was born in Sighet, Hungary, and became a deeply religious student of the Jewish faith whilst still a boy. When the Nazis took over Hungary in March 1944 he was deported to Auschwitz with his parents and three sisters. They were later transferred to Buchenwald, where his parents and youngest sister died. The camp was liberated by the Americans in 1945. Wiesel became a successful novelist and now lives in the USA. He was awarded the Nobel Peace Prize in 1986.

Where is God now?

One day when we came back from work, we saw three gallows rearing up in the assembly place, three black crows. Roll Call. SS all round us, machine guns trained: the traditional ceremony. Three victims in chains — and one of them, the little servant, the sad-eyed angel.

The SS seemed more preoccupied, more disturbed than usual. To hang a young boy in front of thousands of spectators was no light matter. The head of the camp read the verdict. All eyes were on the child. He was lividly pale, almost calm, biting his lips. The gallows threw its shadow over him.

This time the Lagerkapo refused to act as executioner. Three SS replaced him.

The three victims mounted together on to the chairs.

The three necks were placed at the same moment within the nooses.

'Long live liberty!' cried the two adults.

But the child was silent.

'Where is God? Where is He?' someone behind me asked.

At a sign from the head of the camp, the three chairs tipped over.

Total silence throughout the camp. On the horizon, the sun was setting.

'Bare your heads!' yelled the head of the camp. His voice was raucous. We were weeping.

'Cover your heads!'

Then the march past began. The two adults were no longer alive. Their tongues hung swollen, blue-tinged. But the third rope was still moving; being so light, the child was still alive . . .

For more than half an hour he stayed there, struggling between life and death, dying in slow agony under our eyes. And we had to look him full in the face. He was still alive when I passed in front of him. His tongue was still red, his eyes were not yet glazed.

Behind me, I heard the same man asking:

'Where is God now?'

And I heard a voice within me answer him:

'Where is He? Here He is — He is hanging here on this gallows . . .'

At the trial in 1961 of Karl Eichmann, the Nazi war criminal, evidence was given by **Rivka Yosselevska**. She was a young mother from the village of Zagorodski, near Pinsk in the Soviet Union.

Risen from the grave

We turned towards the grave and then he turned around and asked: 'Whom shall I shoot first?' We were already facing the grave. The German asked: 'Whom do you want me to shoot first?' I did not answer. I felt him take the child from my arms. The child cried out and was shot immediately. And then he aimed at me. First he held on to my hair and turned my head around; I stayed standing. I heard a shot, but I continued to stand and then he turned my head again and he aimed the revolver at me and ordered me to watch and then turned my head around and shot at me. Then I fell to the ground into the pit amongst the bodies; but I felt nothing. The moment I did feel, I felt a sort of heaviness and then I thought maybe I am not alive any more, but I feel something after I died. I thought I was dead, that this was the feeling which comes after death. Then I felt that I was choking; people falling over me. I tried to move and felt I was alive and that I could rise. I was strangling. I heard the shots and was praying for another bullet to put an end to my suffering, but I continued to move about. I felt that I was choking, strangling, but I tried to save myself, to find some air to breathe, and then I felt that I was climbing towards the top of the grave above the bodies. I rose, and I felt bodies pulling at me with their hands, biting my legs, pulling me down, down. And yet with my last strength I came up on top of the grave, and when I did, I did not know the place, so many bodies were lying all over, dead people; I wanted to see the end of this stretch of dead bodies but I could not. It was impossible. They were lying, all dying, suffering; not all of them dead, but in their last sufferings; naked, shot, but not dead. Children crying 'Mother', 'Father'; I could stand on my feet.

The Germans were gone. There was nobody there. No one was standing up. I was naked, covered with blood, dirty from the other bodies, with the excrement from other bodies which was poured onto me. I have a scar to this day from the shot by the Germans; and yet, somehow I did come out of the grave. This was something I thought I would never live to recount. I was searching among the dead for my little girl, and I cried for her — Merkele was her name — Merkele! There were children crying 'Mother', 'Father!' — but they were all smeared with blood and one could not recognize the children. I cried for my daughter.

[Later] the Germans ordered that all the corpses be heaped together into one big heap and with shovels they were heaped together, all the corpses, among them many still alive, children running about the place. I saw them. I saw the children. They were running after me, hanging onto me. Then I sat down in the field and remained sitting with the children around me, the children who got up from the heap of corpses.

The Germans came and were going around the place, but they did not approach me, and I sat there watching how they collected the children. They gave a few shots and the children were dead. They did not need many shots. The children were almost dead.

I was praying for death to come. I was praying for the grave to be opened and to swallow me alive. Blood was spurting from the grave in many places, like a well of water, and whenever I pass a spring now, I remember the blood which spurted from the ground, from that grave. I was digging with my fingernails, trying to join the dead in that grave. I dug with my fingernails, but the grave would not open. I did not have enough strength. I cried out to my mother, to my father: 'Why did they not kill me? What was my sin? I have no one to go to. I saw them all being killed. Why was I spared? Why was I not killed?'

And I remained there, stretched out on the grave, three days and three nights.

17. Torture

Nobody can tell how he or she will
physically, intellectually and spiritually
survive the hot knives of torture.

Ngugi wa Thiong'o

To me those things are so base I never
expected another human being can do such
things and I want to believe that even if I
were given the chance of retaliating on those
people who tortured me, I would never,
ever, do the things they did to me.

Joe Seremane *South African church worker
1987*

Speaking of torture . . . some have described
it like being suddenly in hell . . . as if the
most primary fantasies of diabolic terror are
expressed, that fear . . . which we felt when,
as children, we were confronted with the
most brutal forces before which we were
defenceless; experiences with such an
emotional charge, moving such primary
emotions, so terrific, are always of an
important psychological impact.

Fanny Pollarollo *Chilean psychiatrist*

The following was written by an **anonymous Turkish detainee** to a British MP who described him as: 'a very bright and talkative person. He has a great affection for his country and hope for it in the future. He made it clear that whatever was done to him he would struggle for his basic beliefs in democracy, freedom and peace. If it would help to attain these objectives he "would willingly go back to prison again." '

Human dignity will vanquish torture

First the guards marched towards a cell-block with the chant 'How happy 'tis to be a Turk'. Then chants and slogans from that cell-block: 'Human dignity will vanquish torture!' As the chanting went on we could hear erratic footsteps echoing in the hall, and one voice alone yelling the slogan about tortures. That meant a prisoner was being hauled off to the solitaries where he would get the special treatment. The block where the solitary cells are is right across from our windows, so we would learn about these. But the yelling of the single voice was stifled a little later. And one could hear him groan as he went past our block. The corporal was swearing and ordering this one-time officer to strip. But the prisoner would talk back and the corporal started slapping and hitting him (we could hear the sounds). The young man chanted back at him, 'Human dignity will vanquish torture', and the corporal and a few others went berserk.

It was swearing, hitting and tearing off clothes, and the chant getting higher and higher in tone. Then the corporal ordered a private to muffle the man. But as it was, I guess, quite difficult to muffle, beat and strip an uncooperating person, we could hear him mumble under the stifling hand, and once in a while his mouth would go free and he could shout — or shriek rather. For though the tempo of the chant was always in time, his voice had a shrill tone now. This wasn't a normal human voice. But he was still saying the same words, 'Human dignity will vanquish torture'.

One knew the young man didn't feel the blows any more. The thudding of his head against the wall! I think his friends were dumbfounded until it was over. The semi-conscious body was dragged into the cell still moaning 'Human dignity will vanquish torture'.

Once in a while you are woken up by a shrill, unbelievably bitter shriek. A 'No-o-o-o!' that comes from the guts of a cell-mate. This is something that will keep happening to those who have been through weeks of cruel torture.

It was a nightmare for him.
It was a nightmare of us and for all humanity.

When Iran was governed by the Shah, **Reza Baraheni** was a professor of English, a poet and a writer. In 1973 he wrote an article on the Iranian government's cultural policies, for which he was arrested and taken to a prison for students, professors and government employees. After 102 days he was released, and went into exile to the United States. The excerpt which follows is a compilation of two pieces.

A hell made by men

Shouting was coming from all over the place. Sometimes there would be loud moaning or sobbing, and generally when the iron door of the block was opened there would come an open wailing and crying.

Suddenly the door was flung open. I was taken out, blindfolded and handcuffed, pushed into a room, and the blindfold removed. There was a group of people in suits and ties . . . A very well-dressed man with red, nervous eyes started shouting. 'You see this son of a cuckold? He is much more dangerous than all the terrorists, the communists and the socialists. It is because of this son of a bitch that we have all these cells full of students. They are all his students. How dare you write those things against the government?' He took long, hurried, nervous steps towards me and started slapping my face. It seemed he could not stop himself from shouting when he was slapping . . . I was blindfolded again and . . . forced to pass through something which resembled a leather curtain, or perhaps a tunnel. This was used for mystification purposes; the prisoner should be kept in the dark at all times. The curtain led to an iron door, too small even for my size. The leather tunnel, the small iron door and the blindfold gave me the feeling that I was going to be buried alive. So tight and narrow and suffocating did everything seem that I was already gasping for breath. The order came from a metallic voice: 'Take the blindfold off.' One of the guards did so, and I found myself surrounded by four other men in addition to the guards.

The funny thing was that they call each other 'doctor'. It was only later that I came to realise that by using a university title, they provided themselves with a certain type of legitimacy to deal with university students and teachers. The commander of the prison called himself 'professor' . . . There was a bed on the floor. There were also two other iron beds, one on top of the other, in another corner of the room. These two were used to burn the backs, generally the buttocks, of the prisoners. They tie you to the upper bed on your back and with the heat coming from a torch they burn your back in order to extract information. Sometimes the burning is extended to the spine, as a result of which paralysis is certain. There were also all sizes of whips hanging from nails on the walls. Electric prods stood on little stools. The nail-plucking instruments stood on the far side, the gallows on the other side. They hang you upside down and then someone beats you with a club on your legs, or uses the electric prod on your chest or your genitals, or they lower you down, pull your pants up and one of them tries to rape you while you are still hanging upside down.

My hands and feet were tied to the two ends of the bed by the guards. [The interrogator] started to beat me hard on my mouth saying 'Tell me'. He wanted the names of friends, writers and printing-house workers. Then the flogging started. It was a thick plaited whip, made of wire with a knot at the end of it. The whip would go up, curl round and descend with a whacking sound right on the soles of my feet. When the whip came down, it was like a huge hot charcoal, burning and tearing at the soles of the feet, crippling the whole legs. I was screaming at the top of my voice. Now I could understand the meaning of those screams of the other people the night before.

Those screams stayed with me in prison and when I left the prison. Once, months later when I called the interrogator to tell him I wanted to leave Teheran for a few days, the same nauseating, pleading and pitiable screams could be heard over the telephone. Everyone is welcome to ring up and hear some genuine screaming. The number is 320773.

The flogging continued till I fainted. When I regained consciousness [the interrogator] was sitting on one of the stools watching me. 'Why don't you take me to court?' I said. 'This *is* the court. I'm the judge, jury, court and executioner. I'll pull out your tongue and I'll break your fingers one by one so that you won't be able to say anything or write anything.' And he took the little finger of my left hand and broke it. I started screaming and the flogging started again, and I fainted again.

In only a few hours, the torture chamber takes you back to the primeval forest with fear as the only reigning monarch. The meaning of life departs, and you are suspended in a stupid void in which you are totally alone, desperately alone. That gory revelation of pain, that epiphany of historical emasculation and castration haunts a man who has been in a torture chamber in his dreams and awakenings.

After the prisoner comes out there is no way for him to escape the structure of the prisoner's mind. The torture does not end the first day or the first week, even if it may cease to be operational for some time. The torture becomes deeply psychological as times goes on. You are taken out to be shot and you are not. But it takes you two hours of absolute horror to realise that. And then this very action begins to have such an awesome reality in your mind that later, even after you are released, it becomes part and parcel of your maimed subconscious, as if you had genetically inherited it from a subhuman ancestor and could do nothing about it. You hear of people killed under torture, or an agent is thrown in with you who gives you the details about someone else's death at the hands of the agents. Then the next day or night you are taken out and dealt with in the same fashion, with only one difference: they don't kill you this time. The hell is with you until you disappear, and then, somehow, it moves on in the eternity of its own infernal presence, because, after all, it might go on living after you cease to exist.

Having come out of that hell, I know that there is nothing supernatural about it. It is a hell made by one man for another man, and it should be destroyed by man.

Saida Botan Elmi is a Somali married to a judge who left Somalia in 1976 after resigning his post in protest against unjust laws. She was refused permission to join him, and in 1978 was herself arrested and held in solitary confinement for four years. After her release, she escaped from Somalia and now lives in exile in Holland, receiving regular treatment at the International Hospital for Victims of Torture.

My faith helped me

Suddenly I was blindfolded. I was put into a car and driven somewhere. When I entered this place I was aware of a very bright light, that's all. They handcuffed my hands behind my back now and tied my head to my knees. The men there abused and humiliated me. I was struck with what seemed like the butt of a pistol all down my spine. I was kicked from one side to the other. After some time of this, they took me back to the Investigation Centre, still blindfolded and naked.

I was conscious all the time. When I returned, the blindfold was removed. I saw a man I knew well. It was the Minister of Justice, the same man my husband used to work for. When he saw me he fell into a rage — he was furious at the guards for letting me stay conscious. He shouted and screamed at them, and then at me, hitting me and slapping me all over. Then he raped me. The other policemen did this to me, too. They put out their cigarettes on my body and attached wires to my breast.

I don't remember those early days and weeks and months very well. The first day, yes. All the rest is blurred. I was unconscious a lot of the time, or I was too weak or too tired. I can only tell you how it all started. There was no real routine to the torture. I didn't know when to expect it or why. When it happened it was always at night, from nine o'clock to about three in the morning. Perhaps that's when they were bored.

Usually I was blindfolded, so I can't remember the instruments that they used. There was electric shock treatment, with wires attached to my body. And I was put on a chair that seemed to swivel round. Then there was the sack. I was tied up in a sack and taken down to the sea and was continually pushed under the water until I vomited. Then it was done again. When they raped me, many of the officers would do it to me.

This went on for about a year, but I was in solitary confinement for four years. The cells were very small. I couldn't lie down properly. There was no bed or bedding. I could only sit there with my head between my knees, thinking of what would become of me, and of my children and husband, of what had happened to them.

You ask me how I was able to carry on. I nearly went mad towards the end of my time in solitary confinement, when I was no longer able to speak. I suppose that it was my faith that helped me. I always believed that it would one day all be over, that I would be released. You see, I have always been a good Moslem. In prison, they didn't actually stop me from praying, but it was very difficult. When a Moslem prays, she must wash herself. They never allowed me to do this — and you know the state my cells were kept in. But wanting to pray was enough, I believe.

In the 1970s **Kim Keun-Tae** served several short sentences in South Korea for anti-government activities. He is a graduate of Seoul University, and later became chairman of the National Youth Alliance for Democracy, which distributed leaflets, held meetings, and published a journal. He was finally arrested in September 1985, and sentenced to seven years imprisonment. Prior to his trial, he was tortured at police headquarters in Seoul.

The torturers smiled

Whenever I think about what happened in the torture cell, I tremble with anger and humiliation. The police forced me to surrender. They repeatedly said they were going to break me and that is exactly what they did. I was told I was being tortured to drive me to the limits of my physical endurance and to force me to confess. They said they were forced to torture me and anyone else charged with violating the National Security Law. Each time they questioned me about a new fact they tortured me. I was forced to study and memorize what they wanted me to say while I was lying on the torture rack. It goes without saying that my torture was quite deliberately planned and carefully prepared.

Between 4 and 20 September, I was tortured with electric shocks and water. Each time it lasted about five hours. The electric torture was the main thing, and the 'water torture' was for distributing the shocks resulting from the electrical current. They turned the radio up to maximum volume so that nobody could hear my screams. I screamed so much that my throat swelled and often I couldn't speak at all. Whenever this happened they gave me some medicine. I was subjected to 'water torture' twice on 4 September, and on 5 and 6 September to electric torture.

On Friday 13 September, the torturers said to me, 'This is the Last Supper for you. Today, there is going to be a funeral for you.' After this I was tortured twice with electric shocks. On the 20th, there was one session of electric shock torture and one of 'water torture'. On the 25th I was beaten severely and after that day the torturers continued to beat me. I didn't sleep at all during the period of torture and I had to starve for about half of the days.

Because of the torture, I could not eat any food after 13 September. They gave no food on the days of torture. Sometimes, just by giving no food, they made me suffer from psychological pressure and fear, even on days when I wasn't tortured. As an example of psychological torture, a man who seemed to be responsible for my case stopped by the torture cell at 10am on 8 September and said, 'I will torture this guy myself.' A broad-shouldered man who always carried torture tools in his briefcase said, 'Our undertaking business is about to start. Do you know how Lee Jae-mun died here? He died when his internal organs burst. Now it's your turn . . .'

I was subjected to these kinds of barbaric threats and insults whenever I was tortured. During torture they stripped me naked, tied me to the torture rack and would hurl sexual insults at me. When they actually tortured me my eyes were blindfolded. They would put me on a table with a blanket under me and tie my heels, knees, thighs, stomach and chest to the table. They poured water on my head, chest and groin to help conduct the electricity into my body. Then came the electric shocks, at first, light and short, then stronger and longer; the electric shock brought me within the shadow of death.

I was not tortured because I refused to confess; the torture was planned from the start. This is why the torturers did not show any frustration or anger. Some even smiled as they tortured me. When I faced the reality that some people could remain indifferent to a human being struggling with death, my longstanding faith in humanity began to fade away. With torture tools in their hands, the torturers talked to each other about family matters, such as, 'I don't know how my newly wed daughter is doing these days', or 'I wonder how my son did with his physical exam for his college entrance exams'. I do not know how violence such as torture and human love can exist at the same time.

Lucia Morales was a trade union official in Chile when, in 1983, she was arrested by the security police and held for five days, together with her daughter. She was then banished to a small island in the south of the country.

'Mummy, make this stop'

I became desperate, I screamed, I began to cry . . . the thought that my daughter would have to suffer what I had been through was intolerable . . . how can you describe what it means? On the next day they took me to a metal rack and made me lie on it, naked, tied at the wrists and ankles. With lead weights or electrodes they gave me electric shocks to the nipples, the stomach and the region of the vagina.

At one point, I realized that my daughter was in front of me. I even managed to touch her. I felt her hands. 'Mummy, say something, anything to make this stop,' she was saying. I tried to embrace her but they prevented me. They separated us violently. They took her to an adjacent room and there, there I listened in horror as they began to torture her with electricity — my own daughter! When I heard her moans, her terrible screams, I couldn't take any more. I thought I would go mad, that my head and entire body was going to explode in pieces.

It didn't matter to me if they killed me. What caused me most suffering was my daughter — the frightful agony she was going through, poor thing! And you see the electric shock treatment is quite indescribable. When they put those pieces of lead on you you feel a tremendous jolt through your whole body, as if your heart is about to come out of your mouth. I remember when I was back in my cell I could still feel the convulsions from the electric discharges; my arms and legs were quivering. My daughter was given electric shocks on her hands.

I do think that some day justice will have to be done. Justice, not vengeance. I think that there must be something wrong with those people who torture, enjoying watching other people suffer. How sad it must be for them when they suddenly see how they have degraded themselves!

Agostinho Neto (1922–79) joined the Angolan nationalist movement whilst a medical student in Portugal. Imprisoned three times for 'subversive activities', he eventually led the Popular Movement for the Liberation of Angola (MPLA) to victory in the armed struggle and became independent Angola's first President in 1975. In addition to his political work, Neto developed an international reputation as a writer and poet. (The *palmatória* mentioned in the poem below is a wooden paddle with holes in it used by the Portuguese colonialists to hit the palms of people's hands. The impact of the blows draws flesh up into the holes, causing the skin to burst.)

I will say nothing

I never did anything against your country
but you have stabbed ours
I never conspired never spoke with friends
or with the stars or with the gods
never dreamed
I sleep like a stone flung in the well
and am stupid as vengeful butchery
I have never thought I am innocent
I will say nothing I am innocent
I will say nothing I know nothing
even if they beat me
I will say nothing
even if they offer me riches
I will say nothing
even if the *palmatória* crushes my fingers

I will say nothing
even if they offer me freedom
I will say nothing even if they shake my hand
I will say nothing even if threatened with death

An internationally known Kenyan writer, **Ngugi wa Thiong'o**
was head of the Literature Department at the University of
Nairobi when he was arrested in 1977. Brutally treated for
the first months, he was detained without trial for a year
after writing a play critical of the Kenyan regime. After
release he was not allowed to return to his post at the
University, and now lives in exile.

The hour of trial

Even assuming that one was getting the best possible food, the best
possible accommodation and the best possible health facilities, the fact
of being wrongfully held in captivity at the presidential pleasure, the
very act of forcible seizure of one's freedom for an indefinite period
whose termination is entirely dependent on somebody else's political
fears, is in itself torture, and it is continuous to the last second of one's
detention. All other forms of torture, not excepting the physical, pale
besides this cruellest of state-inflicted wounds upon one's humanity.

The detaining authorities are not of course content to just inflict the
wound: they must keep on twisting hot knives into it to ensure its
continued freshness. This takes various forms: physical beating with
the possibility of final elimination; strait-jacketing to ensure total
bodily immobility; sleeping on cold or wet cement floors without a
mat or a blanket so the body can more easily contract disease; denial of
news or books to weaken the intellect; bestial food or a starvation diet
to weaken the body; segregation and solitary confinement to weaken
the heart; such and more are the sadistic ways of prisons and detention
camps. One or a combination of more than one of these instruments
can be used to keep the wound fresh. And for the duration of the
presidential pleasure, the stony dragon remains deaf to all human
cries and groans from its captives.

Saint Man in a deadly combat with the stony dragon: not for
comfort the thought that nobody can tell beforehand how he or she
will cope with the unsought-for combat. Nobody knows how long the
president's pleasure might last. Nobody can tell how he or she will
physically, intellectually and spiritually survive the hot knives of
torture. Many factors come into it: stamina; the occasional measure of
fairness and humaneness in the warders and prison officers; the extent

of the determination by jailers to break their victim; and the degree of a prisoner's awareness of and commitment to the cause that brought him to jail. More important are the moral standards and principles born of that awareness and commitment which the political prisoner has set for himself.

But even when such a prisoner might have all these ideals, it is still difficult for him to tell beforehand his bodily or mental reactions to certain forms of torture. Some people can cope with any amount of physical torture; others, any amount of psychological torture; yet a few others, can withstand all. Whatever the case, he can only tell this at the hour of trial.

SOURCES The editor and publisher are grateful to the following publishers and individuals for their kind permission to reproduce extracts from copyright material. Every effort has been made to trace the copyright owners of each extract. Any omission is unintentional, and the publisher would be glad, if notified, to make due acknowledgement in any future edition.

Abelard, Peter, *Historia Calamitatus*, The Free Press, 1922 ● Abolfathi, Soraya, *Iran Liberation*, Moslem Iranian Students Societies Outside Iran, 1982 ● Adams, Stanley, *Roche versus Adams*, Cape, 1984 ● Aguirre, Luis Perez, from the unpublished papers of an interview with Margaret Hebblethwaite, 1987 ● Akhmetov, Nizametdin, *Newsletter*, Campaign Against Psychiatric Abuse, No. 13, 1986 St Albans, England ● Allen, Clifford, *The Tribunal*, No-Conscription Fellowship, 1917 ● Al-Naqqash, Farida, *Amnesty International*, 1982 ● Anon 1, *Central Board for Conscientious Objectors*, 1945 ● Anon 2, *Barefoot Productions*, Winchester, 1989 ● Anon 3, *Index on Censorship*, 5/1980 ● Anon 4, *Pintag*, Philippine Resource Centre, Hong Kong, 1979 ● Anon 5, *Turkish Peace Association*, 1985 ● Anon 6, *The Forgotten Thousands*, M. Islam, 1973 ● Anon 7, *Turkey: Hall of Mirrors*, Independent Labour Publications, and Campaign for the Defence of the Turkish Peace Movement, 1984 ● Aquino, Benigno, *Pintag*, Philippine Resource Centre, Hong Kong 1979 ● Arango, Jorge Valls, *The Listener*, 26.7.84, interview by Graham Fawcett ● Baraheni, Reza, *Amnesty International* 1973 and *Index on Censorship* 1/1976 ● Baxter, Archibald, *We Will Not Cease*, Gollancz, 1939 ● Bekelle, Mesfin, *Amnesty International*, 1979 ● Berrigan, Daniel, *Sojourners Magazine*, 6/1981 ● Bettelheim, Bruno, *The Informed Heart*, The Free Press, 1960 ● Bielecki, Czeslaw, *Index on Censorship*, 9/1986 ● Biko, Steve, *I Write What I Like*, Bowerdean Press, 1978 ● Birtles, Dorothy, *Newsletter*, Pensioners For Peace, November 1984 ● Boethius, *The Consolation of Philosophy*, V.E. Watts, Penguin, 1969 ● Bone, Edith, *Seven Years Solitary*, Hamish Hamilton, 1957 ● Bonhoeffer, Dietrich, *Letters and Papers From Prison*, SCM Press, 1971 ● Borquez, Adriana, unpublished papers supplied by Quaker Befriending Scheme, UK ● Breytenbach, Breyten, interview in *Index on Censorship*, 3/1983 ● Brightmore, James, *The Tribunal*, No-Conscription Fellowship, 1917 ● Brocklesby, John, unpublished papers in Friends Library, London ● Brockway, Fenner, *Inside the Left*, Allen & Unwin, 1942 ● Brutus, Dennis, *Letters to Martha*, Heinemann, 1968 ● Bukovsky, Vladimir, *To Build a Castle*, Penguin, 1978 ● Bukowinski, Wladyslaw, *Religion in Communist Lands*, Keston College, Spring 1984 ● Bunyan, John, *Grace Abounding to the Chief of Sinners*, Roger Sharrock (ed.) OUP, 1962 ● Campion, Edmund, in *Life*, R. Simpson, Williams & Norgate, 1867 ● Cassidy, Sheila, *Audacity to Believe*, Collins, 1977 ● Catchpool, Corder, *Letters of A Prisoner*, Allen & Unwin, 1941 ● Cavell, Edith, biography by Roland Ryder, Hamish Hamilton, 1975 ● Cheng, Nien, *Life and Death in Shanghai*, Grafton, 1986 ● Chenier, André, poems trans. by V. Loggins, Ohio Univ. Press, 1965 ● Chikane, Frank, *No Life of My Own*, Skotaville Publishers and Catholic Institute for International Relations, 1988 ● Clitherow, Margaret, in *Life*, John Mush, W. Nicholson (ed.), Richardson, 1849 ● Cooper, Thomas, *Autobiography*, Hodder & Stoughton 1872, and Leicester University Press, 1971 ● David, S.A., *Detention, Torture and Murder in Sri Lanka*, Gandhi Society, Sri Lanka, 1983 ● Davitt, Michael, *Leaves From a Prison Diary* (Vol. II), Chapman & Hall, 1895 ● Day, Dorothy, from *The Catholic Worker*, 1957 ● Dimitrov, Georgi, *Selected Articles*, Lawrence & Wishart, 1951 ● Dostoevsky, Fyodor, from *Selected Letters*, Joseph Frank and David Goldstein (eds.), Rutgers University Press, 1987 ● Douglas-Home, William, *Half Term Report*, Longman, 1954 ● Dreyfus, Alfred, *Five Years of My Life*, Fasquelle, 1901 ● Elmi, Saida Botan, *Amnesty*, Amnesty International 2/1988 ● El Sa'adawi, Nawal, *Memoirs from the Women's Prison*, Women's Press, 1986 ● El Sa'adawi, Nawal, *Index on Censorship*, 4/1985 ● English Heritage for J.T. Barker, graffiti, Richmond Castle, Yorks ● Estrella, Miguel, *Le Courrier, Action des Chretiens pour l'Abolition de la Torture* 1984, trans. Ariane Bonzan and Beth Smith ● Esquivel, Adolfo Perez, *Report* and *Reconciliation International*. International Fellowship of Reconciliation, 1980 and 1987 ● Etkind, Michael, private papers, Watford ● First, Ruth, *117 Days*, Penguin, 1982 ● Fischer, Bram, in *The Sun Will Rise*, Mary Benson (ed.), International Defence and Aid, 1981 ● Fox, George, *Journal*, John Nickall (ed.) Religious Society of Friends (Quakers), 1952 ● Frankl, Viktor, *Man's Search for Meaning*, Hodder & Stoughton, 1964 ● Gandhi, Mohandas, *Essays*, S. Radhakrkhnan (ed.), Allen & Unwin, 1939 ● Gardin, Giacomo, in *The Unfulfilled Promise*, Gjon Sinishta, California, 1976 ● Gaspar, Karl, *How Long*, Clarentian Publishers, Philippines, 1985 ● Gerard, John, *Autobiography*, ed. and trans. by Philip Caraman, Longman's, 1951 ● Ginzberg, Eugenia, *Into the Whirlwind*, Collins, 1967 ● Gorbanevskaya, Natalya, *Selected Poems*, D. Weissbort (ed.), Carcanet Press, 1972 ● Gorneau, Etienne-Pierre, in *Last Letters*, Oliver Blanc (ed.), André Deutsch, 1987 ● Gotovac, Vlado, *Index on Censorship*, 6/1981 ● Grigorenko, Peter, *The Grigorenko Papers*, Hurst, 1976 ● Gryn, Hugo, interview BBC Radio 4, July 1987 ● Guerra, Henrique, *Poems from Angola*, Michael Wolfers (ed.), Heinemann, 1979 ● Madam Guyon's Maidservant, *Life of Madam Guyon*, T.C. Upham, Allenson, 1905 ●

Habibi, Suhrab, *Sacrifice*, National Spiritual Assembly of Baha'is, London, 1985 ● Hamlin, John, unpublished papers, correspondence with editor ● Hart, Kitty, *I Am Alive*, Abelard-Schuman, 1961 ● Ha'spari, Shmuel, *The Other Israel*, Israeli Council for Israeli-Palestine Peace, April 1985 ● Hautval, Adelaide, *The Listener*, October 1971 ● Havel, Václaw, *Index on Censorship*, 6/1983 ● Heimler, Eugene, *Night of the Mist*, trans. A. Ungar, Bodley Head, 1959 ● Hermann, Eva, *Der Quaker*, September 1946 ● Hikmet, Nazim, *Poems: Masses and Mainstream*, New York 1954 ● Hillesum, Etty, *A Diary*, Cape, 1983 and estate of Etty Hillesum ● Hockett, William, *Southern Heroes*, F.G. Cartland, Riverside Press, 1895 ● Holladay, Martin, *Hammer and Anvil*, USA, 5/1986 ● Jägerstätter, Franz, *In Solitary Witness*, Gordon Zahn (ed.), Geoffrey Chapman, 1964 ● Janabi, Nabil, *Index on Censorship*, 1989 ● Jara, Victor, in *Victor*, Joan Jara, Cape, 1983 ● Jeanty-Raven, Madam, *Beyond Hatred*, Lutterworth Press, 1969 ● Jowzi, Geeti-oz-Sadat, *Iran Liberation*, Moselm Iranian Students Societies Outside Iran, 1982 ● Juana, unpublished papers, Quaker Befriending Scheme, UK ● Kariuki, Josiah, *Mau Mau Detainee*, Oxford University Press, 1963 ● Kim, Chi Ha, Index on Censorship, trans. J. de Yepes, 4/1975 ● Kim, Keun-Tae, *South Korea*, Amnesty International, 1986 ● King, Martin Luther, *Why We Can't Wait*, Harper Collins, 1963 ● Koestler, Arthur, 'Dialogue With Death' from *Spanish Testament*, Gollancz 1937 ● Kogon, Eugen, *Theory and Practice of Hell*, trans. H. Norden, Secker & Warburg, 1950 ● Kowalska, Anka, *Index on Censorship*, 2/1983 ● Kozlevcar, Joje and Haiderer, Francis, *PACO, Universala Esperanto-Asocio*, Rotterdam, 1975/6 ● Kromberg, Anita, *Report*, International Fellowship of Reconciliation, 1985 ● Laabi, Abdellatif, *Index on Censorship*, 1/1982 ● Laborde, Adriana de, *Nunca Mas*, Faber, 1986 ● Langedul, Christian, *A Martyrology of the Churches of Christ*, vol. 2, G. Underhill (ed.), Hanserd Knollys Society, 1863 ● Laska, Vera, *Women in the Resistance and in the Holocaust*, Greenwood Press, 1983 ● Latimer, Hugh and Ridley, Nicholas, *Foxe's Book of Martyrs*, John Day, 1653 ● Laud, William, printed by Robert Chiswell at the Rose and Crown, St Paul's Churchyard, 1645 ● Lengyel, Olga, *Five Chimneys*, Collins, 1959 and Memorial Library and Art Collection of Second World War, New York ● Levi, Primo, *If This is a Man*, Bodley Head, 1966 ● Lilburne, John, Lancaster University Library, special collection ● Lovelace, Richard, *Palgrave's Golden Treasury*, Collins, 1954 ● Loveless, George, *Victims of Whiggery*, Central Dorchester Committee, 1837 ● Luxemburg, Rosa, *Letters*, S.E. Bronner (ed.), Westview, 1978 ● Magdalena, in *It's Like Holding the Key to Your Own Jail*, Caroline Allison, World Council of Churches, 1986 ● Mager, Andy, *Fellowship*, Fellowship of Reconciliation, 3/1985 ● Mangakis, George, *Index on Censorship*, 1/1972 ● Marin, Guillermo, unpublished papers, correspondence with editor ● Markovski, Venko, *Goli Otok*, East European Quarterly 1984 ● Marten, Howard, 'Conscription and Conscience,' John Graham, Allen & Unwin, 1922 ● Maximilian, in *Early Church History*, E. Backhouse and C. Tylor, Simpkin, Marshall Hamilton & Kent, 1892 ● Mayson, Cedric, *A Certain Sound*, Epworth Press, 1984 ● Michnik, Adam, *Letters From Prison*, Maya Latynski (ed.), University of California Press, 1985 ● Mirga, Roma, *And the Violins Stopped Playing*, as told to Alexander Ramati, Hodder & Stoughton, 1985 ● Moltke, Count Helmuth von, *A German of the Resistance*, Henssel Verlag, Berlin, 1972, by kind permission of Countess Freya von Moltke ● Moore, Howard, *Plowing My Own Furrow*, Norton, 1987 ● Morales, Lucia, *Amnesty*, Amnesty International, 1984 ● More, Sir Thomas, in *Conscience Decides*, Bede Foord, Geoffrey Chapman & Carrel, 1971 ● Müller, Joseph, *Dying We Live*, H. Gollwitzer, K. Kuhn and R. Schneider (eds.), Collins 1958 and Christian Kaiser Verlag, Germany, nd ● Muntsdorp, Janneken, *Martyrs Mirror*, Tielman van Braght, Herald Press, 1979 ● Naude, Beyers, *The Trial of Beyers Naude*, International Commission of Jurists (ed.), Search Press, 1975 ● Nekipelov, Victor, *Institute of Fools*, Farrar, Straus & Giroux, 1980 ● Neto, Agostino, *Sacred Hope*, Tanzania Publishing House, 1974 ● Ngugi, wa Thiong'o, *Detained - A Writer's Prison Diary*, Heinemann, 1980 ● Niemoller, Martin, *Exile in the Fatherland*, Hubert G. Locke (ed.), Eerdmans, 1986 ● Ntuli, Pitika, *Index on Censorship*, 3/1980 ● Paine, Thomas, *The Age of Reason*, Part II (Preface), 1795 ● Pankhurst, Sylvia, *The Suffragette Movement*, Virago, 1977 ● Partnoy, Alicia, *The Little School*, Virago, 1988 ● Paul, St, *New English Bible*, Oxford and Cambridge University Press (Second Edition), 1970 ● Perpetua, in *Acts of the Christian Martyrs*, Herbert Musrillo (ed.), Oxford University Press, 1972 ● Perrin, Henri, *Priest-Workman in Germany*, Sheed & Ward, 1947 ● Polycarp, *The Apostolic Fathers*, trans. K. Lake, Heinemann, 1913 ● Ratushinskaya, Irina, *No, I'm not afraid*, Bloodaxe Books, 1986 ● Reder, Rudolf, *Belzec*, Jewish Commission, Cracow, Poland, 1946 ● Roberts, Rommel, *Reporter*, Quaker Peace and Service, 1984 ● Rowland, James, *We Won't Go*, Alice Lynd (ed.), Beacon Press, 1968 ● Russell, Bertrand, *Autobiography*, Unwin Hyman, 1967 ● Sacco, Nicola and Vanzetti, Bartolomeo, *Letters*, Viking, 1928 ● Sachs, Albie, *Jail Diary of Albie Sachs*, Harvill, 1966 ● Schoenfeld, Howard, *The Pacifist Conscience*, Peter Mayer (ed.), Penguin, 1966 ● Sellar, Richard, *Courage for Conscience*, pamphlet, John Bellows, 1897 ● Sha'at, Zigan, Council for Arab-British Understanding, 7/1989 ● Sharansky, Anatoly, *Sharansky*, Martin Gilbert, MacMillan, 1986 ● Šiklová, Jiřina, *Index on Censorship*, 2/1983 ● Socrates, in *The Last Days of Socrates*,

Plato, trans. by Hugh Tredennick, Penguin, 1954 ● Solzhenitsyn, Alexander, *The Gulag Archipelago*, Collins 1974, and Russian Social Fund for Persecuted Persons and Their Families ● Southwell, Robert, in *Penguin Book of Religious Verse*, R.S. Thomas (ed.), 1963 ● Soyinka, Wole, *The Man Died*, Rex Collings, 1972 ● Steele, Richard, *Reconciliation International*, 11/1981 ● Ten Boom, Corrie, *The Hiding Place*, Hodder & Stoughton, 1971 ● Thien, Nguyen Chi, *Flowers from Hell*, Huynh Sanhthong (ed.), Yale Univ. Press, 1983 ● Thoreau, Henry, *Civil Disobedience*, Ticknor & Fields, 1849 ● Tichborne, Chidiock, *English Recusant Poets*, L.I. Guiney (ed.), Sheed & Ward, 1938 ● Timerman, Jacobo, *Prisoner without a Name, Cell without a Number*, Weidenfeld & Nicolson, 1981 ● de la Torre, Edicio, *Touching Ground, Taking Root*, Socio-Pastoral Institute, Manila, and Catholic Institute for International Relations, 1986 ● Tyndale, William, autograph letter, Religious Tract Society, 1872 ● Uyar, Berin, *Peace News*, 9/1985 ● Ward, Mary, *Life*, vol. II, M. Chambers, Burns Oates, 1885 ● Weir, Ben, *Hostage Bound, Hostage Free*, Westminster Press, 1986 ● Wiesel, Elie, *Night*, Penguin 1981, *Les Editions de Minuit*, Paris, 1958 ● Wolken, Otto, *Auschwitz*, Bernd Naumann, Pall Mall Press, 1966 ● Xu, Wenli, *Index on Censorship*, 5/1986 ● Yang, Jiang, *Six Chapters of My Life downunder*, trans. H. Goldblatt, University of Washington Press, 1984 ● Yosselevska, Rivka, *Women in the Resistance*, V. Laska (ed.), Greenwood Press, 1983 ●

Zed Books Ltd
is a publisher whose international and Third World lists span:

- **Women's Studies**
- **Development**
- **Environment**
- **Current Affairs**
- **International Relations**
- **Children's Studies**
- **Labour Studies**
- **Cultural Studies**
- **Human Rights**
- **Indigenous Peoples**
- **Health**

We also specialize in Area Studies where we have extensive lists in African Studies, Asian Studies, Caribbean and Latin American Studies, Middle East Studies, and Pacific Studies.

For further information about books available from Zed Books, please write to: Catalogue Enquiries, Zed Books Ltd, 57 Caledonian Road, London N1 9BU. Our books are available from distributors in many countries (for full details, see our catalogues), including:

In the USA
Humanities Press International, Inc., 171 First Avenue, Atlantic Highlands, New Jersey 07716.
Tel: (201) 872 1441;
Fax: (201) 872 0717.

In Canada
DEC, 229 College Street, Toronto, Ontario M5T 1R4.
Tel: (416) 971 7051.

In Australia
Wild and Woolley Ltd, 16 Darghan Street, Glebe, NSW 2037.

In India
Bibliomania, C-236 Defence Colony, New Delhi 110 024.

In Southern Africa
David Philip Publisher (Pty) Ltd, PO Box 408, Claremont 7735, South Africa.